BY **Brené Brown**

# Atlas of
# the Heart

to PC and BT,

You ~~don't~~ know me.

love, TJ

# Brené Brown

# Atlas of the Heart

MAPPING MEANINGFUL CONNECTION AND
THE LANGUAGE OF HUMAN EXPERIENCE

Vermilion
LONDON

we are the mapmakers and the travelers

2

Vermilion, an imprint of Ebury Publishing,
20 Vauxhall Bridge Road,
London SW1V 2SA

Vermilion is part of the Penguin Random House group of companies whose addresses can
be found at global.penguinrandomhouse.com

First published in Great Britain in 2021 by Vermilion
First published in the United States in 2021 by Random House, an imprint and division of
Penguin Random House LLC, New York

Grateful acknowledgment is made to the following for permission to reprint previously
published material:
© **HarperCollins Publishers:** Brief excerpts from pp. xxvii and 90-91 of *All About Love* by bell
hooks, copyright © 2000 by Gloria Watkins. Used by permission of HarperCollins Publishers.
© **Routledge, an imprint of Taylor & Francis Group:** Excerpt from *Teaching to Transgress* by
bell hooks, copyright © 1994 by Gloria Watkins. Reprinted by permission of Routledge, an
imprint of Taylor & Francis Group.

ISBN 9781785043772

Printed and bound in Italy by Graphicom

A CIP catalogue record for this book is available from the British Library

The authorised representative in the EEA is Penguin Random House Ireland, Morrison Chambers,
32 Nassau Street, Dublin D02 YH68

Penguin Random House is committed to a sustainable future for our business, our readers and our planet.
This book is made from Forest Stewardship Council® certified paper

# Contents

# Introduction

*Heart is sea,*
*language is shore.*
*Whatever sea includes,*
*will hit the shore.*

— RUMI

# How It Started

I am not a sentimental keeper of things.

Maybe it's because I come from a long line of people who hold on to everything—every receipt and photo and old department store box. From the time I was in my early twenties, I often had the unenviable task of packing up the houses of relatives who could no longer live at home or who had died. If the movie montage version of this chore exists, I've never experienced it. It's miserable.

First, no one in my family is going to admit that they might, at some point, get sick or die. My people die with a look of defiance on their face and shit in every drawer. This leaves me and my sisters packing, crying, cussing, and using every single tool we've learned in therapy to resist turning on one another when we're exhausted. That's actually the only time we laugh—when one of us says "I wish I could take out my rage on y'all" and the other two, without even looking up, say, "Yeah. Same."

There is nothing sweet about packing up. It's hard physical work and an emotional minefield. *Do I keep it? Do I trash it when no one is looking? Should I feel bad? Am I bad? Maybe I should box it all up and let my kids deal with it when it's their turn?*

As far as my own stuff goes, I was Marie Kondo before Marie Kondo was cool. Just like I'm convinced that my car goes faster after I get an oil change, I can feel my house sighing with relief when I take five bags of stuff to the local shelter. There's a lift and a lightness. And a sense of control. The house stands a little straighter without the extra weight, and I feel freer with a little less baggage.

Becoming a parent made the purging tricky. In 1999, when I was pregnant with Ellen, I saw something on TV—a reality show or a movie or something—that showed how a mother had kept all of her son's drawings and used them to decorate for his wedding rehearsal dinner. *Jesus. So much pressure.* From that point forward, every one of the 5,684 pieces of art that my kids brought home became an emotional negotiation about their rehearsal dinner. At some point I realized that unless I was hosting this dinner in a stadium, one box of curated pieces was enough. I saved some, framed and hung pieces all over the house, photographed some of them, and, when no one was looking, put the rest in the garbage. Way down deep where no one could see.

So, given my tendency to throw out everything, I'm always fascinated when I come across an old box of my own stuff. I must have thought something was really important if it warranted saving. If you put all of my memorabilia and artifacts together, you would get the most accurate story of who I was and what I valued at any one point in my life. And you'd probably need no more than a standard issue dining room table to lay it out.

I came across this old college paper several years ago—when I was starting this book. It's not a great or even a very good paper, but it knocked me off balance for a few months. *Why have I been thinking about emotions for so long? Why has this always been so important? Can I even remember a time when I wasn't thinking about emotions?*

As I unpacked a few other things in the box—a lifeguard whistle, poems I'd written, a mixtape from Steve, and a few pictures—my time capsule transported me back to my Flock of Seagulls asymmetrical haircut and a 1974 Volvo 240D with a floorboard that was so rusted out I could see the road pass beneath as I drove. I spent a couple of days with my 1987 self and learned some things that I had either never known or never acknowledged, or things I possibly once knew and pushed way down.

C. Brené Brown
October 9, 1984

# Why We Feel the Pain We Feel

Throughout our lives we must
experience emotions and feelings
that are inevitably painful and
devastating. In order to be able to
cope with these situations, we must
individualy find explanations and
justifications for homing to endure
this pain. Although my explanations
are personnal and based on my
own needs, I feel they are good
guidelines to help others who have
not been able to understand the
reasoning behind sorrow.

Because life's problems follow
a very specific and planned
sequence, it's necessa

I come from a very tough, suck-it-up-get-it-done-and-don't-talk-about-feelings family. Both of my parents had a hard upbringing with a lot of trauma, and despite their own unhappiness, they considered the life they gave us the height of mythical suburban bliss. In their high school years, my dad was the rage-and-grief-fueled football captain and my mom was the head of the drill team and president of half a dozen clubs. She was everything she needed to be to redeem the reputation of what was inconceivable in the *Leave It to Beaver* 1950s—having an alcoholic mother.

When I was growing up, there was a lot of unpredictable behavior and intense emotion in our home. There was intense love and there was intense rage. There was intense laughter and intense hurt. But even the good times were dicey, because they could turn in an instant.

I am the oldest of four, so I often felt the brunt of the madness, along with the responsibility of protecting my siblings from the unpredictable swings. When things were bad, I was the protector. When things were great, I was the protector-in-waiting, always on the outside of the fun, easily teased for being too serious, and always knowing that we were one sideways glance or one smart-ass comment from chaos.

By the time I was in middle school, I had used a combination of my mom's magazines and after-school specials to diagnose myself as "crazy." I know that's a pathologizing word, but back then it was all I had.

First, nothing, I mean *nothing,* was discussed or normalized in my family. Not feelings or fears or periods or friend problems or puberty or money issues or extended family members who struggled with addiction and mental health issues—nothing. *We are all good.* Any question or attempt to understand the things that were clearly *not good* was immediately shut down in punitive ways. For children, it's easy for everything to become a source of shame when nothing is normalized. You assume that if no one is talking about it, it must be just you.

Second, my parents were confusing. My parents were and are good people who did the very best they could with the tools they had. Sometimes those tools weren't enough. Growing up, they seemed to be funny, loving, well liked, smart, great storytellers, and caring neighbors. People loved them. Because they were predictably good outside the house, and wildly unpredictable inside, I assumed it was us. And because I was the oldest, I assumed it was mostly me. And again, it was shaming for all of us when the inside behaviors didn't match the families on TV. Something was wrong and it must be us. We were wrong.

As if all of this wasn't enough to navigate, I had magic powers. And I couldn't talk about them or ask anyone what to do with them. I wasn't allowed to see *The Exorcist, Sybil,* or *Carrie,* but I knew enough about these movies to use them as my reference points for unwell teenage girls. Needless to say, I was worried. Can you imagine how this conversation would have gone over with parents who wanted nothing more than to fit in and be the suburban ideal? *Hey, Mom and Dad, I didn't make the drill team, I don't have a date with a football player to Homecoming, and I got in trouble for saying "shithead" in English. But I do have secret powers.*

At the time, I would have told you that I could predict the future. I couldn't tell you what was going to happen in twenty years, but I could tell you with stunning accuracy what was going to happen in twenty minutes. And when you're young and navigating a tough time at home combined with moving and changing schools in fourth grade, sixth grade, and eighth grade, twenty minutes is all the future you have. So, yes. I could predict the future.

I knew which snarky comment would produce a laugh and which one would set off a fight. And I knew why. I knew that the comment about too much dessert was funny when someone felt good about how they looked and how the same comment would unleash a screaming match if someone didn't feel good about themselves that day or that hour.

I knew everyone's shame triggers and the unwanted identities that elicited their shame. I knew how it was important for everyone to be perceived, when we could poke fun, and how long we had to get the hell out of Dodge if we got that wrong. I knew that everyone in our family was really smart and funny, yet there were flavors of teasing that people used to work out stress or hurt, and once unleashed, that type of teasing wouldn't stop until someone was crying.

I also knew every inch of the supposedly "socially acceptable" place for processing anger, like driving and sporting events. I started out as an athlete but quit as soon as I could. It was too humiliating. Today, when I see *that parent* at my kids' events, I have to put myself in a trance or leave. The irony is that the first time my dad came to one of Ellen's field hockey games, he got out of his folding chair in the middle of the game and started pacing along the fence line. When I went over to ask him what was wrong, he said, "These girls are under too much pressure. These parents and coaches are really piling it on. And someone's going to get hurt with those big sticks." *Who are you?*

The terrifying road rage moments of my childhood left me and my nervous system incapable of handling raging drivers. A couple of years ago, I had a driver pick me up at the airport for a work trip. He got angry when someone passed us on the right side of the freeway, so he started speeding up and slamming on the brakes to prevent that driver from sliding in front of us in the passing lane. I had to say, "I need you to pull over and let me out or stop driving like this." He laughed like I was joking until I put the driving service dispatch operator on speakerphone.

I was eight or nine years old the first time I realized that my superpowers worked outside the house. Our neighborhood swim team coach liked some people and disliked others, and his preferences seemed to change every day. Everyone tried to figure it out—some of the kids even ran experiments— but no one could solve it. Except me. I knew the secret.

This coach liked effort more than natural talent. He liked the kids who tried, even if they didn't win. And, my God, he loved backstroke. So every day when I got to practice, I'd pick the lane with the people who tried the hardest, not the best swimmers but the people who were dying by the time they reached the wall. Luckily, "dying by the time you reach the wall" was a good fit for me. And for free stroke, I'd always swim backstroke. He was a yeller, but I was never once on the receiving end of it.

I also had a really awful piano teacher who would shame and humiliate students. Because of my secret powers, I was never victimized by the teacher, but that wasn't enough. I could barely tolerate watching it happen to others, so I did my best to set the class up for success. One day, as I was showing my friend the scale we were working on, we both started giggling about something (probably how terrible I was at piano). The instructor went nuts and screamed "Why are you laughing?"

We didn't move a muscle.

Finally she said, "One of you is going to the principal's office—who's it going to be?"

It only took me a couple of seconds to work out that my parents would be okay with my getting in trouble, but this girl had an older brother who was constantly in trouble. I had even seen her mom at the school crying and picking him up from the principal's office. I shot straight up. "Me."

She told me to sit back down and set her sights on the girl sitting next to me, who was trembling. I looked at her and said, "No. I will not sit down. It was me." She lost her mind. But I was never afraid. I marched down to the office, gave the principal's assistant my home phone number, and refused to talk to anyone until my parents got there.

I told my parents that I had to stand up for someone who was getting picked on and who was afraid. My dad had me moved out of piano and we stopped for ice cream on the way home. He was proud of me for standing up to a bully. I was proud of myself for accurately predicting how everything would play out, but it wasn't a warm and fuzzy moment for me. The irony was too obvious.

Maybe I couldn't actually predict the future, but I did have top-level observation powers. I understood that people would do almost anything to not feel pain, including causing pain and abusing power, and I understood that there were very few people who could handle being held accountable for causing hurt without rationalizing, blaming, or shutting down.

What surprised me the most when I was growing up was how little other people seemed to understand or even think about the connection between feelings, thinking, and behavior. I remember often thinking, *Oh, God. Do you not see this coming?* I didn't feel smarter or better, just weirder and pained by the amount of hurt that we are capable of causing one another. The observation powers were partly survival and partly how I'm wired.

Everyone, including me, seemed so desperate to feel more connected to their own lives and to one another, but no one was looking in the right places. No one was thinking about how it all works together. Everyone seemed disembodied from their own inner world and disconnected from other people. Too many lonely and secret lives.

As I edged into my late teens and early twenties, my powers waned. Or, it's probably more accurate to say, my power of observation was dulled by a thick layer of beer, cigarettes, dance halls, and behavior that constantly jumped the line between girls-just-want-to-have-fun and self-destructive self-medicating. As it turns out, being able to see what's coming doesn't make it any less painful when it arrives. In fact, knowing probably just upped my anticipatory anxiety and my intolerance for vulnerability. The eggshells weren't on the ground; they were duct-taped to the soles of my shoes. I could never step lightly enough or run fast enough to get away from the cracking, so I made everything around me so loud that it drowned out the sound.

It's awful that the same substances that take the edge off anxiety and pain also dull our sense of observation. We see the pain caused by the misuse of power, so we numb our pain and lose track of our own power. We become terrified of feeling pain, so we engage in behaviors that become a magnet for more pain. We run from anger and grief straight into the arms of fear, perfectionism, and the desperate need for control.

*Oh, God. Did I not see this coming?*

Over the course of several years, I learned that if understanding power and the connections between the way we feel, think, and act was my super-power, numbing was my kryptonite. Inspired by my mom, who, after my parents' divorce, worked several jobs and started therapy, I got help. I got sober and started doing my own work.

It may be just a couple of sentences here, but it was years of terrifying change, hard goodbyes, and boundaries—a truckload of boundaries. When we stop numbing and start feeling and learning again, we have to reevaluate everything, especially how to choose loving ourselves over making other people comfortable. It was the hardest work I've ever done and continue to do.

I learned that taking the edge off is not rewarding, but putting the edge back on is one of the most worthwhile things we can do. Those sharp edges feel vulnerable, but they are also the markers that let us know where we end and others begin.

Understanding and feeling those edges brings grace and clarity. The edges taught me that the more I used alcohol, food, work, caretaking, and whatever else I could get my hands on to numb my anxiety and vulnerability, the less I would understand my feelings, thoughts, and behaviors. I finally realized that trying to outrun and outsmart vulnerability and pain is choosing a life defined by suffering and exhaustion.

Still today, the more I pay attention to my life and the messages from the edges, the more I'm able to choose a way of life that doesn't demand constant vigilance and preparedness. And when there are things outside my control that do demand high alert—COVID, for example—I know running away from the pain and anxiety is way more risky than leaning in and locking eyes with it.

I've learned that power is not bad, but the abuse of power or using power over others is the opposite of courage; it's a desperate attempt to maintain a very fragile ego. It's the desperate scramble of self-worth quicksand. When people are hateful or cruel or just being assholes, they're showing us exactly what they're afraid of. Understanding their motivation doesn't make their behavior less difficult to bear, but it does give us choices. And subjecting ourselves to that behavior by choice doesn't make us tough—it's a sign of our own lack of self-worth.

I know more than I'd like about being subjected to this kind of behavior when I don't want to be, volunteering to experience it just to prove to myself and others that I'm tough, and, sadly, perpetrating it as well. I can get really scary when I'm scared if I'm not paying attention.

I also learned that when you hold someone accountable for hurtful behaviors and they feel shame, that's not the same as shaming someone. I am responsible for holding you accountable in a respectful and productive way. I'm not responsible for your emotional reaction to that accountability. Sadly, I've also learned that sometimes, even when the pain takes your breath away, you have to let the people you love experience the consequences of their own behavior. That one really hurts.

Last, I know I will never have to stop learning these things. Over and over. I've made a lot of progress, but the learning will never stop. I'm just grateful that I can find *and feel* the edges today. I love that saying, "The center will hold." I believe that in the midst of struggle, the center will hold if, and only if, we can feel the edges.

# How It's Going

Although I started honing my power of observation in kindergarten, I officially began studying the connection between how we think, feel, and act over twenty years ago. In addition to researching, I now spend most of my time writing, talking to and learning from social scientists and experts on my podcasts, and working in organizations with leaders who are scaling courage-building skills and creating culture change.

In some ways a lot has changed, and in other ways not enough has changed. For example, today if you ask me to identify the biggest barriers to developing brave leaders or cultivating courage in our families or bringing justice to communities, I'd go right back to what I believed was true about people when I was a kid:

> People will do almost anything to not feel pain, including causing pain and abusing power;

> Very few people can handle being held accountable without rationalizing, blaming, or shutting down; and

> Without understanding how our feelings, thoughts, and behaviors work together, it's almost impossible to find our way back to ourselves and each other. When we don't understand how our emotions shape our thoughts and decisions, we become disembodied from our own experiences and disconnected from each other.

Fifteen years ago, when we first introduced a curriculum based on my shame resilience research, we asked participants in the training workshops to list all of the emotions that they could recognize and name as they were experiencing them. Over the course of five years, we collected these surveys from more than seven thousand people. The average number of emotions named across the surveys was three. The emotions were happy, sad, and angry.

When I think about this data, I think back to a quote from the philosopher Ludwig Wittgenstein that I came across in college: "The limits of my language mean the limits of my world." What does it mean if the vastness of human emotion and experience can only be expressed as mad, sad, or happy? What about shame, disappointment, wonder, awe, disgust, embarrassment, despair, contentment, boredom, anxiety, stress, love, overwhelm, surprise, and all of the other emotions and experiences that define what it means to be human?

Imagine if you had a shooting pain in your left shoulder that was so severe it actually took your breath away. The pain kept you from working, sleeping, and fully engaging in your life. When you finally arrive at the doctor's office and she asks what's going on, there's suddenly tape over your mouth and your hands are tied behind your back. You try yelling through the tape and freeing your hands so you can point to your shoulder, but there's no use. You're just there—inches and minutes from help and possible relief—but you can't communicate or explain the pain. I would imagine in that situation most of us would either fall to the floor in despair or fling ourselves around the room in uncontrollable rage. This is not that different from what can happen to us when we are unable to articulate our emotions. We feel hopeless or we feel a destructive level of anger.

Language is our portal to meaning-making, connection, healing, learning, and self-awareness. Having access to the right words can open up entire universes. When we don't have the language to talk about what we're experiencing, our ability to make sense of what's happening and share it with others is severely limited. Without accurate language, we struggle to get the help we need, we don't always regulate or manage our emotions and experiences in a way that allows us to move through them productively, and our self-awareness is diminished. Language shows us that naming an experience doesn't give the experience more power, it gives *us* the power of understanding and meaning.

Additionally, we have compelling research that shows that language does more than just communicate emotion, it can actually shape what we're feeling. Our understanding of our own and others' emotions is shaped by how we perceive, categorize, and describe emotional experiences—and these interpretations rely heavily on language.

Language speeds and strengthens connections in the brain when we are processing sensory information. But newer research shows that when our access to emotional language is blocked, our ability to interpret incoming emotional information is significantly diminished. Likewise, having the correct words to describe specific emotions makes us better able to identify those emotions in others, as well as to recognize and manage the emotional experiences when we feel them ourselves.

Our ability to accurately recognize and label emotions is often referred to as *emotional granularity*. In the words of Harvard psychologist Susan David, "Learning to label emotions with a more nuanced vocabulary can be absolutely transformative." David explains that if we don't have a sufficient emotional vocabulary, it is difficult to communicate our needs and to get the support that we need from others. But those who are able to distinguish between a range of various emotions "do much, much better at managing the ups and downs of ordinary existence than those who see everything in black and white." In fact, research shows that the process of labeling emotional experience is related to greater emotion regulation and psychosocial well-being.

These benefits seem to be related to the additional information we learn from recognizing what emotion we are feeling. David states that emotions "signal rewards and dangers. They point us in the direction of our hurt. They can also tell us which situations to engage with and which to avoid. They can be beacons, not barriers, helping us identify what we most care about and motivating us to make positive changes." Work by other researchers substantiates David's thinking, indicating that our emotions help us make sense of our surroundings and provide needed input for managing ourselves and responding effectively to others.

# Making Meaning

Eduardo Bericat, a sociology professor at the University of Seville, says "As human beings we can only experience life emotionally." My hope for this book is that together we can learn more about the emotions and experiences that define what it means to be human—including the language that allows us to make sense of what we experience. I want to open up that language portal so even more of us can step through it and find a universe of new choices and second chances—a universe where we can share the stories of our bravest and most heartbreaking moments with each other in a way that builds connection.

I know these universes of new choices and second chances exist because I've discovered them for myself. As I've researched and written about human emotion and experience, my family—including my parents—have cheered me on, read my work, and leaned into learning. The process has been messy and imperfect, but it's been healing and powerful to be a part of a family that now has the language and skill to align the love we feel with the way we actually show up with each other. There are still tough times, and it's easy to default to the old ways, but we've seen what's possible and we're making progress.

In the following chapters, we're going to explore eighty-seven emotions and experiences that have been organized into groups. I say emotions *and* experiences because some of these are not emotions—they're thoughts that lead to emotion. And if you asked ten emotion researchers which ones of these are emotions, you'd probably get ten different answers. The NYU neuroscience professor Joseph LeDoux explains, "It's been said that there are as many theories of emotions as there are emotion theorists."

The matter is complex because human emotions and experiences are studied from the perspective of philosophy, sociology, psychology, neuroscience, medicine, and mental health (to name just a few disciplines), and research topics include studies of facial expression, physiology, brain imaging, genetics, personality traits, cross-cultural analysis, and more. Some researchers place all emotions into one of two categories—low arousal and high arousal—while others like to label them positive and negative. The approaches to understanding emotion are nearly endless.

When the author of a 2015 *Atlantic* article, Julie Beck, asked colleagues to define emotion, she got these varying responses:

- Individual-specific reactions to experiences

- Sensitivity to events

- Your mind's reaction to experience

- The description of intangible human feelings, the powerful internal sensations that color our every experience.

In Beck's article, Alan Fridlund, a social and clinical psychologist at the University of California, Santa Barbara, is quoted as saying, "The only thing certain in the emotion field is that no one agrees on how to define emotion."

While there are many disagreements about the nature of human emotions and experiences, scientific study has narrowed the gaps of what we know to be true. For example, when comparing two studies conducted twenty-two years apart (1994 and 2016) that polled emotion research experts, Paul Ekman (a leading expert himself) concluded that these authorities have come much closer to agreement on many emotion topics. He states that the more recent survey found "broad areas of agreement about the evidence for some of the major issues about the nature of emotion." For example, 80 percent of emotions experts now agree that there are universal voice and facial expression signals that reflect our emotional experience.

One area that remains under debate is how many human emotions and experiences exist. Ekman believes there is clear evidence for seven universal emotions (although he really talks about these as emotion "families"). He also believes that there are ten additional emotions that are close to having sufficient evidence for being universal and eleven more on which the jury is still out. Emotion researchers Alan Cowen and Dacher Keltner believe that at least twenty-seven or twenty-eight emotions are required to convey the range of human experience.

Based on my research on the importance of emotional nuance, I have chosen to take a broader approach. These nuances matter, particularly when we are trying to accurately convey our experiences to others. Therefore, the emotions and experiences categorized in this book span beyond what many researchers would call "basic."

The list of emotions and experiences that I present in this book first emerged from a content analysis of comments from an online course I was teaching that had several main sections on emotion and story. From 2013 to 2014, 66,625 participants were enrolled in the course and there were more than 550,000 comments. The comments were de-identified (no names) and exported to spreadsheets. After going through the human subjects approval process, I analyzed the data using two questions:

What are the emotions and experiences that emerge the most often, and which emotions and experiences do people struggle to name or label?

This yielded approximately 150 emotions and experiences. From here, we invited a group of experienced therapists who work in diverse mental health settings to a focus group process that I led. The therapists' experience ranged from addiction and community mental health to college counseling to inpatient psychiatry and individual and group psychotherapy. We posted all 150 of the emotions and experiences on the walls of the room, and the clinicians were asked to physically tag them with red, yellow, or green stickers based on this criteria:

*In my experience working with clients, the ability to name this emotion or experience is essential to being able to process it in a productive and healing manner.*

Let me just say how much I love my job! This was such an amazing experience. Here's a picture of me with the therapists after we finished our group process.

BACK ROW LEFT TO RIGHT: Wesley Clayton, Gabriel Ramirez

FRONT ROW LEFT TO RIGHT: Debbie Sieck, Helen Stagg, Sarah Luna, Brené Brown, Ashley Brown Ruiz, Chinyere Eigege, Cheryl Scoglio, Sasha Coles

Emotions and experiences that received all green stickers were automatically included on the list. We debated and discussed the yellow and red stickers, and those were not included unless defining them offered clarity to the emotions and experiences that were marked green.

Over a three-year period, I worked closely with Dr. Ronda Dearing, our senior director of research, reviewing close to fifteen hundred academic publications. As we started researching the emotions and experiences that made the list, there were times that we would add a word that was helpful to define for comparative reasons—especially if we have a tendency to confuse the words in question (e.g., jealousy and envy). I couldn't have done this work without her.

At first the terms were in alphabetical order, but in 2020, our summer college interns told us that learning about the emotions and experiences was most effective when the terms were in groups that highlighted the subtle and not-so-subtle differences between experiences. They explained that grouping them based on how they relate and compare to one another reflects more of our lived experiences and enhances learning. When interns teach, we listen and learn. Thank you, Ellen and Prerna!

Once we had the final list, we used the course data to better understand how people actually use language when describing their feelings. How we talk about our experiences is often not even close to how those experiences are discussed by researchers. My commitment is to deliver work that is empirically based and accessible and that resonates with our lived experiences and lived language.

I know what a privilege it is to have spent my education and career working closely with research participants, practitioners (therapists, counselors, organizers, leaders, and others) and educators (from kindergarten teachers to doctoral professors). Without this diverse group of people, I'd have no career, which is why I consider them my most important audience when I'm researching and writing.

I figure that if these groups have the courage to share their experiences and stories with me, I'm going to do my best to present the research findings in ways that are meaningful for them and their work, including using accessible language and stories.

If the research participants, practitioners, and educators don't get what I'm saying, or find it irrelevant because of how it's presented, I've failed. This is not the way I'm trained—there is absolutely no emphasis on accessibility in academia—but I'm a social worker before I'm anything else, and "meeting people where they are" is an ethical mandate from this perspective. Sometimes I'm successful, sometimes I need to do better. Sometimes I fail. And when I fail, I hear about it. Thankfully.

I want this book to be an atlas for all of us, because I believe that with an adventurous heart and the right maps, we can travel anywhere and never fear losing ourselves. Even when we don't know where we are.

# You Are Here

In most of my books, I've shared the line "I am a mapmaker and a traveler." It's my way of telling you that I don't have the answers. I have data, and I use that data to chart a course that I'm sharing with you and trying to navigate at the same time. I don't have it figured out, and most of my research has surprised me and kicked my ass.

I stumble and fall a lot as I try to put what I learn into practice. This book is no exception. In the three years that we've been working on this research, I learned that I was misusing language and that I had a profound misunderstanding of several of these concepts. I also came across new research that shifted my thinking on emotions and how I'll talk about them in the future.

This research also taught me that there are times when I can't even offer you a map. I simply don't have access to some of the places you've been and many of the places you'll need to go. This is one of those times. For this work, we are all the mapmakers and the travelers.

When I settled on using a map metaphor for the book, the first person I called was Dr. Kirk Goldsberry, my friend and colleague at the University of Texas at Austin. Kirk is a mapmaker and a cartography scholar. He knows and loves maps. He also knows and loves basketball. Realizing that the accuracy of his shots depended on his court position, he used his cartography skills to analyze and present spatial basketball data to readers in new ways. He was the vice president for strategic research for the San Antonio Spurs, the lead analyst for Team USA Basketball, and a visiting researcher at the Harvard Institute of Quantitative Social Sciences. Kirk is best known for his sports writing, including his book *Sprawlball: A Visual Tour of the New Era of the NBA*.

Kirk explained that there are two ways to make a map: actual exploration to collect your own data, and using data provided by other people. Either way, maps are about layers. If you're using existing data, you might start with elevation, then use a different set of data to layer on roads, then perhaps use hydrography data to find the lakes, streams, and rivers, and so on. He helped me understand that while different maps may use different layers, the one thing that all maps do is provide readers with orientation.

But mapmaking is not as easy as simply stacking data on top of data. There's an art and science to how cartographers prioritize and integrate the data. And, according to Kirk, 50 to 60 percent of the challenge of mapmaking is labeling the map in a way that appropriately prioritizes the right information. He explained, "The interaction between the layers is the story of the map. It is the narrative structure of what we see when we read a map. The layers tell us the hierarchy of what's most important."

When he said that, I could immediately picture a Texas state map on which Houston, Austin, Dallas, and San Antonio immediately grab your attention and Luckenbach and Hondo require a solid squint and some finger tracing. The labeling tells me which cities are the biggest and where they are in relation to one another.

Kirk told me, "Maps are the most important documents in human history. They give us tools to store and exchange knowledge about space and place." I know I'm a map geek, but when he said that, I got goosebumps. We are meaning makers, and a sense of place is central to meaning-making.

*Where am I?*

*How did I get here from there?*

*How do I get there from here?*

These questions are central to understanding the physical world, and they're central to understanding our internal worlds. Whether we're looking at a map of Texas or reflecting on a tough conversation with someone we love, we need landmarks to orient us, and we need language to label what we're experiencing. And, just like a map, the interaction between the layers of our emotions and experiences tells our story.

But rather than elevation and roads and water, **human emotions and experiences are layers of biology, biography, behavior, and backstory.** As you make your way through this book, you'll see that in order to recognize, name, and make sense of our feelings and experiences, we have to:

1. Understand how they show up in our bodies and why (biology)

2. Get curious about how our families and communities shape our beliefs about the connection between our feelings, thoughts, and behavior (biography)

3. Examine our go-to (behaviors), and

4. Recognize the context of what we're feeling or thinking. *What brought this on?* (backstory)

These are the questions that help us make meaning of our lives.

So often, when we feel lost, adrift in our lives, our first instinct is to look out into the distance to find the nearest shore. But that shore, that solid ground, is within us. The anchor we are searching for is connection, and it is internal. To form meaningful connections with others, we must first connect with ourselves, but to do either, we must first establish a common understanding of the language of emotion and human experience.

# Atlas of
# the Heart

# #1

# Places We Go When Things Are Uncertain or Too Much

Stress, Overwhelm, Anxiety, Worry, Avoidance, Excitement, Dread, Fear, Vulnerability

# Stressed and Overwhelmed

The restaurant is packed. It's loud, every table is full, and people are lined up out the door. There's at least one angry person at every table who is desperately trying to wave down a waiter.

"We never got our bread!"
"We need more tea!"
"We've been waiting on our salads for twenty minutes!"
"We need our check unless you don't want us to pay for this crappy service!"

You can hear the kitchen manager's booming voice through the swinging doors:

"The food on the line is dying—let's go, let's go!"
"We've got desserts ready for table 10 and bread ready for tables 3, 4, and 8."

But only one waiter showed up for the shift. And it's me. And I can't speak, for some reason. And I'm wearing a bathing suit and huge fins that make it hard to walk and impossible to run.

This is one of my least favorite recurring bad dreams. I hate it because, after six years of waiting tables and bartending for a high-pressure, high-expectation restaurant group through college and grad school, I know that feeling all too well. We made a lot of money, but we worked our asses off. And the pressure left a mark.

Still today, if Steve is in the kitchen and I walk behind him, I'll shout, "Behind you!" And if I spy someone leaning against the counter during a family kitchen clean-up after dinner, I have to stop myself from saying, "Hey! If you have time to lean, you have time to clean." The language and habits of that job were survival, and they stuck.

Weirdly—or maybe not—the majority of my current leadership team have significant restaurant experience. Maybe we attract one another, or maybe I'm just drawn to the capacity for grind. If you work on our team and you step over a sugar packet on the floor because picking that up is someone else's job—you're not a good fit.

**Stressed** and **overwhelmed** remind me of two restaurant terms that my team and I often use today: "in the weeds" and "blown." Back in the day, if I walked into the kitchen and told another waiter "I'm in the weeds"—the response would be, "What do you need?" I might say, "Can you take bread to tables 2 and 4, and re-tea tables 3 and 5, please?"

Being in the weeds and pulling out of the weeds happened to everyone on almost every shift. It was just part of the job, and you learned to manage it.

Walking into the kitchen and saying "I'm blown"—well, that's completely different. The kitchen gets really quiet. No one asks what you need. Normally, someone runs to the hostess stand to find out what tables you're running that shift—they don't even assume you know at this point. The kitchen manager, who would never get involved in an "in the weeds" situation, pulls all the tickets for your guests to evaluate what's happening and immediately assigns your tables to other waitstaff.

When you're blown, you can either step outside or into the cooler or go to the bathroom (and cry). Whatever you need. You're expected back in ten minutes, ready to go, but for ten minutes, there's a complete takeover. In six years, it happened to me twice, both times due to pure exhaustion at the end of triple shifts that I was working because tuition was due. Stressed is being in the weeds. Overwhelmed is being blown.

## Stressed

**We feel stressed when we evaluate environmental demand as beyond our ability to cope successfully. This includes elements of unpredictability, uncontrollability, and feeling overloaded.**

Stressful situations cause both physiological (body) and psychological (mind and emotion) reactions. However, regardless of how strongly our body responds to stress (increases in heart rate and cortisol), our emotional reaction is more tied to our cognitive assessment of whether we can cope

# 66

# **Stressed** is being in the weeds. **Overwhelmed** is being blown.

with the situation than to how our body is reacting. I found this really interesting because I always assumed that my emotions responded to my body freaking out. But really, my emotions are responding to my "thinking" assessment of how well I can handle something.

Just as getting in and out of the weeds is a part of every waitstaff shift in a restaurant, navigating stressors is a daily part of living. However, daily stress can take a toll. In fact, chronic exposure to stressors can be detrimental to health. High levels of perceived stress have been shown to correlate with more rapid aging, decreased immune function, greater inflammatory processes, less sleep, and poorer health behaviors.

## Overwhelmed

If stress is like being in the weeds, feeling overwhelmed is like being blown. **Overwhelmed means an extreme level of stress, an emotional and/or cognitive intensity to the point of feeling unable to function.** I love this definition of "overwhelmed" from the Merriam-Webster online dictionary: "completely overcome or overpowered by thought or feeling."

We all know that feeling that washes over us and leaves us completely unsure of what to do next. Even when people ask "How can I help?" or

"What needs to be done?"—responding with organized thoughts feels impossible. This is also when I can get really crappy and think to myself, *If I had the wherewithal to figure out what comes next and how we need to approach all of this, I wouldn't be walking around in circles crying and talking to myself.*

Feeling stressed and feeling overwhelmed seem to be related to our perception of how we are coping with our current situation and our ability to handle the accompanying emotions: *Am I coping? Can I handle this? Am I inching toward the quicksand?*

Jon Kabat-Zinn describes overwhelm as the all-too-common feeling "that our lives are somehow unfolding faster than the human nervous system and psyche are able to manage well."

This really resonates with me: *It's all unfolding faster than my nervous system and psyche can manage it.*

When I read that Kabat-Zinn suggests that mindful play, or no-agenda, non-doing time, is the cure for overwhelm, it made sense to me why, when we were blown at the restaurant, we weren't asked to help problem-solve the situation. We were just asked to engage in non-doing. I'm sure experience taught the managers that doing nothing was the only way back for someone totally overwhelmed.

The non-doing also makes sense—there is a body of research that indicates that we don't process other emotional information accurately when we feel overwhelmed, and this can result in poor decision making. In fact, researcher Carol Gohm used the term "overwhelmed" to describe an experience where our emotions are intense, our focus on them is moderate, and our clarity about exactly what we're feeling is low enough that we get confused when trying to identify or describe the emotions.

In other words: *On a scale of 1 to 10, I'm feeling my emotions at about 10, I'm paying attention to them at about 5, and I understand them at about 2.*

This is not a setup for successful decision making. The big learning here is that feeling both stressed and overwhelmed is about our narrative of emotional and mental depletion—there's just too much going on to manage effectively.

# Anxiety

For me, **anxiety** feels like what I lovingly call the "Willy Wonka shit tunnel." There's a frightening scene in the original Willy Wonka film that starts out as a sweet boat ride through a magical land of supersized candy and turns into an escalating scene of fear and loss of control. As the boat enters a dark tunnel, the mood turns. The boat starts going faster and faster while terrible images flash on the walls, including a close-up of a millipede crawling over someone's face, a chicken getting its head cut off, and a lizard eating a bug. None of it makes narrative sense; it's just scary and confusing.

All of this is happening while the passengers—children and their parents—are freaking out and Willy Wonka, played by the incredible, wild-eyed Gene Wilder, is maniacally reciting this poem at an increasingly frenetic rate:

> *There's no earthly way of knowing*
> *Which direction we are going.*
> *There's no knowing where we're rowing*
> *Or which way the river's flowing.*
> *Is it raining?*
> *Is it snowing?*
> *Is a hurricane a-blowing?*
> *Not a speck of light is showing*
> *So the danger must be growing.*
> *Are the fires of hell a-glowing?*
> *Is the grisly reaper mowing?*
> *Yes! The danger must be growing*
> *For the rowers keep on rowing.*
> *And they're certainly not showing*
> *Any signs that they are slowing!*

That's what anxiety feels like to me. Escalating loss of control, worst-case-scenario thinking and imagery, and total uncertainty.

## Let. Me. Off. The. Boat.

As the team and I reviewed the research, what I learned about language and how some of these experiences work together felt like a life jacket for me—something that would keep me afloat if I had to jump off that boat before it headed into the shit tunnel. I hope it does for you too.

**elizabeth_gilbert_writer**

You are afraid of Surrender because you don't want to lose control.

but you never had control; all you had was anxiety.

**The American Psychological Association defines anxiety as "an emotion characterized by feelings of tension, worried thoughts and physical changes like increased blood pressure."** Anxiety can be both a state and a trait. To better understand this, let's get clear on what these terms mean. The best explanation I've come across is from *The Oxford Review Encyclopaedia of Terms*. Here's how they explain it:

- A trait is considered to be something that is part of an individual's personality and therefore a long-term characteristic of an individual that shows through their behavior, actions, and feelings. It is seen as being a characteristic, feature, or quality of an individual. For example, someone who says "I am a confident person" or "I am just an anxious person" is stating that these attributes are part of who they are.

- A state, on the other hand, is a temporary condition that they are experiencing for a short period of time. After the state has passed, they will return to another condition. For example, someone who says "I am feeling quite confident about this interview" or "I feel nervous about doing this" is describing states.

I loved their closing sentence, which may be the understatement of the decade: "However, working out what is really a trait and what is a state can often be difficult and is the content of much scientific argument at times."

So, when we say that anxiety can be both a state and a trait, it means that some of us feel anxious mainly in response to certain situations, while some of us can be naturally more predisposed to anxiety than others.

Generalized anxiety disorder is different from both trait and state anxiety. According to Johns Hopkins Medicine, "generalized anxiety disorder is a condition of excessive worry about everyday issues and situations." It lasts longer than six months, and "in addition to feeling worried, you may also feel restlessness, fatigue, trouble concentrating, irritability, increased muscle tension, and trouble sleeping."

Approximately one-third of U.S. adults will be affected by an anxiety disorder in their lifetime; however, it is estimated that fewer than half of people with diagnosable anxiety disorders seek any type of professional treatment. It's very difficult to work through an anxiety disorder without professional help.

I'd describe myself as having frequent state anxiety with trait rising, and I know that therapy has been essential for me in terms of recognizing and understanding my reactions and developing techniques for working through my feelings of anxiety. I've also had to give up caffeine, commit to eight to nine hours of sleep a night, and exercise almost every day.

An intolerance for uncertainty is an important contributing factor to all types of anxiety. Those of us who are generally uncomfortable with uncertainty are more likely to experience anxiety in specific situations as well as to have trait anxiety and anxiety disorders.

Our anxiety often leads to one of two coping mechanisms: worry or avoidance. Unfortunately, neither of these coping strategies is very effective.

Worrying and anxiety go together, but worry is not an emotion; it's the thinking part of anxiety. **Worry is described as a chain of negative thoughts about bad things that might happen in the future.**

What really got me about the worry research is that those of us with a tendency to worry believe it is helpful for coping (it is not), believe it is uncontrollable (which means we don't try to stop worrying), and try to suppress worry thoughts (which actually strengthens and reinforces worry). I'm not suggesting that we worry about worry, but it's helpful to recognize that worrying is not a helpful coping mechanism, that we absolutely can learn how to control it, and that rather than suppressing worry, we need to dig into and address the emotion driving the thinking.

**Avoidance, the second coping strategy for anxiety, is not showing up and often spending a lot of energy zigzagging around and away from that thing that already feels like it's consuming us.** And avoidance isn't benign. It can hurt us, hurt other people, and lead to increased and mounting anxiety. In her book *The Dance of Fear,* Dr. Harriet Lerner writes, "It is not fear that stops you from doing the brave and true thing in your daily life. Rather, the problem is avoidance. You want to feel comfortable, so you avoid doing or saying the thing that will evoke fear and other difficult emotions. Avoidance will make you feel less vulnerable in the short run, but it will never make you less afraid."

The entire premise of this book is that language has the power to define our experiences, and there's no better example of this than anxiety and excitement.

Anxiety and **excitement** feel the same, but how we interpret and label them can determine how we experience them.

Even though **excitement is described as an energized state of enthusiasm leading up to or during an enjoyable activity,** it doesn't always feel great. We can get the same "coming out of our skin" feeling that we experience when we're feeling anxious. Similar sensations are labeled "anxiety" when we perceive them negatively and "excitement" when we perceive them positively. One important strategy when we're in these feelings is to take a deep breath and try to determine whether we're feeling anxiety or excitement. Researchers found that labeling the emotion as excitement seems to hinge on interpreting the bodily sensations as positive. The labels are important because they help us know what to do next.

**Dread occurs frequently in response to high-probability negative events; its magnitude increases as the dreaded event draws nearer.** Because dread makes an anticipated negative event even worse, we often prefer to get unpleasant things over with quickly, even if doing them sooner means that they will be more unpleasant (e.g., a more painful procedure now is preferred to a less painful procedure later).

I felt so called out when I read this. I can convince myself that an experience is going to be disastrous and work myself into a dread-frenzy. It's terrible, because even if it goes well, I'm so dread-exhausted that I can't enjoy it.

For anxiety and dread, the threat is in the future. For fear, the threat is now—in the present. **Fear is a negative, short-lasting, high-alert emotion in response to a perceived threat, and, like anxiety, it can be measured as a state or trait.** Some people have a higher propensity to experience fear than others.

Fear arises when we need to respond quickly to physical or psychological danger that is present and imminent. Because fear is a rapid-fire emotion, the physiological reaction can sometimes occur before we even realize that we are afraid. The typical responses are fight, flight, or freeze.

In the research, you can find many lists of what elicits fear in us. The items range from rodents and snakes, to the inability to see our surroundings, to observing our children in peril. However, no matter how much the lists vary, one item is on every list I've seen: the fear of social rejection. We can never forget that we experience social pain and physical pain in the same part of our brains, and the potential exposure to either type of pain drives fear.

To close this section, I want to go back to my friend and mentor Dr. Harriet Lerner. She writes, "Throughout evolutionary history, anxiety and fear have helped every species to be wary and to survive. Fear can signal us to act, or, alternatively, to resist the impulse to act. It can help us to make wise, self-protective choices in and out of relationships where we might otherwise sail mindlessly along, ignoring signs of trouble."

Like all of the experiences in this book, both our anxiety and our fear need to be understood and respected, perhaps even befriended. We need to pull up a chair and sit with them, understand why they're showing up, and ask ourselves what there is to learn. Dismissing fear and anxiety as not useful to our quest for connection is as dangerous as choosing to live in constant fear and anxiety.

# Vulnerability

**Vulnerability is the emotion that we experience during times of uncertainty, risk, and emotional exposure.** It first emerged in my dissertation research, and it has been validated by every study I've done since.

Through our research and training, we've asked tens of thousands of people to give us examples of vulnerability from their own lives. These are a few of the answers that directly pierce the emotion:

- The first date after my divorce

- Talking about race with my team

- Trying to get pregnant after my second miscarriage

- Talking about my feelings

- Starting my own business

- Watching my child leave for college

- Remembering that leaders don't have all the answers, but ask important questions

- Apologizing to a colleague about how I spoke to him in a meeting

- Sending my son to orchestra practice knowing how badly he wants to make first chair and knowing there's a really good chance he will not make the orchestra at all

- Waiting for the doctor to call back

- Giving and getting feedback

- Getting back up to bat after striking out

While these are uncomfortable and difficult experiences, there is no evidence that they are indicators of weakness. In fact, this is one of the biggest myths of vulnerability. We've found that across cultures, most of us were raised to believe that being vulnerable is being weak. This sets up an unresolvable tension for most of us, because we were also raised to be brave. There is no courage without vulnerability. Courage requires the willingness to lean into uncertainty, risk, and emotional exposure.

In my most recent research on courage and leadership, the ability to embrace vulnerability emerged as the prerequisite for all of the daring leadership behaviors. If we can't handle uncertainty, risk, and emotional exposure in a way that aligns with our values and furthers our organizational goals, we can't lead.

In a world where perfectionism, pleasing, and proving are used as armor to protect our egos and our feelings, it takes a lot of courage to show up and be all in when we can't control the outcome. It also takes discipline and self-awareness to understand what to share and with whom. Vulnerability is not oversharing, it's sharing with people who have earned the right to hear our stories and our experiences.

Vulnerability is not weakness; it's our greatest measure of courage.

# "
# Vulnerability
is not weakness;
it's our greatest
measure of
## courage.

# #2

# **Places We Go When We Compare**

---

Comparison, Admiration, Reverence, Envy,
Jealousy, Resentment, Schadenfreude,
Freudenfreude

# Comparison

Swimming is the trifecta for me—exercise, meditation, and alone time. When I'm swimming laps you can't call me or talk to me, it's just me and the black stripe. The only thing that can ruin a swim is when I shift my attention from my lane to what's happening in the lanes next to me. It's embarrassing, but if I'm not paying attention, I can catch myself racing the person next to me, or comparing our strokes, or figuring out who has the best workout set. When I go into comparison, I completely lose the meditation and alone time I need. And I once hurt my shoulder trying to race a twentysomething triathlete in the next lane.

I have this picture hanging in my study as a reminder to focus on my journey and to stop checking the lanes next to me. It applies to my time in the pool and everything else—how I parent, my work, my relationships—everything! Researching comparison helped me understand that, like it or not, I'm probably going to check the lanes next to me. But what I do next is up to me. Let's dive in. *Sorry, I had to.*

**Comparison** is actually not an emotion, but it drives all sorts of big feelings that can affect our relationships and our self-worth. More often than not, social comparison falls outside of our awareness—we don't even know we're doing it. This lack of awareness can lead to us showing up in ways that are hurtful to ourselves and others. All of the experiences in this section are connected to comparison, and the goal is to raise our awareness about how and why they happen so we can name them, think about them, and make choices that reflect our values and our heart. We're going to start with comparison then get into more specific experiences.

Researchers Jerry Suls, René Martin, and Ladd Wheeler explain that "comparing the self with others, either intentionally or unintentionally, is a pervasive social phenomenon," and how we perceive our standings or rankings with these comparisons can affect our self-concept, our level of aspiration, and our feelings of well-being. They describe how we use comparison not only to evaluate past and current outcomes, but to predict future prospects. This means significant parts of our lives, including our future, are shaped by comparing ourselves to others.

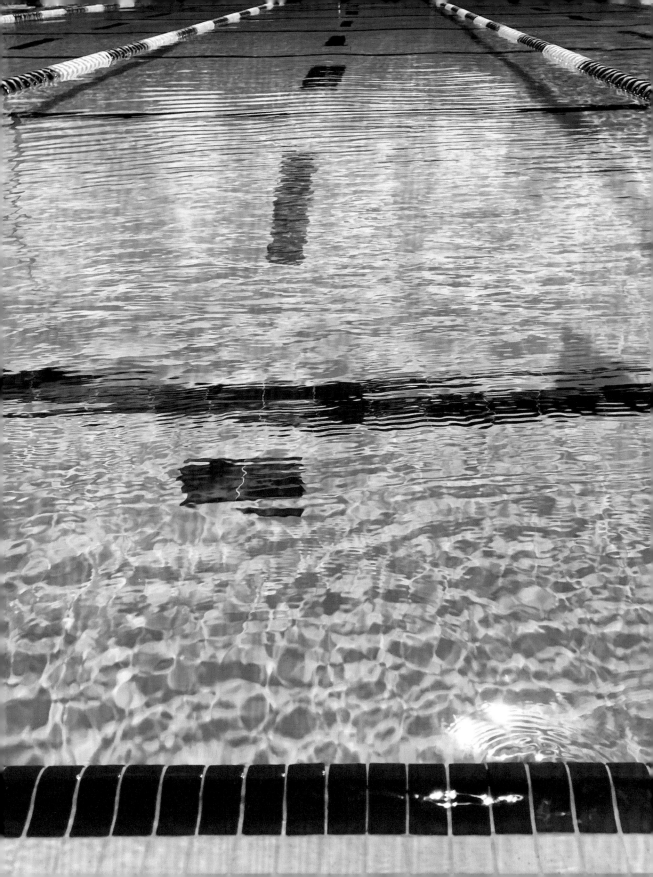

I've collected data on comparison for years, starting with the research that informed *The Gifts of Imperfection*. Guidepost #6 in the list of guideposts for wholehearted living is "cultivating creativity and letting go of comparison." Comparison is a creativity killer, among other things.

**Here is my definition of comparison**:

**Comparison is the crush of conformity from one side and competition from the other—it's trying to simultaneously fit in and stand out.**

Comparison says, "Be like everyone else, but better."

At first it might seem that conforming and competing are mutually exclusive, but they're not. When we compare ourselves with others, we are ranking around a specific collection of "alike things." We may compare things like how we parent with families who have totally different values or traditions from ours, but the comparisons that get us really riled up are the ones we make with the folks living next door, or on our child's soccer team, or at our school. We don't compare our house to the mansions across town; we compare our yard to the yards on our block. I'm not swimming against Katie Ledecky's times, I'm just interested in the stranger in the lane next to me.

When we compare, we want to be the best or have the best of our group. The comparison mandate becomes this crushing paradox of "Fit in and stand out!" It's not be yourself and respect others for being authentic, it's "Fit in, but win." I want to swim the same workout as you, and beat you at it.

Many researchers talk in terms of upward and downward comparisons. Specifically, Alicia Nortje writes, "When we engage in upward social comparison, we compare ourselves to someone who is (perceived to be or performing) better than we are. In contrast, when we engage in downward social comparison, we compare ourselves to someone who is (perceived to be or performing) worse than we are. The direction of the comparison doesn't guarantee the direction of the outcome. Both types of social comparison can result in negative and positive effects."

Most of us assume that upward comparisons always leave us feeling "not enough" and downward comparisons make us feel "better than." But researcher Frank Fujita writes, "Social comparisons can make us happy or unhappy. Upward comparisons can inspire or demoralize us, whereas downward comparisons can make us feel superior or depress us. In general, however, frequent social comparisons are not associated with life satisfaction or the positive emotions of love and joy but are associated with the negative emotions of fear, anger, shame, and sadness." These are important findings because, regardless of the different outcomes, in the end, comparing ourselves to others leads us to fear, anger, shame, and sadness.

Here's what makes all of this really tough: Many social psychologists consider social comparison something that happens *to us*.

Fujita writes, "From this perspective, when we are presented with another person who is obviously better or worse off, we have no choice but to make a social comparison. 'It can be hard to hear an extremely intelligent person on the radio, or see an extremely handsome one in the grocery store, or participate on a panel with an expert without engaging in social comparison no matter how much we would like not to' (Goethals, 1986, p. 272) . . . Even if we do not choose whether or not to make a comparison, we can choose whether or not to let that comparison affect our mood or self-perceptions."

Whenever I find myself in comparison mode, I think back to an *Unlocking Us* podcast conversation that I had with my friend Scott Sonenshein about his wonderful book *Stretch*. Scott is an organizational psychologist, a researcher, and a professor at Rice University. In the book and on the podcast, Scott talks about the popular comparison cliché "the grass is always greener on the other side" and the idea that people spend a lot of time and money trying to get their grass pristine because they want to outdo their neighbors.

As someone who can fall prey to comparing myself and my life to edited and curated Instagram feeds, I laughed so hard when he told me that due to the physics of how grass grows, when we peer over our fence at our neighbor's grass, it actually does look greener, even if it is truly the same lushness as our own grass. I mean, does it get better than that? The grass actually

> **Comparison** is the crush of conformity from one side and competition from the other—it's trying to simultaneously fit in and stand out.

Comparison says,

'Be like everyone else, but better.'

*does* look greener on the other side, but that means nothing comparatively because it's all perspective.

So the bad news is that our hardwiring makes us default to comparison—it seems to happen to us rather than be our choice.

The good news is that we get to choose how we're going to let it affect us. If we don't want this constant automatic ranking to negatively shape our lives, our relationships, and our future, we need to stay aware enough to know when it's happening and what emotions it's driving. My new strategy is to look at the person in the lane next to me, and say to myself, as if I'm talking to them, *Have a great swim.* That way I acknowledge the inevitable and make a conscious decision to wish them well and return to my swim. So far, it's working pretty well.

Below are some of the ways we respond to others, often when comparing to our own situations. The more we know, the more we can choose connection over comparison.

# Admiration and Reverence

**We feel admiration when someone's abilities, accomplishments, or character inspires us, or when we see something else that inspires us, like art or nature.** Interestingly, admiration often leads to us wanting to improve ourselves. It doesn't, however, make us want to be like the person or thing we admire—we just want to be better versions of ourselves. For example, I admire many female athletes. I don't want to be a professional on tour, but they do inspire me to be the best athlete I can be. *Okay, sometimes I want to be a professional on tour. But the senior tour.*

**Reverence, which is sometimes called adoration, worship, or veneration, is a deeper form of admiration or respect and is often combined with a sense of meaningful connection with something greater than ourselves.** I can't think of this word without thinking of church. This research definition is probably why: "Reverence is a cardinal virtue characterized by the capacity of feeling deep respect, love, and humility for something sacred or transcendent."

What's interesting is that while admiration fosters self-betterment, reverence seems to foster a desire for connection to what we revere—we want to move closer to that thing or person.

A bonus word for our list is **irreverent**. After reading all the research related to reverence, I was curious about how it was defined, because I see it all the time on Netflix. It must be a key tag for their algorithm. They have tags for irreverent comedies, irreverent sitcoms, irreverent adult animation, irreverent stand-up, irreverent British comedies, and more.

I normally do *not* like any of the shows with the "irreverent" tag. I looked it up in the *Cambridge English Dictionary* online—their definition was, not surprisingly, very straightforward: "not showing the expected respect for official, important, or holy things." I'm not sure, but I think my adult experiences with unchecked authority leave me wary of reverence, and my upbringing, where social conformity was important, leaves me uncomfortable with irreverence. Translation: I sometimes laugh at irreverent humor. Then I feel bad.

# Envy and Jealousy

Let me be the first to say that I've been using these words all wrong. And I'm pretty sure it's because, like most people, I don't like to say that I'm feeling envious—even when I am. I'd rather offer a friendly, "Man, that's amazing. I'm so jealous." But as it turns out, I'm probably not jealous when I say that, I'm envious. But I don't like the way that sounds. Here's what I've learned.

There are several debates about the inner workings of envy and jealousy, but there seems to be a consensus that these are two significantly different emotions, starting with these definitions:

**Envy occurs when we want something that another person has.**

**Jealousy is when we fear losing a relationship or a valued part of a relationship that we already have.**

According to researchers Richard H. Smith and Sung Hee Kim,

> Envy typically involves *two* people and occurs when one lacks something enjoyed by another. The target of envy may be a person or a group of persons, but the focus of envy is that one lacks something compared with a specific target, whether it be a target individual or target group.

> Jealousy typically involves *three* people and occurs when one fears losing someone to another person. Envy and jealousy result from different situations, generate distinct appraisals, and produce distinctive emotional experiences.

## Envy

A 2015 study found that 90 percent of recalled episodes of envy can be attributed to one of three categories:

1. Attraction (e.g., physical attractiveness, romantic attraction, social popularity);

2. Competence (e.g., intelligence, knowledge); and

3. Wealth (e.g., financial status or lifestyle).

There's not full agreement in the research, but it appears that some envy comes with hostility. (*I want that, and I don't want you to have it. I also want you to be pulled down and put down.*) Some experiences of envy don't include hostile feelings. (*I want that, but you can have it too, and I don't want you to be put or pulled down.*)

The fact that hostility and a desire for denigration are sometimes part of envy makes it tough to own that emotion. What would we say? *I'm envious, but not the bad kind. Swear.*

**"**

**Envy** occurs when we want something that another person has.

**Jealousy** is when we fear losing a relationship or a valued part of a relationship that we already have.

# Jealousy

Jealousy doesn't seem to be a singular emotion but rather a cognitive evaluation in response to feeling anger, sadness, and/or fear. In other words, we *think* jealousy in response to how we *feel*.

According to researchers Mingi Chung and Christine Harris, jealousy typically involves a triad—two people in a relationship and a rival; the rival is usually another person, but occasionally it is something else, such as loss of valuable relationship time to a favored activity. They write, "The core form of jealousy primarily involves threats to relationship rewards including loss of a loved one's attention, affection, or resources to another."

We mostly think of jealousy in the context of romantic relationships, but jealousy also applies to parent/child interactions, sibling relationships, friendships, and coworker relationships. In children, jealousy most often relates to loss of parental attention or perceived special treatment of a sibling that they believe to be unfair. In adults, there are the familiar scenarios like our partner flirting with someone at a party or a close friend suddenly spending a lot of time with a new friend. But sometimes we might even feel a pang of jealousy when a partner or friend spends a lot of time alone, doing something that doesn't involve us. We might feel anger, or sadness, or fear, but what goes through our mind is that we are jealous. And the reason for our jealousy (and the accompanying emotion) is that the other person or activity is threatening to take time away from our relationship.

While jealousy is frequently considered more socially acceptable than envy, it can often lead to more dire consequences. For example, some research has found that high levels of jealousy are directly related to problem drinking and to interpersonal violence when drinking. Other research has found that frequent experiences of jealousy combined with problematic alcohol use are related specifically to higher levels of physical assault and sexual coercion.

But is all jealousy dangerous? No. It's normal to feel some level of jealousy, and research shows that in small doses and expressed appropriately, it's a normal part of healthy relationships. I love how the poet Maya Angelou frames it. "Jealousy in romance is like salt in food. A little can enhance the savor, but too much can spoil the pleasure and, under certain circumstances, can be life-threatening."

Last, it's interesting to note that people who are more satisfied in their romantic relationships are *less* likely to be jealous about potential relationship threats; however, they are *more* likely to react negatively to actual relationship breaches.

Even after learning about these distinctions, it still feels hard to use the word "envious." Maybe it's because envy can have that hostility component? Also, I wonder if, unconsciously, we don't use the term because it's one of the "seven deadly sins," and two of the ten commandments are warnings against envy. *Is it in our upbringing and our culture to feel shame about feeling envy?*

Additionally, the term "jealous" has worked its way into our vocabulary in a way that can sound almost complimentary or admiring: "Your vacation pics are great. I'm so jealous!" And who can get mad when we use "jelly" for jealous—it's funny and sounds benign in a sticky-sweet way. *I love those shoes—I'm so jelly.* No one would wonder if you're thinking, *I want those, I don't want you to have those, and you're going down.*

Regardless of whether we choose to change our language or not, understanding the nuances of that language can help us ask ourselves the right questions when we're experiencing jealousy or envy. If we're feeling afraid or sad or angry or we're deep in "coveting mode"—we have the tools now to ask ourselves: *Am I fearful of losing something I value to another person, or do I want something someone else has? If I want something that someone else has, do I want to see them lose it, or is it not about that? If I'm scared I'm losing something important to me, what kind of conversation do I need to have with that person?*

# Resentment

Understanding **resentment**—how it works in my life, where it comes from, and how I stay out of it—has been one of my lifelong struggles. This is not something that's easy for me to share with you, because, on top of struggling with resentment, I'm judgmental toward my own resentment. Let me explain. We know from the research that *unwanted identity* is the most powerful elicitor of shame. If you want to know what's likely to trigger shame for you, just fill in this sentence stem: It's really important for me *not* to be perceived as _____.

"Resentful" and "bitter" are definitely on my list. So, I struggle with feeling resentment and I struggle with how struggling with resentment makes me feel.

For years, I assumed that resentment was a form of anger related to my perfectionism. I mostly felt resentful toward people whom I perceived to be not working or sacrificing or grinding or perfecting or advocating as hard as I was. You want to see me go into full-tilt resentment, just watch someone tell me, "Yeah. I stopped working on it—it's not exactly perfect, but it's good enough" or "I know it's due tomorrow, but I'm wiped out so I'm packing it in" or "I don't get involved in those issues—they really don't affect me."

Ugh. IT IS ON.

I've spent decades working on my perfectionism, and that helped, but resentment remained an issue. Then, all of a sudden, in one sentence—my life changed. I was interviewing the emotions researcher and writer Marc Brackett for our *Unlocking Us* podcast, and we were chatting before the actual recording started. Out of the blue, I said, "Before we start, I've got a personal question. Is resentment part of the anger family?"

Without hesitation, Marc replied, "No. Resentment is part of envy."

Oh, holy shit.

*I'm not mad because you're resting. I'm mad because I'm so bone tired and I want to rest. But, unlike you, I'm going to pretend that I don't need to.*

*I'm not furious that you're okay with something that's really good and imperfect. I'm furious because I want to be okay with something that's really good and imperfect.*

*Your lack of work is not making me resentful, my lack of rest is making me resentful.*

My life changed. Maybe it's unfair to say that it changed in one sentence because I've been curious and committed to figuring out my resentment for twenty-six years—maybe it's a case of "when the student is ready, the teacher appears." And why twenty-six years? Because I remember the moment I saw resentment in another person and thought, "Oh, no. She's so unlikable. So awful. But so painfully relatable. I don't want to be that person."

It was 1995, and I was alone at the movie theater watching *Home for the Holidays*. It's a funny, smart movie, directed by Jodie Foster, about adult children gathering at their parents' house on Thanksgiving Day. Two siblings, played by Holly Hunter and Robert Downey, Jr., are unconventional free spirits who have both moved away and maintained a close relationship. Then there's the sister, played brilliantly by Cynthia Stevenson, who never left, who takes care of the parents (more than they'd like), who is paralyzed by perfectionism, and whose rigidity makes her the brunt of family jokes. She's bitter and resentful and exhausted.

After dinner goes very wrong, and a turkey ends up in the perfect sister's lap, she and her obnoxiously uptight family leave. Then there's a scene when Cynthia Stevenson's character is in the basement of her house, working out on her StairMaster, and Holly Hunter's character comes over to apologize for Thanksgiving turning into a circus. The resentful sister goes off about how she's the only one who grew up and how the other two shirked all of the responsibilities that she now has to bear alone. After she says something really cruel to Holly Hunter's character, she looks down at her Stair-Master and signals for her sister to leave: "Do you mind? This is the only thing I do all day that I like."

*Yikes.* I don't think I've ever been that bad, but as I said, it was painfully relatable. And scary to think that I could even be on that trajectory. Now when I start to feel resentful, instead of thinking, *What is that person doing wrong?* or *What should they be doing?* I think, *What do I need but am afraid to ask for?* While resentment is definitely an emotion, I normally recognize it by a familiar thought pattern: *What mean and critical thing am I rehearsing saying to this person?*

**"**

While **resentment**
is definitely an emotion,
I normally recognize
it by a familiar
thought pattern:
*What mean and critical
thing am I rehearsing
saying to this person?*

Here's our definition:

**Resentment is the feeling of frustration, judgment, anger, "better than," and/or hidden envy related to perceived unfairness or injustice. It's an emotion that we often experience when we fail to set boundaries or ask for what we need, or when expectations let us down because they were based on things we can't control, like what other people think, what they feel, or how they're going to react.**

# Schadenfreude

**Schadenfreude** is a compound of the German words *schaden,* meaning harm, and *freude,* meaning joy. It's pronounced *sha-din-froy-da.* And the world is full of it these days. The German language is known for accurately capturing nuanced emotions, often with compound words that make the meaning very clear. **In the case of "schadenfreude," it simply means pleasure or joy derived from someone else's suffering or misfortune.**

All of us on the research team were confident that no English equivalent existed, and the articles we read seemed to agree; however, I recently read a piece in *The Irish Times* in which a reader made the argument that "epicaricacy" captures the same meaning. It means rejoicing at, taking fun in, or getting pleasure from the misfortune of others. The word is derived from the ancient Greek *epi* (upon), *kharis* (joy), and *kakos* (evil).

"Epicaricacy" is far less fun to say than "schadenfreude," and other than that article, I've never heard it used and can't even find it in most dictionaries.

"Schadenfreude," on the other hand, is a word I hear a lot. In an article in *The Wall Street Journal,* the reporter Ben Cohen explains, "It is an old German word whose usage in English dates to the 1850s, spiking in American publications after World War II but then fading, according to Google data. It returned nearly a half century later, some linguists say, because of a 1991 episode of *The Simpsons.*"

More recently the term made a guest appearance on *Ted Lasso* when one of the characters was rejoicing in another character's misfortune until Ted Lasso declared the office a "schadenfreude-free zone."

While schadenfreude may be fun to say and it's an increasingly used term in the United States, it's a tough emotion. There's a cruelty and insecurity about it. Taking pleasure in someone else's failings, even if that person is someone we really dislike, can violate our values and lead to feelings of guilt and shame. But, make no mistake, it's seductive, especially when we're sucked into groupthink.

It's easy to build counterfeit connection with collective schadenfreude. I say "counterfeit" because when we see someone who we don't like, we disagree with, or is outside our group stumble, fall, or fail, it's tempting to celebrate that suffering together and to stir up collective emotion. That kind of bonding might feel good for a moment, but nothing that celebrates the humiliation or pain of another person builds lasting connection.

> " Nothing that celebrates the **humiliation** or pain of another person builds lasting connection.

Schadenfreude involves counter-empathy—our emotional reaction is incongruent with another person's emotional experience. When someone else is suffering and we feel joy, there is decreased activity in the area of the brain that processes empathy and increased activity in the reward centers. In other words, when we feel schadenfreude, it shuts down the area of our brain that we use when feeling empathy and lights up the areas of the brain that make us feel good and that entice us to engage in similar behaviors in the future.

I think it's important to point out, especially in this political and social climate, that when we feel relieved, grateful, or even happy that someone who has done something hurtful, unethical, or unjust is held accountable, that's not schadenfreude and normally doesn't stem from counter-empathy. On the contrary, it can stem from empathy for the aggrieved. It's similar to the distinction that when we hold someone accountable and they respond to that accountability by feeling shame, it does *not* mean we've shamed them.

When we are relieved or happy to see someone held accountable for wrongdoing, we're not automatically celebrating their suffering, but more often we're grateful for the healing that accountability brings to those who have been affected by the wrongdoing.

Schadenfreude has trait-like properties, meaning that some people have a tendency to take greater pleasure in others' misfortune across a range of scenarios. It is positively correlated with envy, aggression, narcissism, and anger, and negatively correlated with empathy and conscientiousness.

We often don't talk about our schadenfreude because it can make us feel shame and/or guilt. This came up a lot during the pandemic when vaccinated people struggled with feeling outside their values over their schadenfreude toward antivaccination folks who were diagnosed with COVID. I wrestled with it myself. I remember thinking one day, *Is this who I want to be? Someone who celebrates people getting sick or dying—regardless of the circumstance?* I would justify it for a minute by thinking: *But they're threatening my health and the health of people I love.* In the end, I couldn't make it work with my values. But I'm still angry, and without a viable accountability strategy, it's hard not to let the shitty emotions take over.

Researchers Richard H. Smith and Wilco W. van Dijk grabbed my attention with this line about schadenfreude: It's "an emotion typically born out of inferiority rather than superiority." I would add that it doesn't always have to be about inferiority; schadenfreude is also born out of fear, powerlessness, and/or a sense of deservedness.

# Freudenfreude

**To end on a positive note, let's talk a little about freudenfreude, which is the opposite of schadenfreude—it's the enjoyment of another's success. It's also a subset of empathy.**

In a paper in *World Journal of Psychiatry and Mental Health Research,* the psychologist Catherine Chambliss examines the role that freudenfreude and schadenfreude play in depression. She writes, "When others report success to us, they generally hope for an empathic response of shared joy (Freudenfreude). If instead they get a negative, competitive reaction, they may respond with confusion, disappointment, irritation, or all three. Ongoing lack of Freudenfreude eventually can pose a fatal challenge to a relationship, and in turn, relationship failure often produces depression. We suspected that depressed folks might exhibit deficiencies in Freudenfreude."

I'm sharing this research with you because I think it's invaluable to understand. As Steve and I support our kids in learning how to cultivate meaningful connection with the people in their lives, we've always told them that good friends aren't afraid of your light. They never blow out your flame and you don't blow out theirs—even when it's really bright and it makes you worry about your own flame. When something good happens to you, they celebrate your flame. When something good happens to them, you celebrate their flame. To illustrate, we'd have our kids hold their hands out, palms flat and open, and say, "If this is your flame and the wind picks up, good friends cup their hands around your flame to prevent it from going out. And you do the same for them."

"No flame blower-outers" was our way of saying "more freudenfreude, less schadenfreude."

One last thing from this article: shoy and bragitude.

In an intervention designed by researchers to increase freudenfreude, they coined two new terms to describe behaviors that were very effective:

1.  Shoy: intentionally sharing the joy of someone relating a success story by showing interest and asking follow-up questions.

2.  Bragitude: intentionally tying words of gratitude toward the listener following discussion of personal successes.

I love these terms and the practical advice. When someone shares something great that's happened to them, we can show interest and ask questions. When someone demonstrates joy when we share ours, we can express gratitude: "Thank you for celebrating this with me. It means so much that you're happy for me."

Something about freudenfreude reminds me of a leadership lesson I learned in Abby Wambach's book *Wolfpack.* Abby is a two-time Olympic gold medalist soccer player and FIFA World Cup Champion. She was the United States' leading scorer in the 2007 and 2011 Women's World Cup tournaments and the 2004 and 2012 Olympics. In *Wolfpack,* Abby writes about the "Point and Run." She explains that every time she scored a goal, the first thing she would do is point to the person who made the assist or the coach who called the play. And the run was about celebrating another person's victory. She writes, "You will not always be the goal scorer. When you are not, you better be rushing toward her."

## #3

# Places We Go When Things Don't Go as Planned

Boredom, Disappointment, Expectations, Regret, Discouragement, Resignation, Frustration

# Boredom

**Boredom is the uncomfortable state of wanting to engage in satisfying activity, but being unable to do it.** When we're bored we experience a lack of stimulation, time seems to pass very slowly, and if we're working on tasks, they seem to lack challenge and meaning.

What's unique about boredom is that, depending on the situation, it can wind us up and leave us feeling irritable, frustrated, or restless, or, rather than getting us worked up, it can leave us feeling lethargic. When we have more control and autonomy over the boring tasks, it's more likely that boredom will leave us feeling lethargic. If we have little autonomy and control over the boring tasks, we are more likely to feel frustration.

This resonates with me. If I assign myself something to do and it's really boring, I normally end up mindlessly scrolling on social media. If, however, I'm asked to do something by someone else and it turns out to be boring, I can get really frustrated and irritated.

While most of us think of boredom as a negative feeling, it turns out that not all experiences of boredom are bad. In fact, if it weren't for boredom, you wouldn't be reading this book or any book by me. Let me explain the research first. A recent study showed that simple, boring tasks or mundane activities can allow our minds to wander, daydream, and create. The lack of stimulation that defines "being bored" gives our imagination room to play and grow.

A big part of my book writing routine is watching super predictable, formulaic mysteries—even ones I've seen ten times. These shows would bore me to tears if I were in a normal mental space. But when I'm coding data and writing, something weird happens. It's like the shows lull the easily distracted part of my brain into a rhythmic stupor, setting free the deeper, meaning-making part of my brain to engage and start making connections between things that don't seem connectable. I actually sit on my couch with a notepad next to me because the more bored I get, the more ideas bubble to the surface.

This has been my process for thirty years, which is why, from the time my kids were little, I never rushed to alleviate their boredom. If I could wait out the "I'm *soooo* bored" episodes, things would eventually turn quiet and I'd find them doing something really important, like daydreaming or creating. I've seen Ellen turn a boring day into a fully choreographed song and dance routine to the *Wicked* soundtrack, and Charlie go from "Ugh. I don't know what to do" to writing an illustrated book about rocks.

As researcher and writer Sherry Turkle says, "Boredom is your imagination calling to you."

## Disappointment and Regret

**Disappointment** and **regret** can range from mild discomfort to deep hurt. And, in my experience as a researcher and a human being, we underestimate both in terms of the disconnection and pain they can cause within us and in our relationships. Thankfully, there are tools and practices that can help us better understand what's behind these experiences and how to better set ourselves up for less hurt when possible.

66

# Boredom is your imagination calling to you.

— *Sherry Turkle*

**"**

Disappointment is **unmet expectations.** The more significant the expectations, the more significant the disappointment.

# Disappointment

**There are many definitions of disappointment, but this one emerged from our data and I think it's as clear and clean as it gets:**

**Disappointment is unmet expectations. The more significant the expectations, the more significant the disappointment.**

Because disappointment and regret are so interwoven into our experiences of vulnerability and shame, I talk about them to some degree in all of my books. For *Rising Strong,* I did a deep research dive into both because it's a book about the stories we tell ourselves when we're hurting, and you can bet that these emotions are often front and center in these narratives. With disappointment, it always starts with expectations. I've found two categories of expectations in my work: expectations that are unexamined and unexpressed (aka stealth expectations) and examined and expressed expectations.

## Unexamined and Unexpressed Expectations (aka Stealth Expectations)

Every day, sometimes every hour, we are consciously and unconsciously setting expectations of ourselves and the people in our lives—especially those closest to us. The unconscious, unexamined, and unexpressed expectations are the most dangerous and often turn into disappointment. In fact, the research tells us that disappointment is one of the most frequently experienced emotions, and it tends to be experienced at a high level of intensity. **When we develop expectations, we paint a picture in our head of how things are going to be and how they're going to look.** Sometimes we go so far as to imagine how they're going to feel, taste, and smell. That picture we paint in our minds holds great value for us. We set expectations based not only on how we fit in that picture, but also on what those around us are doing in that picture. This means that our expectations are often set on outcomes totally beyond our control, like what other people think, what they feel, or how they're going to react. The movie in our mind is wonderful, but no one else knows their parts, their lines, or what it means to us.

When the picture or movie fails to play out in real life, we feel disappointed. And sometimes that disappointment is severe and brings shame and hurt and anger with it. It's a setup for us and for the people involved. Disappointment takes a toll on us and our relationships. It requires considerable emotional bandwidth. Researcher Eliane Sommerfeld explains that we come away from the experience of disappointment feeling bad about ourselves and the other person. Our negativity is tinged with astonishment and surprise, and, at the same time we're trying to forgive, we're concealing emotions. We're trying to think positively and urging ourselves to move on. It's exhausting. I speak from experience. Here's a story that I shared in *Rising Strong.*

For Steve and me, stealth expectations and disappointment have been the sources of some of our most difficult arguments and hurt feelings. About ten years ago, we noticed a pattern where one of us would feel disappointment, resentment, and anger at the end of a weekend spent trying to jointly juggle our family's hectic soccer–birthday party–sleepover–school project schedules along with our own personal obligations.

It was so much easier when we were flying solo with the kids over the weekends—but how on earth could it be easier for Steve to hold down the fort when I'm out of town? Why is it simpler for me to navigate a busy weekend when he's out of town or on call at the hospital for hours on end? The arguments we had after we spent weekends together often ended with one of us feeling disappointed and angry, and slipping into blaming mode. Our frustration would turn into hurtful jabs: You're not helpful. You don't make it any easier. You just make it harder. *So painful.*

I finally said to Steve, "I'm tired of this argument about it being easier without the other one here. It totally hurts my feelings. I feel like I don't belong here. Something about the story we're telling ourselves is not true. I don't believe it." He confessed that it also hurt his feelings, so we started examining the patterns.

It took a lot of trial and error—and several near meltdowns—until Steve finally said, "When it's just me with the kids, I have no expectations for getting my own stuff done. I give up my to-do list so I can actually enjoy the craziness." It was that simple.

This fight was all about stealth expectations.

To this day, when I'm on my own for a weekend with the kids, I clear the expectations deck. Back then, however, when Steve and I were both home, we set all kinds of wild expectations about getting stuff done. What we never did was reality-check our expectations or make them explicit. We just tended to blame each other for our disappointment when our expectations weren't realized.

Now, before weekends, vacations, or even busy school or workweeks, we talk about expectations. We specifically ask each other, "What do you want this weekend to look like?"

I might say, "This is going to be a busy weekend. I'm down for whatever we need to do, but I would like to swim at least one day and play pickleball for a couple of hours on Saturday."

Steve might say, "Let's try to grab dinner, just the two of us, on Saturday night after we drop off Charlie. I'd like to play water polo for a couple of hours on Sunday. What time is pickleball?"

That doesn't mean stealth expectations no longer trip us up. They do. But now we help each other. We help each other reality-check our expectations, we ask each other a lot of questions about what we think will happen or what we want to happen, and we often ask ourselves and each other: *What's this about? What are you not saying?*

These are vulnerable conversations, but worth the discomfort. For example, with Steve, I want him to have a great weekend, and I know he feels the same way about me. I've learned that my expectations often come down to fear, a need for certainty, or a need for rest and play. It's just so hard to ask sometimes. But it doesn't stop me from expecting.

We're also trying to teach our kids how to reality-check, communicate, and dig into the intentions driving their expectations. We try to model the questions: *What expectations do you have going into this? What do you want to happen? Why? What will that mean to you? Do you have a movie in your head?* And in this perception-driven world, the big question is always: *Are you setting goals and expectations that are completely outside of your control?*

Unexamined and unexpressed expectations can also lead to serious disappointment at work. In *Dare to Lead,* I write about the power of "painting done." When I hand off an assignment at work, I will often say "Let me paint done"—and if I don't, you can be assured that the person on my team will say "I'm on it. But I need you to paint done."

"Painting done" means fully walking through my expectations of what the completed task will look like, including when it will be done, what I'll do with the information, how it will be used, the context, the consequences of not doing it, the costs—everything we can think of to paint a shared picture of the expectations. It's one of the most powerful tools we have.

Here are some other examples of unchecked and unexpressed expectations that came up in the research for *Rising Strong.*

**It's going to be a great holiday! I've got everything planned to the minute.** Is this a setup for success? What do you need from this gathering and why? Have you talked about your needs, or are you assuming everyone is on board? Have you shared your plans and talked about why they're important to you? Have you asked the other people what they want and need?

**My sister-in-law is going to love her gift and be so impressed with dinner.** You have no control over her response. None. Is there something you need for yourself or your relationship that a gift and dinner won't deliver? If there's no response, or a response that isn't what you expected, will you still feel good about buying the gift and preparing dinner?

**I can't wait to share my project presentation with the team tomorrow. They're going to be blown away and really appreciate how hard I've worked.** Is there a way to feel validated other than your team's saying something? It's dangerous to put your self-worth in other people's hands. Again, no matter what you do, you can't control other people's responses.

These are recipes for disappointment and hurt.

I know that asking for what we need and talking openly about our expectations is vulnerable. I'll pass on some advice that I got from a therapist early on in my marriage. I told this therapist that I was really pissed off because earlier that week, I had woken up on my birthday and there was nothing in the house celebrating my day. It was my first birthday after we were married and there were no signs taped to the wall or notes on the kitchen table—nothing. I told her that we did these kinds of things in my family and it really hurt my feelings that Steve didn't do it for me. I was sure it was because he was too busy in his residency.

The therapist asked me if I had shared my expectations with Steve, or explained to him how we did it in our family and asked him to celebrate with me that way because it meant a lot to me. I rolled my eyes and said, "If I have to ask, it's not worth it."

She tilted her head and said, "If you're not asking for what's important to you, maybe it's because you don't think *you* are worth it."

*Shut up. You don't know me. You're fired.*

Communicating our expectations is brave and vulnerable. And it builds meaningful connection and often leads to having a partner or friend who we can reality-check with. Steve and I still laugh about this one:

We were packing for spring break at Disney World when Steve, who was looking in my bag, said, "Babe, should we reality-check expectations for the week?"

Somewhat frustrated, I replied, "No. I think we're good, *babe.*"

Steve pointed to the three books I had stuffed into my carry-on bag and said, "Tell me about those."

As I started to explain that I wanted to sleep late, relax, and read some good mysteries over the course of our week away, I suddenly heard what I was saying. *Who am I kidding? We're going to be at Disney World with five kids for seven days!* The only thing I'd be reading was the sign that says YOU MUST BE THIS TALL TO RIDE. Sure enough, we were out the door by eight o'clock every morning of that vacation and I didn't read a thing, but we had a great time—once I had reality-checked my expectations with Steve's help.

## Examined and Expressed Expectations

Sometimes our expectations are realistic, clearly communicated, and self-aware. By "self-aware," I mean we're not unconsciously trying to get needs met without directly asking for what we need—we understand the *why* behind the expectation. When we are intentional and thoughtful about our expectations, and things don't turn out how we thought they would, disappointment still hurts. Potentially, a lot. One reason it can sting is precisely because we were vulnerable and asked for what we needed or shared what we were excited about.

Very early in my shame research, I interviewed a woman named Elizabeth. It's been fifteen years and I still think about her story.

After Elizabeth was told she was a "shoo-in" for a promotion in her office, she learned that she did not get the position. She said, "I was most ashamed because I'd told everyone how much it meant to me. I'd talked about it with everyone—my husband, my kids, my neighbors, my mom, my colleagues. It's not that I told everyone I was going to get it; I was so honest about how much I wanted it. Instead of just feeling sad and disappointed, I felt sad, disappointed, and ashamed."

When someone shares their hopes and dreams with us, we are witnessing deep courage and vulnerability. Celebrating their successes is easy, but when disappointment happens, it's an incredible opportunity for meaningful connection.

Think how powerful it might have been for Elizabeth to hear, "You had such courage to apply for that promotion and even more courage to be honest about how much you wanted it. I'm so proud to be your daughter/son/mentor/friend/parent."

When we've self-examined and shared expectations with someone and we feel they've let us down, it's important to keep the lines of communication open, circle back, and talk about our feelings and move to accountability. *"I let you know how important this was to me . . ."*

**"**

When someone shares their hopes and dreams with us, we are witnessing **deep courage** and **vulnerability.** Celebrating their successes is easy, but when **disappointment** happens, it's an incredible opportunity for meaningful connection.

There is research that shows that one way to minimize disappointment is to lower our expectations. True, optimism can sometimes lead to increased disappointment, and I believe these findings are accurate, but there is a middle path—a way to maintain expectations and stay optimistic—that requires more courage and vulnerability: Examine and express our expectations.

There are too many people in the world today who decide to *live* disappointed rather than risk *feeling* disappointment.

This can take the shape of numbing, foreboding joy, being cynical or critical, or just never really fully engaging. Sometimes, when I'm in one of those moods where I just want to pull the covers over my head and stay in bed—and there were many of those days during quarantine—I promise myself that I'm going to get less excited about things so I feel less disappointed. Then I always remember this interview I did with a man early on in my research. He was in his sixties, and I'll never forget how he looked at me when he said:

> I used to think the best way to go through life was to expect the worst. That way, if it happened, you were prepared, and if it didn't happen, you were pleasantly surprised. Then I was in a car accident and my wife was killed. Needless to say, expecting the worst didn't prepare me at all. And worse, I still grieve for all of those wonderful moments we shared and that I didn't fully enjoy. My commitment to her is to fully enjoy every moment now. I just wish she was here now that I know how to do that.

I don't like the vulnerability of leaning into good things, or the uncomfortable experience of examining and expressing my expectations. But I consider it more about discomfort than pain, which is what I heard in this man's voice.

I've heard people say that disappointment is like a paper cut—painful, but not long-lasting. I do believe we can heal disappointment, but it's important not to underestimate the damage it inflicts on our spirit. When I was researching *Daring Greatly,* I watched the magnificent Japanese animated film *Spirited Away,* written and directed by Hayao Miyazaki. There's a scene in the film where a young boy named Haku, who has taken the form of a dragon, is being attacked by a relentless swarm of birds. The attackers are actually

**"**

There are too many people in the world today who decide to **live** disappointed rather than risk **feeling** disappointment.

origami birds, and they cut into Haku, leaving him battered and bloodied. Disappointments may be like paper cuts, but if those cuts are deep enough or if we accumulate them over a lifetime, they can leave us seriously wounded. Yes, it takes courage to reality-check, communicate, and dig into the intentions behind our expectations, but that exercise in vulnerability helps us maintain meaningful connection with ourselves and others.

# Regret

**Both disappointment and regret arise when an outcome was not what we wanted, counted on, or thought would happen.** With disappointment, we often believe the outcome was out of our control (but we're learning more about how this is not always the case). **With regret, we believe the outcome was caused by our decisions or actions.**

Interestingly, research shows that in the short term, we tend to regret bad outcomes where we took action. However, when we reflect back over the long term, we more often regret the actions we didn't take—what we didn't do—and we think of those as missed opportunities.

As I reference in *Rising Strong,* I think one of the most powerful lines about regret comes from George Saunders's 2013 commencement address at Syracuse University.

Saunders talked about how when he was a child, a young girl was teased at his school and, although he didn't tease her and even defended her a little, he still thought about it. He said:

> So here's something I know to be true, although it's a little corny, and I don't quite know what to do with it: What I regret most in my life are failures of kindness. Those moments when another human being was there, in front of me, suffering, and I responded . . . sensibly. Reservedly. Mildly.

While a meta-analysis (a study of studies) focusing on regret indicates that approximately 90 percent of regrets fall into one of six categories: education, career, romance, parenting, self-improvement, and leisure, I've heard many research participants echo Saunders in regretting failures of kindness. I know that some of my own biggest regrets include failures of kindness, including failures of self-kindness.

While some people disagree with me, I firmly believe that regret is one of our most powerful emotional reminders that reflection, change, and growth are necessary. In our research, regret emerged as a function of empathy. And, when used constructively, it's a call to courage and a path toward wisdom.

The idea that regret is a fair but tough teacher can really piss people off. "No regrets" has become synonymous with daring and adventure, but I disagree. The idea of "no regrets" doesn't mean living with courage, it means living without reflection. To live without regret is to believe we have nothing to learn, no amends to make, and no opportunity to be braver with our lives.

One reason we may avoid regret is the fact that it can be accompanied by an element of self-blame and even guilt. Maybe we don't like the accountability that often comes with regret.

When I was writing *Rising Strong,* a friend of mine sent me a picture of a tough-looking kid who had NO RAGRETS tattooed across his chest. I later found out that the image was from the film *We're the Millers*. It's such a perfect metaphor for what I've learned: If you have no regrets, or you intentionally set out to live without regrets, I think you're missing the power of regret to teach us. In the film, a character played by Jason Sudeikis challenges the guy with the tattoo: "You have no regrets? Like not even a single letter?" So funny.

In our work, we find that what we regret most are our failures of courage, whether it's the courage to be kinder, to show up, to say how we feel, to set boundaries, to be good to ourselves, to say yes to something scary. Regret has taught me that living outside my values is not tenable for me.

Regrets about not taking chances have made me braver. Regrets about shaming or blaming people I care about have made me more thoughtful.

Sometimes the most uncomfortable learning is the most powerful.

# Discouraged, Resigned, and Frustrated

**Discouraged, resigned,** and **frustrated** are also ways that we feel when things aren't going or didn't go as desired.

Here's a simple way to think about the differences between some of the emotional experiences we have looked at in this chapter:

**Disappointed:** *It didn't work out how I wanted, and I believe the outcome was outside of my control.*

**Regretful:** *It didn't work out how I wanted, and the outcome was caused by my decisions, actions, or failure to act.*

**Discouraged:** *I'm* **losing** *my confidence and enthusiasm about any* **future** *effort—I'm losing the motivation and confidence to persist.*

**Resigned:** *I've* **lost** *my confidence and enthusiasm about any* **future** *effort—I've* **lost** *the motivation and confidence to persist.*

**Frustrated:** *Something that feels out of my control is preventing me from achieving my desired outcome.*

Things to note here:

Feeling discouraged and resigned is about effort rather than outcome. With discouragement, we're *losing* the motivation and confidence to continue with our efforts. With resignation, we've *lost* the motivation to keep trying.

Frustration sometimes overlaps with anger. Both anger and frustration can result when a desired outcome is blocked. The main difference is that with frustration, we don't think we can fix the situation, while with anger, we feel there is something we can do.

"

The idea of **'no regrets'** doesn't mean living with courage, it means living without reflection.
To live without regret is to believe we have nothing to learn, no amends to make, and no opportunity to be **braver with our lives.**

# #4

# Places We Go When It's Beyond Us

Awe, Wonder, Confusion, Curiosity, Interest, Surprise

# Awe and Wonder

If I had influence with the good fairy who is supposed to preside over the christening of all children, I should ask that her gift to each child in the world be a sense of wonder so indestructible that it would last throughout life, as an unfailing antidote against the boredom and disenchantments of later years, the sterile preoccupation with things that are artificial, the alienation from the sources of our strength.

— RACHEL CARSON, *The Sense of Wonder:*
*A Celebration of Nature for Parents and Children*

Both **awe** and **wonder** are often experienced in response to nature, art, music, spiritual experiences, or ideas. In the midst of these moments, we can feel overwhelmed by the vastness of something that is almost incomprehensible—it almost feels like what we're witnessing can't be true—like we're seeing something that doesn't fit with how we move through and understand our everyday lives.

Even seeing things we may fail to notice on a regular basis, like a starry sky or a butterfly in the garden, can stop us in our tracks on occasion. Both awe-inspiring events and the experiences that leave us filled with wonder often make us feel small compared to our expansive universe. Small, but connected to each other and to the largeness itself.

We often use "awe" and "wonder" interchangeably, which makes sense because as you can see, the experiences share a lot in common. But there is a primary difference between our experiences of these incredible emotions that's worth understanding. **I love how researchers Ulrich Weger and Johannes Wagemann explain it. They write, "Wonder inspires the wish to understand; awe inspires the wish to let shine, to acknowledge and to unite." When feeling awe, we tend to simply stand back and observe, "to provide a stage for the phenomenon to shine."**

Awe and wonder are essential to the human experience. **Wonder fuels our passion for exploration and learning, for curiosity and adventure.** Researchers have found that awe "leads people to cooperate, share resources, and sacrifice for others" and causes them "to fully appreciate the value of others and see themselves more accurately, evoking humility." Some researchers even believe that "awe-inducing events may be one of the fastest and most powerful methods of personal change and growth."

And we don't need to stand on a cliff and see the Northern Lights to feel awe or wonder—although this is absolutely on my bucket list. Sometimes I feel like my dog, Lucy, is staring into my soul and I feel a huge sense of wonder. How did I end up with an actual Ewok living in my house? How did this happen? It's unreal. And as a parent, simple moments with my children have rendered me speechless with awe. I thought this would change as they got older, but even with a sixteen-year-old and a twenty-two-year-old, the awe still takes my breath away on a regular basis.

# AWE

HOW IT *LOOKS*

HOW IT *FEELS*

WHAT IT *DOES* TO US

# WONDER

HOW IT *LOOKS*

HOW IT *FEELS*

WHAT IT *DOES* TO US

Comic art by GAVIN AUNG THAN

# Confusion

"I need time for my confusion." Confusion can be a cue that there's new territory to be explored or a fresh puzzle to be solved.

— ADAM GRANT, *Think Again:*
*The Power of Knowing What You Don't Know*

If I ever start a punk band—which is not out of the question—I've already nailed the name: The Zone of Optimal Confusion. It's perfect on so many levels.

The concept of *optimal confusion* is key to understanding why **confusion** is good for us and why it's categorized as an *epistemic emotion*—an emotion critical to knowledge acquisition and learning.

It turns out that confusion, like many uncomfortable things in life, is vital for learning. According to research, confusion has the potential to motivate, lead to deep learning, and trigger problem solving. A study led by Sidney D'Mello found that when we're trying to work through our confusion, we need to stop and think, engage in careful deliberation, develop a solution, and revise how we approach the next problem.

It doesn't sound like a big deal, but how often do we observe people (and ourselves) dismissing new data or information that challenges our ideas, in order to avoid confusion or the risk of being wrong? If you ask me, stopping to think, engaging in careful deliberation, and revising old thinking are rare and courageous actions. And they require dealing with a healthy dose of confusion. And that's uncomfortable.

In an article in *Fast Company,* Mary Slaughter and David Rock with the NeuroLeadership Institute write, "To be effective, learning needs to be *effortful.* That's not to say that anything that makes learning easier is counterproductive—or that all unpleasant learning is effective. The key here is *desirable difficulty.* The same way you feel a muscle 'burn' when it's being strengthened, the brain needs to feel some discomfort when it's learning. Your mind might hurt for a while—but that's a good thing." Comfortable learning environments rarely lead to deep learning.

So, we have "the zone of optimal confusion" and "desirable difficulty" (another great band name), but what happens when things get too confusing? Based on D'Mello's research, too much confusion can lead to frustration, giving up, disengagement, or even boredom. Learning strategies most often used to help resolve confusion were seeking help, finding the most important information, monitoring progress, and planning a strategy.

# Curiosity and Interest

I've done a lot of research on curiosity, starting with *Rising Strong* and most recently while working on *Dare to Lead*. It turns out that curiosity is an irreducible component of courageous leadership. Personally, understanding what it means to be curious and what gets in the way has rearranged how I parent, teach, and lead.

Curiosity and interest are both important parts of our need for meaning-making, but are they the same thing, or are they totally different experiences? It depends on whom you ask. Researchers don't agree—there's no consensus. However, in our research we found a clear distinction between how we use the words and what they mean to us.

Let's start by looking at some examples of how we use the words. We often say things like:

- I want my kids *to be* curious and *to show* interest.

- I'm looking for employees *who are* curious and *demonstrate* interest in our work.

- I value curiosity in a person.

- They show interest in the topic.

What starts to take shape, as we look at how we talk about these terms, is the difference between thinking and feeling, and between who we are and what we're doing.

Here's what emerged from our data:

**Curiosity** seems to be both a trait and a state. You can be a curious person and, regardless of having this trait or not, you can feel curious about something in the moment. **Interest** is more of a state ("interested" is not who we are but how we are at a specific time).

Curiosity seems to involve both feeling (emotion) and thinking (cognition), while interest is really more about thinking.

Definitions:

**Interest is a cognitive openness to engaging with a topic or experience.**

**Curiosity is recognizing a gap in our knowledge about something that interests us, and becoming emotionally and cognitively invested in closing that gap through exploration and learning. Curiosity often starts with interest and can range from mild curiosity to passionate investigation.**

In addition to the state and trait differences, the big things to understand here are the heart and head investments. With interest, our mind is open to seeing what's there, but with curiosity, we've acknowledged a gap in what we know or understand, and our heart and head are both invested in closing that gap. There is a thinking challenge and an emotional experience of the satisfaction or potential satisfaction of closing the gap.

In *Rising Strong,* I talk about George Loewenstein's groundbreaking 1994 article "The Psychology of Curiosity" and his introduction of the "information gap" perspective. Loewenstein, a professor of economics and psychology at Carnegie Mellon University, proposed that curiosity is the feeling of deprivation we experience when we identify and focus on a gap in our knowledge.

What's important about this perspective is that it means we have to have some level of knowledge or awareness before we can become curious. We aren't curious about something we are unaware of or know nothing about. This has huge implications for education. Loewenstein explains that simply encouraging people to ask questions doesn't go very far toward stimulating curiosity. He writes, "To induce curiosity about a particular topic, it may be necessary to 'prime the pump'"—to use intriguing information to get folks interested so they become more curious and to create opportunities for exposure to new ideas and experiences.

Curiosity doesn't exist without interest, but we can be interested and not have our interest grow to curiosity.

An increasing number of researchers believe that curiosity and knowledge building grow together—the more we know, the more we want to know.

Choosing to be curious is choosing to be vulnerable because it requires us to surrender to uncertainty. We have to ask questions, admit to not

> "
> Choosing to be **curious** is choosing to be vulnerable because it requires us to surrender to **uncertainty.** We have to ask questions, admit to not knowing, risk being told that we shouldn't be asking, and, sometimes, make discoveries that lead to **discomfort.**

knowing, risk being told that we shouldn't be asking, and, sometimes, make discoveries that lead to discomfort.

Our "childlike" curiosity is often tested as we grow up, and we sometimes learn that too much curiosity, like too much vulnerability, can lead to hurt. As a result, we turn to self-protection—choosing certainty over curiosity, armor over vulnerability, knowing over learning. But shutting down comes with a price—a price we rarely consider when we're focused on finding our way out of pain.

Einstein said, "The important thing is not to stop questioning. Curiosity has its own reason for existence." Curiosity's reason for existing is not simply to be a tool for acquiring knowledge; it reminds us that we're alive. Researchers are finding evidence that curiosity is correlated with creativity, intelligence, improved learning and memory, and problem solving.

# Surprise

**Similar to findings by researchers Sascha Topolinski and Fritz Strack, my team and I define surprise as an interruption caused by information that doesn't fit with our current understanding or expectations. It causes us to reevaluate.**

We can think of surprise as "a bridge between cognition and emotion." But it's a short bridge! Surprise is the shortest-duration emotion, rarely lasting more than a few seconds.

In addition to being a short bridge, surprise is also an amplifier. Once our thinking brain works out the unexpected thing that's happening, we move into emotion. There's evidence that surprise amplifies subsequent emotion, with more surprising events resulting in stronger emotional reactions.

SPOILER SPOILER ALERT: I'm pretty sure this research explains why I do *not* like surprises. I'm not a fan of having to manage amplified emotion while in the spotlight. But it's not just my introversion and the spotlight piece, I don't like surprises in movies or TV series either. I know many of y'all will find this egregious, but I normally read the entire plot of any potentially stressful movie before I watch it. People assume that ruins it for me, but it doesn't. I can actually enjoy it better without being thrown off the surprise bridge into amplified emotion. No, thank you.

However, I do understand why the research shows that surprising news is more likely to be shared, surprising advertisements are more likely to be noticed, and people are more likely to return to a restaurant that was surprisingly better than expected. If I find a restaurant or a product that is surprisingly great, I'll talk about it to anyone who will listen.

There's a strong relationship between **surprise** and **unexpectedness**. In fact, several of the definitions of "surprise" use the word "unexpected." However, in our lived experience, we don't use the words synonymously. We normally use "surprise" for experiences that link quickly to emotion. When we use the term "unexpected," the experience starts with thinking (just like surprise), but it often stays cognitive rather than bridging to emotion.

As you can see, "unexpected" doesn't convey emotion the way "surprise" does!

Comic art by GAVIN AUNG THAN

67

# #5

# Places We Go When Things Aren't What They Seem

Amusement, Bittersweetness, Nostalgia, Cognitive Dissonance, Paradox, Irony, Sarcasm

**What happens when we feel two competing emotions at the same time?**

**Can two seemingly contradictory thoughts both be true?**

Welcome to being human! Competing emotions and contradictory thoughts are messy and can feel uncomfortable, vulnerable, even irritating. But it's important to remember that this push-pull is a reflection of our complexity, and if we're willing to stay with it and stay curious, complexity is one of our greatest teachers.

The problem starts when we don't have the skills or experience to tolerate the uncertainty and ambiguity and we give in to the cravings for neat, mutually exclusive categories. There's nothing more limiting than tapping out of tension and oversimplifying the thoughts and feelings that have the power to help us understand who we are and what we need.

Adam Grant has been the top-rated professor at the Wharton School of the University of Pennsylvania for seven years. As an organizational psychologist, he is a leading expert on how we can find motivation and meaning, and live more generous and creative lives. Adam is a number one *New York Times* bestselling writer, and his latest book, *Think Again: The Power of Knowing What You Don't Know,* might be my new favorite.

I love talking to, learning from, and debating with Adam. We've been on each other's podcasts and it's always fun. You can hear our brains grinding over the airwaves.

In *Think Again,* Adam writes about the problem of oversimplifying and the importance of complexity:

> As consumers of information, we have a role to play in embracing a more nuanced point of view. When we're reading, listening, or watching, we can learn to recognize complexity as a signal of credibility. We can favor content and sources that present many sides of an issue rather than just one or two. When we come across simplifying headlines, we can fight our tendency to accept binaries by asking what additional perspectives are missing between the extremes.

"

There's nothing more limiting than tapping out of tension and oversimplifying the **thoughts** and **feelings** that have the power to help us **understand who we are** and what we need.

This applies when we're the ones producing and communicating information, too. New research suggests that when journalists acknowledge the uncertainties around facts on complex issues like climate change and immigration, it doesn't undermine their readers' trust. And multiple experiments have shown that when experts express doubt, they become more persuasive. When someone knowledgeable admits uncertainty, it surprises people, and they end up paying more attention to the substance of the argument.

While Adam didn't write this about our emotions, thoughts, and behaviors, the same wisdom applies. When we gather information from our emotions, thoughts, and behaviors, especially the layered, messy ones, the tension can serve us. When we're communicating our feelings and thoughts to ourselves and others, we might want to consider sharing our uncertainties.

When someone tells me, "I'm not sure how I feel. I'm sad, but weirdly I'm also relieved"—my first thought isn't *Yikes. They have no idea how they feel!* Or *Hmmm, they don't have a lot of self-awareness.* My first thought is normally *Oh, man. I get that, and I get how those feelings can coexist. That makes sense.* The uncertainty feels like self-awareness to me.

When someone tells me, "Well, I'm not sure what I think about that policy. I used to be a fierce proponent of it, but I'm learning more and I'm not as sure as I used to be"—my first thought isn't *What a flip-flopper!* My first thought is normally *Wow. That's rare. What are you learning? I'm curious.* Again, it's counterintuitive, but acknowledging uncertainty is a function of grounded confidence, and it feels like humility to me.

# Amusement

The etymology of "amusement" is interesting. The word dates from the late 1500s, when it meant a pleasurable diversion from work or duty.

According to researchers, amusement is connected to humor and includes elements of unexpectedness, incongruity, and playfulness. It's typically seen as a brief spike in a person's level of cheerfulness, lasting only a few seconds. **The definition of amusement that aligns with our research is "pleasurable, relaxed excitation."** Amusement differs from happiness in that happiness is a general sense of pleasure, whereas amusement appeals specifically to one's sense of humor.

There are two themes that clearly help distinguish amusement from other positive emotions, like contentment, gratitude, interest, joy, love, or pride:

1. An awareness of incongruity (there's something unexpected about what causes us to be amused—we weren't expecting that punch line or that behavior or that timing);

2. When we feel amusement, we feel playful with those around us.

Is amusement important at work? Research shows that breaks involving amusement may help replenish depleted cognitive resources, and that the replenishment continues through difficult tasks.

After reading the research on amusement, I started thinking about how people say "I did *not* find that amusing," and why it's sometimes said in a judgmental voice.

I don't have any data to support this supposition, but I wonder if what we're saying is "That unexpected thing that you did or said that was supposed to be funny was not funny." It's almost like *You failed at your attempt to be funny. That was neither playful nor pleasurable.* It takes me straight back to my parents reading a note from my teacher and me trying to make a joke about what really happened in the classroom. I can still hear my mom saying, "I'm not amused."

# Bittersweet

The bittersweet side of appreciating life's most precious moments is the unbearable awareness that those moments are passing.

— MARC PARENT, *Believing It All*

**Bittersweet is a mixed feeling of happiness and sadness.** As someone who feels bittersweet about a lot of things—especially related to Ellen and Charlie—I was curious about this emotion. With very few exceptions, developmental milestones leave me feeling bittersweet. I'm proud of Ellen and excited about her new apartment in a different city, and I share Charlie's happiness about his new driver's license, but I'm also sad when I walk by Ellen's room in our house, and I'm sad that I don't get to drive Charlie and his friends to school every morning (which is when you overhear the best conversations).

I asked folks across my social media channels to share some examples of experiences that felt bittersweet for them, and we received more than forty thousand beautiful, heartfelt comments. I don't think I was fully aware of the depth of humanity that lives in the curves of this emotion. Here are some of the most commonly shared experiences and a few notes on the context:

- Watching children grow up
- Leaving a job
- Divorce/Ending a relationship
- Graduating
- Letting go of friendships that aren't working
- Moving
- Death of a loved one
- Teachers watching students graduate
- Retiring
- Coming home from vacation

# "

The **bittersweet** side of appreciating life's most precious moments is the unbearable awareness that those moments are passing.

— *Marc Parent*

What all of the comments have in common is sadness about letting go of something, mixed with happiness and/or gratitude about what's been experienced and/or what's next.

Several things that are important to keep in mind about feeling bittersweet:

- It's not the same as ambivalence (when we're unsure whether we're happy or sad), it's feeling both at the same time.

- One line of research indicates that multiple emotions, such as happiness and sadness, may be rapidly vacillating below our consciousness, but our interpretation may be a more integrated emotional experience.

- It's possible that feeling bittersweet may be more frequently experienced or recognized by people who have a more nuanced ability to interpret their emotional states.

- Developmental research shows that the experience of mixed emotion is not present in very young children, and that it develops gradually. At around age seven or eight, children report experiencing positive and negative emotions simultaneously, and by age ten or eleven, they can recognize and understand the tension caused by experiencing mixed emotions.

# Nostalgia

There's nothing wrong with celebrating the good things in our past. But memories, like witnesses, do not always tell the truth, the whole truth, and nothing but the truth. We need to cross-examine them, recognizing and accepting the inconsistencies and gaps in those that make us proud and happy as well as those that cause us pain.

— STEPHANIE COONTZ, historian

The term "nostalgia" has a dark past, and I'm not so sure there's a consensus about the term today.

Adrienne Matei, a Vancouver-based journalist and editor, has written a brilliant essay on the history and global translation of the word. Matei explains:

> In the late 1600s, Swiss medical student Johannes Hofer noticed a pattern in his patients who were living far from home. Those who were obsessed with returning to their estranged locations became physically, sometimes fatally, sick. To reflect this phenomen[on], he coined the medical term "nostalgia" in 1688, which he created by combining the Greek words *nostos* (homecoming) and *alga* (pain).
>
> The disease's reported symptoms included loss of appetite, fainting, heightened suicide risk, and, according to Swiss doctor Albert Van Holler, hallucinations of the people and places you miss. . . . It ran so rampant among Swiss mercenaries fighting far-flung wars that playing "Khue-Reyen"—an old Swiss milking song that seemed to send soldiers into a contagiously nostalgic frenzy—was punishable by death.

Matei goes on to explain how cures for nostalgia included being burned with a hot poker and punishments included being buried alive. As I mentioned, it's a powerful essay, and I encourage you to read it—you can find the link in the notes section.

Nostalgia was considered a medical disease and a psychiatric disorder until the early nineteenth century. Today, researchers describe **nostalgia** as a frequent, primarily positive, context-specific bittersweet emotion that combines elements of happiness and sadness with a sense of yearning and loss. The researchers also tell us that feeling nostalgic involves putting ourselves at the center of a story in which we're reminiscing about people we are close to or about important events in our lives. Interestingly, nostalgia is more likely to be triggered by negative moods, like loneliness, and by our struggles to find meaning in our current lives.

There is some research that shows that nostalgia can serve us psychologically, by increasing positive feelings and helping us "navigate successfully the vicissitudes of daily life." I don't doubt that the bittersweet recalling or romanticizing of our history can relieve pain or help us deal with the hard parts of life, but at what cost?

Across our research, nostalgia emerged as a double-edged sword, a tool for both connection and disconnection. It can be an imaginary refuge from a world we don't understand and a dog whistle used to resist important growth in families, organizations, and the broader culture and to protect power, including white supremacy.

What's spoken: *I wish things were the way they used to be in the good ol' days.*

What's not spoken: *When people knew their places.*

What's not spoken: *When there was no accountability for the way my behaviors affect other people.*

What's not spoken: *When we ignored other people's pain if it caused us discomfort.*

What's not spoken: *When my authority was absolute and never challenged.*

So, is nostalgia good, helpful, bad, dangerous, or detrimental? The answer is yes. Which is why we're lucky to have this fascinating research from Sandra Garrido.

Garrido presents evidence that nostalgia can be a part of both healthy and unhealthy coping strategies, depending on an individual's personality and coping style. In her study, she found that for individuals who are prone to depression or rumination, nostalgia tends to be associated with negative emotional outcomes.

The level of divisiveness, uncertainty, and anxiety in the world today leads a lot of us to struggle with **rumination,** which Garrido explains is an "involuntary focus on negative and pessimistic thoughts." It's important to note that she also differentiates rumination from **reflection,** which is "highly adaptive and psychologically healthy."

Rumination is also different from worry. According to researchers, worry is focused on the future, while rumination focuses on the past or on things about ourselves that we're stuck on.

Researchers believe that rumination is a strong predictor of depression, makes us more likely to pay attention to negative things, and zaps our motivation to do things that would improve how we feel.

This combination of rumination and nostalgia emerged from our research as destructive and disconnecting. If you're wondering how dangerous the combination can be, think back to the insurrection at the U.S. Capitol on January 6, 2021, or examine the strategy used by every authoritarian leader in history: Exploit fears by photoshopping a picture of yesteryear to be everything people wanted it to be (but never was), seduce people into believing that a make-believe past could exist again, and give them someone to blame for ruining the picture and/or not being able to restore the mythical utopia.

Stephanie Coontz, whose quote opens this section, explains that it's important to reality-check our nostalgic ideas by uncovering and examining the tradeoffs and contradictions that are often deeply buried in all of our memories. *Were the comfort and safety of that past existence real? If so, were they at someone else's expense?*

**We define nostalgia as a yearning for the way things used to be in our often idealized and self-protective version of the past.**

# Cognitive Dissonance

My favorite book on cognitive dissonance is *Mistakes Were Made (but Not by Me): Why We Justify Foolish Beliefs, Bad Decisions, and Hurtful Acts* by Carol Tavris and Elliot Aronson. Talk about feeling called out! I learned a ton about how we put a spit shine on almost everything we do and remember. Or, as Aronson wrote in a more recent book, how "human beings engage in all kinds of cognitive gymnastics aimed at justifying their own behavior."

The Tavris and Aronson book's dedication reads: "For Leon Festinger, creator of the theory of cognitive dissonance, whose ingenuity inspired this book."

Before we jump in, I want to share an abbreviated version of a story about Festinger from their book. When I first read this story, it felt impossible to believe. After surviving the past five years in the United States, it now feels sadly plausible. We see these double-down behaviors every day, especially in the antiscience movement.

Tavris and Aronson explain that in 1954, the social psychologist Leon Festinger and two associates infiltrated a doomsday cult to find out what would happen when the leader's prophecy failed to be fulfilled. The leader had promised her followers that the world would end on December 21, 1954, but that they would be picked up by a flying saucer and transported to safety at midnight on December 20. Tavris and Aronson explained, "Many of her followers quit their jobs, gave away their houses, and disbursed their savings in anticipation of the end. Who needs money in outer space? Others waited in fear or resignation in their homes."

Festinger predicted that "the believers who had not made a strong commitment to the prophecy . . . would quietly lose their faith" in the leader when the world didn't end, and "those who had given away their possessions and waited with other believers for the spaceship" would double down on their belief in her mystical abilities. He predicted that even if the prophecy did not materialize, the followers who lost the most would demonstrate their increased commitment by doing "whatever they could to get others to join them." At the time, this hypothesis blew the doors off every existing theory about motivation and human behavior. It was unthinkable that people would double down once proven wrong.

But by 4:45 a.m., when the spaceship was a no-show, their leader shared a new vision of the world: Because of their strong faith, they had been spared. As hypothesized by Festinger, the most invested members responded by calling the media with the great news, and they became even more invested evangelists for the group.

Luckily, the doomsday leader's prediction failed, but Festinger's prediction didn't, and he changed the way we think about human behavior. Tavris and Aronson write:

> The engine that drives self-justification, the energy that produces the need to justify our actions and decisions—especially the wrong ones—is the unpleasant feeling that Festinger called "cognitive dissonance." **Cognitive dissonance is a state of tension that occurs when a person holds two cognitions (ideas, attitudes, beliefs, opinions) that are psychologically inconsistent with each other,** such as "Smoking is a dumb thing to do because it could kill me" and "I smoke two packs a day." Dissonance produces mental discomfort that ranges from minor pangs to deep anguish; people don't rest easy until they find a way to reduce it. In this example, the most direct way for a smoker to reduce dissonance is by quitting. But if she has tried to quit and failed, now she must reduce dissonance by convincing herself that smoking isn't really so harmful, that smoking is worth the risk because it helps her relax or prevents her from gaining weight (after all, obesity is a health risk too), and so on. Most smokers manage to reduce dissonance in many such ingenious, if self-deluding, ways.
>
> Dissonance is disquieting because to hold two ideas that contradict each other is to flirt with absurdity, and, as Albert Camus observed, we are creatures who spend our lives trying to convince ourselves that our existence is not absurd. At the heart of it, Festinger's theory is about how people strive to make sense out of contradictory ideas and lead lives that are, at least in their own minds, consistent and meaningful. The theory inspired more than three thousand experiments that, taken together, have transformed psychologists' understanding of how the human mind works.

When we're faced with information that challenges what we believe, our first instinct is to make the discomfort, irritation, and vulnerability go away by resolving the dissonance. We might do this by rejecting the new information, decreasing its importance, or avoiding it altogether. "The greater the magnitude of the dissonance, the greater is the pressure to reduce dissonance."

In these challenging moments of dissonance, we need to stay curious and resist choosing comfort over courage. It's brave to invite new information to the table, to sit with it and hear it out. It's also rare these days.

As Adam Grant writes, "Intelligence is traditionally viewed as the ability to think and learn. Yet in a turbulent world, there's another set of cognitive skills that might matter more: the ability to rethink and unlearn."

# Paradox

> The paradox is one of our most valuable spiritual possessions . . . only the paradox comes anywhere near to comprehending the fullness of life.
>
> — CARL JUNG

While cognitive dissonance pushes us to resolve the tension of conflicting information, **paradox** challenges us to straddle the tension of two conflicting elements and recognize that they can both be true. From its Greek origins, the term "paradox" is the joining of two words, *para* (contrary to) and *dokein* (opinion). The Latin term *paradoxum* means "seemingly absurd but really true."

**A paradox is the appearance of contradiction between two related components.** Although light and darkness seem to be opposites, you can't have one without the other—the opposing elements of a paradox are inextricably linked. Even though the elements seem contradictory, they actually complement and inform each other in ways that allow us to discover underlying truths about ourselves and the world.

Here's an example of a paradox from my work:

*Vulnerability is the first thing we look for in other people, and the last thing we want to show them about ourselves.*

"

In these challenging moments of dissonance, we need to stay **curious** and resist choosing **comfort** over **courage.** It's brave to invite new information to the table, to sit with it and hear it out. It's also rare these days.

How can both of those statements be true? If we dig into the tension of that statement, it reveals truths about us:

- We're drawn to authentic, imperfect people, but we're scared to let people see who we really are.

- I want to experience your vulnerability, but I don't want to be vulnerable.

- Vulnerability is courage in you and inadequacy in me.

- I'm drawn to your vulnerability but repelled by mine.

Embracing the paradox teaches us how to think deeper and with more complexity. It invites us to reality-check the validity of the statements above. It moves us away from oversimplifying how systems, organizations, and humans work.

Paradox is not an emotion. Much like cognitive dissonance, it starts with thinking but brings in emotion as we start to feel the tension and pull of different ideas. In the case of paradox, our brain wants to solve the puzzle. However, paradoxes can't be fully resolved using rationality and logic—we need to allow the seeming contradictions to coexist in order to gain deeper understanding. In this way, paradoxes force us to think in expansive ways and lean into vulnerability.

About 90 percent of the work I do these days is in organizations, working with leaders. The idea of embracing paradox has been fundamental to building organizational cultures for at least two decades now. In Jim Collins and Bill Lazier's book *BE (Beyond Entrepreneurship) 2.0,* Jim writes,

> False dichotomies are undisciplined thought. In the words of F. Scott Fitzgerald, "The test of a first-rate intelligence is the ability to hold two opposed ideas in the mind at the same time, and still retain the ability to function." Builders of greatness are comfortable with paradox. They don't oppress themselves with what we call the "Tyranny of the OR," which pushes people to believe that things must be either A OR B, but not both. Instead, they liberate themselves with the "Genius of the AND." Undisciplined thinkers force debates

into stark "Tyranny of the OR" choices; disciplined thinkers expand the conversation to create "Genius of the AND" solutions. In our research, we found myriad permutations of "Genius of the AND" dualities. For example:

Creativity AND Discipline

Innovation AND Execution

Humility AND Audacity

Freedom AND Responsibility

In line with Jim's argument, a large body of research shows that rejecting paradox can result in conflict and turmoil. Conversely, engaging with a paradox and accepting the competing elements as both valid can foster creativity, innovation, and productivity.

Paradoxes: hard and good.

# Irony and Sarcasm

I don't love putting these two words together. *My attempt at sarcasm.*

I don't like going on the record about knowing the difference between sarcasm and irony because it means I can't defend my clever use of sarcasm by saying "I was just being ironic." *My attempt at irony.*

**Irony and sarcasm are forms of communication in which the literal meaning of the words is different, often opposite, from the intended message. In both irony and sarcasm, there may be an element of criticism and humor. However, sarcasm is a particular type of irony in which the underlying message is normally meant to ridicule, tease, or criticize.**

Both irony and sarcasm are easily misunderstood, especially when you're talking to someone you don't know well, when there's already some heightened emotion in the exchange, or when you're emailing or texting.

As explained in an overview of neurological findings related to irony and sarcasm, "researchers suggest that the successful comprehension of irony depends on the perceiver's ability to infer other people's mental states, thoughts, and feelings." Which is exceptionally difficult over text and email.

Research on intent behind delivery of sarcastic communication has been mixed, with some studies indicating that sarcasm is intended to soften the blow and other research showing that sarcasm is intended to be more hurtful than direct criticism. Recipients of sarcastic communication have varying interpretations of intent, which do not always map onto the intended meaning.

One of the things that I learned early in my work is the developmental requirements for understanding irony and sarcasm. While we sometimes think of our kids as being more than capable of sarcasm, the research tells us that understanding the subtleties of irony and sarcasm is a developmental process that involves coordination of multiple brain areas. According to Ruth Filik and her colleagues, "children do not seem to distinguish between irony and sarcasm until the age of nine or ten, when they master second-order mental state reasoning." Another group of researchers finds that "Although middle-school-age children can correctly discern the sarcastic speaker's meaning and attitude, appreciation of sarcasm's humor develops through adolescence," and development of full understanding of the nuances of both communication styles continues into adulthood.

I was raised in a family where sarcasm was confused with intellectual ability and craft. When I was a kid, there were many instances when teasing and sarcasm were too hurtful or went too far or went on for too long. I remember reading when I was pregnant with Ellen that the word "sarcasm" comes from a Greek word meaning "to tear flesh." We didn't do it perfectly, but Steve and I set an intention to watch our use of sarcasm around and with the kids. It can go wrong too quickly and often ends up in shame and tears.

I will confess, however, that my dear friend Chaz and I can have so much fun with each other while trading ironic and sarcastic comments. When I read that these behaviors can sometimes enhance close relationships and highlight closeness, I wasn't surprised. We've been friends for more than thirty years, and the verbal sparring is great fun. I asked him why he thinks it works, and we agreed that we're very careful and don't use sarcasm and irony to express emotions and thoughts that we're afraid to talk about. We have plenty of hard conversations, and we're diligent about not weaponizing words. Sarcasm and irony are reserved for playfulness only.

I think that's the biggest watch-out with irony and sarcasm: *Are you dressing something up in humor that actually requires clarity and honesty?*

# #6

# Places We Go When We're Hurting

Anguish, Hopelessness, Despair, Sadness, Grief

# Anguish

Anguish . . . It's one of those words you understand the meaning of just by the way that it sounds. It has this gnarling rasp to it as you twist your mouth around to say it . . . kind of like what feeling it does to your insides. It's an awful, drawn out, knotted up word. It's also one of the things I feel without you.

— RANATA SUZUKI

Poets, artists, and writers approach the topic of anguish without apology, often capturing it in a way that leaves us with a sense of shock, heartbreak, and foreboding. We may not be clear on what we're seeing or reading or hearing, but we are certain that we don't want to move in closer, we don't want to know or relive that emotion, that experience.

This painting by August Friedrich Albrecht Schenck hangs in the National Gallery of Victoria in Melbourne, Australia. While little is known about its artist, it has twice been voted one of the NGV's most popular works—first in 1906 and then again a century later in 2011. The pained mother surrounded by a murder of crows is hard to take in.

On the other end of the art-and-science spectrum, social science researchers seem to steer clear of the concept of anguish altogether. Many study around the construct, while others put it on a continuum that includes less extreme emotions like sadness. Yet what emerged from my work is that anguish is an emotion and an experience that is singular and must be understood and named, especially for those of us who have experienced it, will experience it, or may bear witness to it.

**Anguish is an almost unbearable and traumatic swirl of shock, incredulity, grief, and powerlessness.** Shock and incredulity can take our breath away, and grief and powerlessness often come for our hearts and our minds. But anguish, the combination of these experiences, not only takes away our ability to breathe, feel, and think—it comes for our bones. Anguish often causes us to physically crumple in on ourselves, literally bringing us to our knees or forcing us all the way to the ground.

The element of powerlessness is what makes anguish traumatic. We are unable to change, reverse, or negotiate what has happened. And even in those situations where we can temporarily reroute anguish with to-do lists and tasks, it finds its way back to us.

About ten years ago, I received a call from someone I love very much. In the span of ninety seconds, they shared that they had spent the night contemplating suicide, then disclosed a major trauma that I did not know about—a violence that tore through my memories and reorganized my history and my life. I was standing on a sidewalk outside my church when I took the call. The kids had run inside to find friends, and Steve was a few feet in front of me, watching me after I said, "I wonder why this person is calling so early on a Sunday—I better answer it." As I listened, I dropped my purse so I could brace myself against the wall, clenching my cellphone in the other hand and sliding down the brick wall. Pure anguish.

After helping me stagger to the car, Steve got the kids from inside the church and drove me home. For months, it was a dance of desperate attempts to fix, change, and help, followed by more anguish. Then ultimately I got help.

Today, a decade later, I no longer fall to the ground when I think about that call, but it still evokes anguish and I am not the same. I'm still me at my

**" Anguish** not only takes away our ability to breathe, feel, and think—it comes for our bones. Anguish often causes us to **physically crumple** in on ourselves, literally bringing us to our knees or forcing us all the way to the ground.

The element of powerlessness is what makes anguish

traumatic. We are unable to change, reverse, or negotiate what has happened. And even in those situations where we can temporarily reroute anguish with to-do lists and tasks, it finds its way back to us.

core, but it took time and help and processing for the bones to come back, and they're slightly different than they were before.

Another example comes from a story that a graduate student named Gabriella shared with me several years ago when we were talking about my research and the experience of anguish. Gabi told the story of being in high school and spending the weekend helping her best friend, Carmen, prepare for her quinceañera. A quinceañera is a coming-of-age celebration in many Latinx communities. It's a special milestone for girls who are turning fifteen (*quince* in Spanish). The celebration often starts with a religious service followed by a party. These gatherings range from small get-togethers in the girl's home to huge parties in hotel ballrooms. Sometimes there are even "courts," which are similar to bridal parties.

Gabi and Carmen had been best friends since middle school, and Gabi wanted to be by Carmen's side for what she knew would be an emotional weekend. Carmen's mother had died of ovarian cancer when Carmen was twelve. Gabi told me that she was pretty sure that if it had been up to Carmen, she would have skipped the quinceañera, but Carmen's family insisted.

The night before the celebration, Carmen and Gabi were in Carmen's room, sitting on the bed texting with friends. They heard a quiet knock on the door—it was Carmen's dad, accompanied by her older brother and her older sister. Gabi could tell by the look on their faces that something serious was happening. Carmen's father stopped at the door, and her brother and sister gently pushed past him until they were standing just inside the room. Carmen stood up and looked at her father, who had one foot in her room and one foot in the hall.

He looked unsure, and this made Carmen visibly nervous. "What is it, Papa?" she asked. Her father, eyes cast down and hands slightly trembling, handed Carmen a wooden box. Carmen held the box, nervously looking at her father and her siblings.

Her sister said, "Open it, Carmen. It's okay." Carmen gave Gabi a knowing look, and then opened the box. In it was the tiara that her mother and her sister had worn at their quinceañeras. Both Carmen and Gabi had been expecting this moment, and they both felt relieved that it had arrived and would soon be past. They had even talked through what to say and how to act with Carmen's father, who Carmen guessed would be in tears.

But then, unexpectedly, Carmen's father handed Carmen an envelope.

Carmen's father could barely speak: "Your mother wrote you this note the week before she died. She wanted you to open it the day before your quinceañera." Carmen grabbed the letter and immediately fell to the floor.

Gabi said, "She just sank. And moaned. It was like she was being hurt and sucked into the ground."

Before Gabi could understand what was happening, Carmen's brother and her sister had both dropped to their knees and were also on the floor, crying and burying their heads in their hands. Carmen's father held on to the door frame for a minute but ended up on the floor with his children.

Gabi and I talked about how what we think is a familiar grief—a grief we've come to know and understand and even integrate into our lives—can surprise us again and again, often in the form of anguish. This is especially true when something sparks shock and incredulity in us, like the letter that Carmen's mother had written to her.


It's often hard to find our way back into our bodies after experiencing anguish. This is why so much effective trauma work today is not only about reclaiming our breath, our feelings, and our thinking, but also getting our bones back and returning to our bodies.

When we experience anguish and we don't get help or support, we can find it difficult to get up off the floor and reengage with our lives. We go through the motions, but we are still crumpled. I tried doing that for several months until I realized that I needed to talk with someone to help process that phone call and my anguish.

There is another alternative to not addressing the trauma of anguish—we can convince ourselves that we're okay and keep ourselves upright by hanging our crumpling anguish on rigidity and perfectionism and silence, like a wet towel hanging on a rod. We can become closed off, never open to vulnerability and its gifts, and barely existing because anything at any moment could threaten that fragile, rigid scaffolding that's holding up our crumpling selves and keeping us standing.

The human spirit is resilient, and just as we can reclaim our ability to breathe and feel and think, we can rebuild the bones that anguish rips away. But it takes help and time.

I don't remember when or where I first saw *Dark Elegy,* but I knew then that I'd never forget it. And I haven't.

When I started working on this book, I reached out to the artist and asked if I could share her work as an example of anguish. She generously said yes.

A note from Suse Ellen Lowenstein:

> On December 21, 1988, while coming home for the holidays, our older son Alexander was murdered along with 258 others aboard Pan Am flight 103 over Lockerbie, Scotland. A total of 270 people lost their lives in that terrorist act, 259 aboard the jumbo jet and 11 on the ground. Alexander was 21 years young.
>
> *Dark Elegy* is made up of 75 larger than life size pieces, each portraying a mother or wife at that moment when they first heard the awful news of the death of their loved one.
>
> What makes this memorial so unique, even more so than the sheer number of pieces or the personal and individual loss each mother portrays, is the fact that it was created by one of those affected rather than by an outsider portraying someone else's tragedy. I am one of the depicted figures.
>
> Although the concept of my sculpture, *Dark Elegy,* was spawned out of this, my personal tragedy, it has always been dedicated to all victims of terrorism.

*Dark Elegy* is a universal appeal for peace and dignity for all victims of senseless hate and vengeance called terrorism and will be a beacon for all peace-loving people.

# Hope, Hopelessness, and Despair

We need hope like we need air. To live without hope is to risk suffocating on hopelessness and despair, risk being crushed by the belief that there is no way out of what is holding us back, no way to get to what we desperately need. But hope is not what most of us think it is. It's not a warm, fuzzy emotion that fills us with a sense of possibility. Hope is a way of thinking—a cognitive process. Yes, emotions play a role, but hope is made up of what researcher C. R. Snyder called a "trilogy of goals, pathways, and agency."

We experience **hope** when:

1.  We have the ability to set realistic **goals** (*I know where I want to go*).

2.  We are able to figure out how to achieve those goals, including the ability to stay flexible and develop alternative **pathways** (*I know how to get there, I'm persistent, and I can tolerate disappointment and try new paths again and again*).

3.  We have **agency**—we believe in ourselves (*I can do this!*).

# We need **hope** like we need air.

*Dark Elegy*
Sculptures by Suse Ellen Lowenstein
Photograph by Karen Walrond

**"**

**Hope** is a function of struggle—
we develop hope not during the easy or comfortable times, but through adversity and **discomfort.**

Hope is a function of struggle—we develop hope not during the easy or comfortable times, but through adversity and discomfort. Hope is forged when our goals, pathways, and agency are tested *and* when change is actually possible. Unfortunately, there are times when hope isn't sufficient to combat entrenched systemic barriers. It doesn't matter how much hope we have if the deck is stacked or the rules apply to some but not others—that is actually a recipe for hopelessness and despair. We think we should be able to overcome an obstacle; however, the system is rigged so there is no possible positive outcome.

It's also important to know that hope is learned. According to Snyder, children most often learn the habit of hope from their parents. To learn hopefulness, children need relationships that are characterized by boundaries, consistency, and support. Children with high levels of hopefulness have experience with adversity. They've been given the opportunity to struggle, and in doing that they learn how to believe in themselves and their abilities.

As someone who struggles watching my kids struggle, I can tell you—this is hard. I remind myself of the saying "Prepare the child for the path, not the path for the child." One thing that bolsters my commitment to letting my kids figure out on their own things that are both developmentally appropriate and possible is thinking about the alternatives: hopelessness and despair.

## Hopelessness and Despair

Everything about these words is hard. First, they are both emotions and experiences that can lead to feelings of desperation and can pose serious threats to our well-being. Second, it is really difficult to separate these two constructs and talk about them as different experiences, yet they are. In the despair research, the word "hopeless" is often used synonymously with "despair." But in the research on hopelessness, we see very few mentions of the concept of despair. Let's break it down.

While hope is not an emotion, hopelessness and despair are emotions. **Hopelessness arises out of a combination of negative life events and negative thought patterns, particularly self-blame and the perceived inability to change our circumstances.**

Let's look back at C. R. Snyder's work and *reverse* his trilogy of goals, pathways, and agency to better understand hopelessness.

Hopelessness stems from not being able to set realistic goals (we don't know what we want), and even if we can identify realistic goals, we can't figure out how to achieve them. If we attempt to achieve the goals, we give up when we fail, we can't tolerate disappointment, and we can't reset. Last, we don't believe in ourselves or our ability to achieve what we want.

Hopelessness is serious. In more than thirty years of research, Aaron Beck and his colleagues have established that experiences of hopelessness are strongly and specifically related to suicidality.

There are two ways to think about despair and its relationship to hopelessness: **Hopelessness** can apply to a specific situation (such as feeling hopeless about finishing school or feeling hopeless about our financial future) or to life more generally.

**Despair is a sense of hopelessness about a person's entire life and future. When extreme hopelessness seeps into all the corners of our lives and combines with extreme sadness, we feel despair.**

I once heard theologian Rob Bell define despair as "the belief that tomorrow will be just like today." When we are in struggle and/or experiencing pain, despair—that belief that there is no end to what we're experiencing—is a desperate and claustrophobic feeling. We can't figure a way out of or through the struggle and the suffering.

When I look at examples of hope practices in our research, I see commitments to new ways of thinking about what we want to achieve and why. We need to learn how to reality-check our goals and the pathways to them, and how to take the shame out of having to start over many, many times when our first plan fails. I used to ask my graduate students to submit a semester-long goal the second week of school. After doing this for years, I knew I could expect 90 percent of the goals to be unrealistic. Setting realistic goals is a skill and a prerequisite for hope.

When we don't have these skills, small disappointments can grow into hopelessness and despair. If we didn't learn hope from our parents, we can still learn it as adults. But it's going to require skilled help and support—a therapist or maybe even a coach.

We all fear pain and struggle, but they are often necessary for growth, and, more important, they don't present the level of danger that hopelessness and despair bring to us. We can't ignore hopelessness and despair in ourselves or others—they are both reliable predictors of suicidal thoughts, suicide attempts, and completed suicide, especially when hopelessness is accompanied by emotional pain.

In addition to cultivating a hope practice—getting intentional about setting goals, thinking through pathways, and developing a strong belief in ourselves and what we can accomplish—we can also look to Martin Seligman's research on resilience, especially what many people call his 3 Ps: personalization, permanence, and pervasiveness.

**Personalization:** When we experience despair and hopelessness, we often believe that we are the problem and forget to think about larger issues and context. Self-blame and criticism don't lead to increased hopefulness; they're quicksand. Realizing that outside factors play a role in our struggles can give us a different lens on our experience.

**Permanence:** This one is tough, because thinking that our struggle will never end is built in to the experiences of despair and hopelessness. This is the "Tomorrow will be no different from today" thinking. One way to build resilience is to practice thinking about the temporary nature of most setbacks as a part of how we look at adversity on a daily basis. We can't afford to wait to build this skill until we're up against something huge in our lives.

Permanence can be tough for me, so I've developed the habit of asking myself, "I'm really scared, worried, overwhelmed, stressed about what's happening. Will this issue be a big deal in five minutes? Five hours? Five days? Five months? Five years?"

I've been doing it for about a year—I started it during the pandemic—and now I try not to sink into fear until I've asked and answered these questions. If nothing else, it pulls my thinking brain online instead of letting my fear brain run the show.

**Pervasiveness**: Sometimes, when we're struggling, we fall into the trap of believing that whatever we're up against has stained or changed every single thing in our life. Nothing good is left. I recently found myself dealing with a crisis at work that, for a moment, felt like the end of the world. I felt as if this thing had swallowed me whole and nothing was left. Then I got a text that said "hey mom do you know where my new goggles are?"

The first thing I thought was, *Ah, the three Ps. There's a part of my life—the biggest, most important part—that hasn't even been touched by this.* My second thought was: *I need to apologize to my mom for walking past my stack of shit on the bottom of the stairs every day for seventeen years. Those goggles have been on the stairs for a week.*

# Sadness

As I was writing this book, I posted a question on Instagram, Facebook, LinkedIn, and Twitter to all of the folks in our social media community: *What is your favorite sad movie?* At last count we'd received more than a hundred thousand enthusiastic responses. The films that came up over and over include (in no particular order):

*Life Is Beautiful*
*Terms of Endearment*
*Beaches*
*The Joy Luck Club*
*The Color Purple*
*Steel Magnolias*
*Brokeback Mountain*
*P.S. I Love You*
*Inside Out*
*Up*
Every movie ever made where a dog dies.

I can't even type this list without getting a lump in my throat. I've seen lots of these—in fact, I've seen most of the ones that people mentioned. Except

"

When I'm really **scared,
worried, overwhelmed,
stressed** about what's
happening, and trying
to find perspective, I ask
myself: *Will this issue be
a big deal in five minutes?
Five hours? Five days?
Five months? Five years?*

for the ones where dogs die. I was caught off guard in fourth grade with *Where the Red Fern Grows* and *Old Yeller*. Both in the same year. That won't happen again.

Not only was I curious about the films, I became obsessed with analyzing the descriptors and the reasons that people loved their films:

> "Beautifully devastating."
> "So relatable."
> "What it means to be human."
> "I bawl every time I see this but it's also an incredibly joyful film."
> "It's been different movies depending on the season of my life."
> "I felt less alone."
> "If I need to release some tears."
> "When I need a good cry."
> "I don't really *like* the sadness, but I'm so affected by this movie."
> "This film is the best in people and the worst."

I'm not going to tell you that sadness is wonderful and we need it. I'm going to say that sadness is *important* and we need it. Feeling sad is a normal response to loss or defeat, or even the perception of loss or defeat. To be human is to know sadness. Owning our sadness is courageous and a necessary step in finding our way back to ourselves and each other.

Here are four things that I think are important to know about sadness:

**1. Sadness and depression are not the same thing.** Sadness is sometimes referred to as "depressed mood." However, sadness is a common but not essential feature of clinical depression. Technically, depression is a cluster of symptoms that persist over a period of time. These symptoms can include lack of interest in pleasant activities, loss of appetite, excessive fatigue and/or insomnia, and difficulty concentrating.

**2. Sadness and grief are not the same thing.** Although sadness is one part of grief, grief involves a whole group of emotions and experiences. (I'll tell you more about grief soon.)

" To be human is
to know **sadness**.
Owning our sadness
is **courageous** and
a necessary step
in finding our way
back to ourselves and
each other.

**3. There are positive aspects to sadness.** Joseph P. Forgas, a professor of psychology at the University of New South Wales in Sydney, Australia, writes:

> Though much has been made of the many benefits of happiness, it's important to consider that sadness can be beneficial, too. Sad people are less prone to judgmental errors, are more resistant to eyewitness distortions, are sometimes more motivated, and are more sensitive to social norms. They can act with more generosity, too.

Forgas goes on to explain, "Evolutionary theory suggests that we should embrace all of our emotions, as each has an important role to play under the right circumstances. So, though you may seek ways to increase happiness, don't haphazardly push away your sadness. No doubt, it's there for good reason."

Additionally, some scholars have speculated that one function of sadness is to cause the person to evaluate their life and consider making changes in their circumstances following a negative event, as well as to recruit help and support from others.

My research has taught me that acknowledging and naming our own sadness is critical in the formation of compassion and empathy. In our saddest moments, we want to be held by or feel connected to someone who has known that same ache, even if what caused it is completely different. We don't want our sadness overlooked or diminished by someone who can't tolerate what we're feeling because they're unwilling or unable to own their own sadness.

**4. There's a reason we love sad movies.** Researchers Julian Hanich and colleagues investigated the sad-film paradox: How can a negative emotion such as sadness go together with "aesthetic liking" and even pleasure? Their findings totally align with the hundred-thousand-plus comments from our community: We like to be moved. We like to feel connected to what it means to be human, to be reminded of our inextricable connection to one another. Sadness moves the individual "us" toward the collective "us."

Their study revealed a "highly significant positive correlation between sadness and enjoyment." However, this association is sequential. Sadness leads

"

In our **saddest** moments, we want to be held by or feel **connected to someone** who has known that same ache, even if what caused it is completely different. We don't want our sadness overlooked or diminished by someone who can't tolerate what we're feeling because they're unwilling or unable to own their own sadness.

to feeling moved, which in turn leads to enjoyment. "Hence sadness primarily functions as a contributor to and intensifier of the emotional state of being moved."

Look back at that list of movies. They were *moving*. I felt deeply *moved* by them.

# Grief

> Grief does not obey your plans, or your wishes. Grief will do whatever it wants to you, whenever it wants to. In that regard, Grief has a lot in common with Love.
>
> — ELIZABETH GILBERT

**Grief** is often thought of as a process that includes many emotions, rather than a singular emotion. For a long time, we thought about the grief process in terms of linear stages, but almost all of the recent research actually refutes the idea that grief progresses in predictable, sequenced stages.

Robert A. Neimeyer, a psychology professor at the University of Memphis and a clinician, is one of the world's most prolific grief researchers. I often share his work with professionals looking for training in grief work and with individuals who are grieving. Neimeyer writes, *"A central process in grieving is the attempt to reaffirm or reconstruct a world of meaning that has been challenged by loss."*

In my research, three foundational elements of grief emerged from the data: loss, longing, and feeling lost.

**Loss**—While death and separation are tangible losses associated with grief, some of the participants described losses that are more difficult to identify or describe. These included the loss of normality, the loss of what could be, and the loss of what we thought we knew or understood about something or someone.

**Longing**—Related to loss is longing. Longing is not conscious wanting; it's an involuntary yearning for wholeness, for understanding, for meaning, for the opportunity to regain or even simply touch what we've lost. Longing is a vital and important part of grief, yet many of us feel we need to keep our longings to ourselves for fear we will be misunderstood, perceived as engaging in magical or unrealistic thinking, or lacking in fortitude and resilience.

**Feeling lost**—Grief requires us to reorient every part of our physical, emotional, and social worlds. When we imagine the need to do this, most of us picture the painful struggle to adjust to a tangible change, such as someone dying or moving away. But this is a very limited view of grief.

The more difficult it is for us to articulate our experiences of loss, longing, and feeling lost to the people around us, the more disconnected and alone we feel. Talking about grief is difficult in a world that wants us to "get over it" or a community that is quick to pathologize grief.

The Center for Complicated Grief at Columbia is another tremendous resource. Their definitions (below) are very helpful when thinking about grief. I think the most important line is "When a person adapts to a loss grief is not over." It doesn't mean that we're sad the rest of our lives, it means that "grief finds a place" in our lives. Imagine a world in which we honor that place in ourselves and others rather than hiding it, ignoring it, or pretending it doesn't exist because of fear or shame.

I keep thinking back to a conversation I had on *Unlocking Us* with the grief expert David Kessler. I'll never forget him saying this: "Each person's grief is as unique as their fingerprint. But what everyone has in common is that no matter how they grieve, they share a need for their grief to be witnessed. That doesn't mean needing someone to try to lessen it or reframe it for them. The need is for someone to be fully present to the magnitude of their loss without trying to point out the silver lining."

Professor Neimeyer's work supports this need for real connection in healing. He writes, "Most people who struggle with complicating loss feel a great press to 'tell the story,' to find someone willing to hear what others cannot, and who can join them in making sense of the death without withdrawing into awkward silence or offering trite and superficial advice regarding the questions it poses."

This need for connection, for storytelling and story catching, is what makes group therapy and support groups such powerful healing experiences for those who are grieving.

Working through complicated grief, however, requires a mental health professional with training in complicated grief work.

*The Center for Complicated Grief*

**Acute grief** occurs in the initial period after a loss. It almost always includes strong feelings of yearning, longing, and sadness along with anxiety, bitterness, anger, remorse, guilt, and/or shame. Thoughts are mostly focused on the person who died and it can be difficult to concentrate on anything else. Acute grief dominates a person's life.

**Integrated grief** is the result of adaptation to the loss. When a person adapts to a loss grief is not over. Instead, thoughts, feelings, and behaviors related to their loss are integrated in ways that allow them to remember and honor the person who died. Grief finds a place in their life.

**Complicated grief** occurs when something interferes with adaptation. When this happens, acute grief can persist for very long periods of time. A person with complicated grief feels intense emotional pain. They can't stop feeling that their loved one might somehow reappear and they don't see a pathway forward. A future without their loved one seems forever dismal and unappealing. . . . Grief dominates their thoughts and feelings with no respite in sight. Relationships with family and friends flounder. Life can seem purposeless, as if nothing matters without their loved one. Others begin to feel frustrated, helpless, and discouraged. Even professionals may be uncertain about how to help. People often think this is depression, but complicated grief and depression are not the same thing.

*Based on the research of Tashel Bordere*

**Disenfranchised grief** is a less-studied form of grief: grief that "is not openly acknowledged or publicly supported through mourning practices or rituals because the experience is not valued or counted [by others] as a loss." The grief can also be invisible or hard to see by others. Examples of disenfranchised grief include loss of a partner or parent due to divorce, loss of an unborn child and/or infertility, the multitude of losses experienced by a survivor of sexual assault, and loss of a loved one to suicide. As an illustrative example of disenfranchised grief, Tashel Bordere explains that sexual assault survivors suffer from numerous losses, many of which are invisible to others. Some of these losses include loss of one's prior worldview, loss of trust, loss of self-identity and self-esteem, loss of freedom and independence, loss of a sense of safety and security, and loss of sexual interest.

# #7

# Places We Go with Others

Compassion, Pity, Empathy, Sympathy, Boundaries, Comparative Suffering

# Compassion and Empathy

Across the research and clinical practice community, there are compelling debates happening right now about the role that compassion and empathy play in how we connect with people who are struggling. Some people argue that compassion is the best response, some people argue that it's empathy, and some people think we need both for different reasons. Everyone is trying to answer this question:

*What's the most effective way to be in connection with and in service to someone who is struggling, without taking on their issues as our own?*

It's an important debate that is frustratingly hijacked on occasion by folks who come up with new, arbitrary definitions for emotions that are completely different from how we all use the terms. They change the meaning, then argue that the emotion is "bad" based on their new definitions. For example, someone might say that empathy is taking on all the feelings of another person, then argue that empathy is bad. Unfortunately, this approach is often misleading and self-serving and puts no value on how we use the word. I would argue that a lot of this linguistic shell-gaming is about wanting to be contrarian. There's nothing more seductive and clickable than a discovery that something we believe to be good is bad: "Empathy is bad for you."

When it comes to language, I'm a populist. How we, the collective, use language matters as much as, if not more than, arbitrary definitions that don't center lived experiences. If research is going to serve people, it has to reflect their experiences.

There are significant differences between compassion and empathy that are vital to understand if we want to cultivate connection with others. There are also different definitions and types of empathy. I'm going to try to sort it out here using a combination of our research and that being done by other experts in the field.

**"**

**Compassion** is fueled by understanding and accepting that we're all **made of strength and struggle**—no one is immune to pain or suffering. Compassion is not a practice of 'better than' or 'I can fix you'—it's a practice based in the beauty and pain of shared humanity.

## The Relationship Between Compassion and Empathy

Here's what I've learned: **Compassion is a daily practice and empathy is a skill set that is one of the most powerful tools of compassion.** The most effective approach to meaningful connection combines compassion with a specific type of empathy called *cognitive empathy*. Let's get into it.

**Our working definition of compassion first emerged from the data about ten years ago. It's been revised over time, but the core has remained the same and has stood the test of new data: Compassion is the daily practice of recognizing and accepting our shared humanity so that we treat ourselves and others with loving-kindness, and we take action in the face of suffering.** A very similar definition can be found in the research literature: Compassion is a "virtuous response that seeks to address the suffering and needs of a person through relational understanding and action." What the majority of definitions share, including these, is that compassion includes action. It's not just feeling, it's doing.

Compassion is fueled by understanding and accepting that we're all made of strength and struggle—no one is immune to pain or suffering. Compassion is not a practice of "better than" or "I can fix you"—it's a practice based in the beauty and pain of shared humanity.

In her book *The Places That Scare You,* the American Buddhist nun Pema Chödrön writes:

> When we practice generating compassion, we can expect to experience our fear of pain. Compassion practice is daring. It involves learning to relax and allow ourselves to move gently toward what scares us. . . . In cultivating compassion we draw from the wholeness of our experience—our suffering, our empathy, as well as our cruelty and terror. It has to be this way. Compassion is not a relationship between the healer and the wounded. It's a relationship between equals. Only when we know our own darkness well can we be present with the darkness of others. Compassion becomes real when we recognize our shared humanity.

This paragraph completely rearranged my parenting approach. I went from always wanting to fix things and make them better to literally sitting in the dark with my kids. Before I fully understood that the "action" part of compassion wasn't making things better or fixing, I would race to flip on the metaphorical lights when my kids were suffering. Now, I try to sit with them in the dark and show them how to feel the discomfort. Talk about moving gently toward what scares us. It's so painful, but now that I've been doing it for the past decade, I can see how my kids are developing that sense of shared humanity. I've even had the incredible fortune of witnessing them moving toward others in pain without trying to solve.

But I'm not going to lie. It's still really hard. Sitting in the dark with them is not one bit easier in the moment than it was ten years ago. Everything in my body is screaming, "Make it better! Fix it!" Maybe this is an example of how understanding emotion can be a life raft in a sea of turbulent feelings. Sometimes I have to desperately cling to what I know, rather than act on what I'm feeling in the moment.

# Pity

While compassion is not rescuing, it's also not pity. In fact, **pity** is the *near enemy* of compassion. In her book *Fierce Self-Compassion,* University of Texas researcher Kristin Neff writes, "'Near enemy' is a useful Buddhist concept referring to a state of mind that appears similar to the desired state—hence it is 'near'—but actually undermines it, which is why it's an enemy." "Far enemies" are the opposite of emotions or experiences—the far enemy of compassion might be cruelty. What's interesting is that near enemies are often greater threats than far enemies because they're more difficult to recognize.

As we build our understanding of emotion and experiences, the concept of near enemy is invaluable. To better understand how this works, let's look at compassion and pity. In *Bringing Home the Dharma,* Jack Kornfield writes,

The near enemy of compassion is pity. Instead of feeling the openness of compassion, pity says, "Oh, that poor person. I feel sorry for people like that." Pity sees them as different from ourselves. It sets up a separation between ourselves and others, a sense of distance and remoteness from the suffering of others that is affirming and gratifying to the self. Compassion, on the other hand, recognizes the suffering of another as a reflection of our own pain: "I understand this; I suffer in the same way." It is empathetic, a mutual connection with the pain and sorrow of life. Compassion is shared suffering.

**There's nothing worse than feeling pitied, and we have the research to show us why it feels so isolating. Pity involves four elements: a belief that the suffering person is inferior; a passive, self-focused reaction that does not include providing help; a desire to maintain emotional distance; and avoidance of sharing in the other person's suffering.**

And, addressing the big question about being with people without taking on their pain, Kornfield goes on to say,

Another enemy of compassion is despair. Compassion does not mean immersing ourselves in the suffering of others to the point of anguish. Compassion is the tender readiness of the heart to respond to one's own or another's pain without despair, resentment, or aversion. It is the wish to dissipate suffering. Compassion embraces those experiencing sorrow, and eliminates cruelty from the mind.

# Empathy

**Empathy, the most powerful tool of compassion, is an emotional skill set that allows us to understand what someone is experiencing and to reflect back that understanding.** Empathy has a huge upside. Researchers Peter Paul Zurek and Herbert Scheithauer explain that empathy helps interpersonal decision making; facilitates ethical decision making and moral judgments; enhances short-term subjective well-being; strengthens relational bonds; allows people to better understand how others see them; and enhances prosocial and altruistic behavior.

66

**Empathy** is a tool of **compassion.** We can respond empathically only if we are willing to be present to someone's pain. If we're not willing to do that, it's not real empathy.

Most researchers agree that there are at least two elements to empathy: *cognitive empathy* and *affective empathy*. Cognitive empathy, sometimes called perspective taking or mentalizing, is the ability to recognize and understand another person's emotions. Affective empathy, often called experience sharing, is one's own emotional attunement with another person's experience.

Based on my work, I believe meaningful connection requires a combination of compassion and cognitive empathy or perspective taking.

In simple terms, the empathy I'm talking about is understanding what someone is feeling, not feeling it for them. If someone is feeling lonely, empathy doesn't require us to feel lonely too, only to reach back into our own experience with loneliness so we can understand and connect. Affective empathy, feeling something along with the person who is struggling, is a slippery slope toward becoming overwhelmed and not being able to offer meaningful support.

There are several models of and theories on empathy, but the one that aligns the most closely with our data is Theresa Wiseman's research. She studied empathy across helping professions and developed four attributes. We added a fifth attribute from Kristin Neff, whose work on self-compassion has been a life changer for me (more on that to come).

Theresa Wiseman's Attributes of Empathy:

1.  Perspective taking: What does that concept mean for you? What is that experience like for you?

2.  Staying out of judgment: Just listen, don't put value on it.

3.  Recognizing emotion: How can I touch within myself something that helps me identify and connect with what the other person might be feeling? Check in and clarify what you are hearing. Ask questions.

4.  Communicating our understanding about the emotion: Sometimes this is elaborate and detailed, and sometimes this is simply, "Shit. That's hard. I get that."

5.  Practicing mindfulness (from Kristin Neff): This is not pushing away emotion because it's uncomfortable, but feeling it and moving through it.

Again, empathy is a tool of compassion. We can respond empathically only if we are willing to be present to someone's pain. If we're not willing to do that, it's not real empathy.

A few researchers argue that empathy is a skill set that can be used to hurt people as well as in the service of compassion. I disagree. If you're connect-

**"**

We need to dispel the myth that **empathy** is 'walking in someone else's shoes.' Rather than walking in your shoes, I need to learn how to listen to the story you tell about what it's like in your shoes *and* **believe you even when it doesn't match my experiences.**

ing to how I feel so you can leverage my emotions, we shouldn't call that empathy—it makes no sense. We should call that manipulation or exploitation. Language matters. Don't use a word that has an almost universally positive connotation to describe a dangerous behavior that is hurtful. Use a word that issues a caution and demands accountability. *Much more to come on this in the final chapter.*

# Sympathy

Empathy is not **sympathy**—in fact, using the near enemy concept, we can definitely consider sympathy the near enemy of empathy. Rather than being a tool for connection, sympathy emerged in the data as a form of disconnection. Sympathy is removed: When someone says "I feel sorry for you" or "That must be terrible," they are standing at a safe distance. Rather than conveying the powerful "me too" of empathy, it communicates "not me," then adds, "But I do feel sorry for you." Sympathy can even be a trigger for shame, which we will discuss in the next chapter.

Researchers found that cancer patients on the receiving end of sympathy describe it as an unwanted, superficial, pity-based response that, although well intended, is focused on the observer's discomfort rather than on alleviating the patient's distress. Patients prefer empathic and compassionate responses from others, seeing these responses as more helpful and more genuine than sympathy responses.

Sympathy and pity are first cousins. They're the emotions of: *We feel bad for you. From way over here where the kind of misery you're experiencing doesn't happen.* Lulu Wang, the writer and director of one of my favorite films, *The Farewell,* tweeted, "Let's be clear. Empathy and pity are not the same thing. When non-POC non-female tell our stories, they may think they're creating empathy, but they unconsciously channel pity, which can often look like empathy but it's not. The difference is hierarchy."

This is one reason we need to dispel the myth that empathy is "walking in someone else's shoes." Rather than walking in your shoes, I need to learn how to listen to the story you tell about what it's like in your shoes *and* believe you even when it doesn't match my experiences.

The minute I try to put myself in your place rather than try to understand the situation from your perspective, our empathic connection unravels. Either I get sucked into the vortex of my own emotional difficulties, or, because my experience doesn't match yours, I doubt what you're telling me.

We see this empathic miss all the time when we share our experiences with people whose identities afford them more physical, social, and emotional safety. "I'm imagining not being called on in a meeting and I don't think it's so painful," says the man to the woman who is often overlooked, or the white woman to the Black woman who is routinely ignored—versus hearing what that experience felt like for the person sharing the story and responding by saying, "Feeling invisible is painful."

I also want to talk about the concept of **compassion fatigue**. This is a term used to refer to the emotional exhaustion or burnout that can occur among caregivers. The term comes up most frequently in research focusing on medical professionals (doctors, nurses), but is also used as related to other clinical professions (psychologists, therapists, social workers) and non-clinical service professions (customer service, teaching).

There's compelling research that shows that compassion fatigue occurs when caregivers focus on their own personal distress reaction rather than on the experience of the person they are caring for. Focusing on one's own emotional reaction results in an inability to respond empathically to the person in need. In this view, the more appropriate term, rather than "compassion fatigue," might be "empathic distress fatigue." We're not hearing the story, we're inserting ourselves in the story.

Last, the number one question I get when I'm teaching empathy is "How can I be empathic with someone if I haven't had their experience?" It's a great question, because it exposes a dangerous myth about empathy. Empathy is not relating to an experience, it's connecting to what someone is feeling about an experience. When I'm working with groups, I often ask participants to raise their hands if they know joy, hurt, heartbreak, shame,

# EMPATHY MISSES

**1. Sympathy Versus Empathy**

*I feel sorry for you.*

The person who responds with sympathy ("I feel so sorry for you") rather than empathy ("I get it, I feel with you, and I've been there"). The subtext of this response is distance: These things don't happen to me or people like me. If you want to see a shame cyclone turn deadly, throw one of these at it: "Oh, you poor thing" or "Bless your heart."

**2. Judgment**

*You "should" feel shame!*

The person who hears the story and actually feels shame for you. The friend gasps and confirms how horrified you should be. Then there is an awkward silence. Then you have to make this person feel better by convincing them that you're not a terrible person.

**3. Disappointment**

*You've let me down.*

The person who needs you to be the pillar of worthiness and authenticity. This person can't help you because they are too disappointed in your imperfections. You've let this person down.

**4. Discharging Discomfort with Blame**

*This feels terrible. Who can we blame? You?*

Because shame is visceral and contagious, we can feel it for other people. This person immediately needs to discharge the discomfort and vulnerability of the situation by blaming and scolding. They may blame/scold you: "What were you thinking?" Or they may look for someone else to take the fall: "Who was that guy? We'll kick his butt." Caution: Parents can fall easily into this when a child shares a shaming story with them. "How did you let this happen?"

### 5. Minimize/Avoid
*Let's make this go away.*

We minimize and avoid when we want hard feelings to go away. Out of their own discomfort, this person refuses to acknowledge that you're in pain and/or that you're hurting: "You're exaggerating. It wasn't that bad. You rock. You're perfect. Everyone loves you."

### 6. Comparing/Competing
*If you think that's bad!*

This person confuses connecting with you over shared experiences with the opportunity to one-up you. "That's nothing. Listen to what happened to me one time!"

### 7. Speaking Truth to Power
*Don't upset people or make them uncomfortable.*

You hold someone accountable for language, comments, or behavior that marginalizes or dehumanizes others, and it causes discomfort or conflict. When this person observes this or hears your story of what happened, they respond with, "I can't believe you said that to your boss!" or "I can't believe you went there!" or "You can't talk about that stuff with people" versus an empathic response of "That must have been hard—you were really brave" or "It's hard to stand up for what you believe in—thank you."

### 8. Advice Giving/Problem Solving
*I can fix this and I can fix you.*

Sometimes when we see pain our first instinct is to fix it. This is especially true for those of us whom people seek out to help with problem-solving. In these instances, rather than listen and be with people in their emotion, we start fixing.

From *The Gifts of Imperfection* (2020)
Comic art by **GAVIN AUNG THAN**

grief, love, etc. At the end, after all of the hands have been raised to every emotion, I say, "You're qualified." You don't need to be the expert or experience what they've experienced.

You need to connect to your own experiences in a "thinking" way that creates emotional resonance: *Oh, yeah. I know that feeling. I'm not going to fall into it right now, but I know it and I can communicate with you in a way that makes you know you're not alone.*

# Boundaries

Boundaries are a prerequisite for compassion and empathy. We can't connect with someone unless we're clear about where we end and they begin. If there's no autonomy between people, then there's no compassion or empathy, just enmeshment.

This has probably been one of the most significant, soul-shaking learnings of my career. For a couple of years, it made no sense to me at all.

Why did all of the compassion practitioners—therapists, counselors, monks—that I interviewed talk about the importance of boundaries? Why did the lack of boundaries and judgment seem to go hand in hand in the data?

In *The Gifts of Imperfection,* I write, "The heart of compassion is really acceptance. The better we are at accepting ourselves and others, the more compassionate we become. Well, it's difficult to accept people when they are hurting us or taking advantage of us or walking all over us. This research has taught me that if we really want to practice compassion, we have to start by setting boundaries and holding people accountable for their behavior."

I was recently struggling with a boundary issue (yes, still) and I told my therapist that I refuse to go back to saccharine—that I like solid better. Before I really understood how impossible it is to be compassionate to myself or others when people are taking advantage of me and when I'm prioritiz-

**"**

# Boundaries

are the distance
at which I can
**love** you and me
simultaneously.

*— Prentis Hemphill*

ing being liked over being free, I was much sweeter but less authentic. Now I'm kinder and less judgmental. But also firmer and more solid. Occasionally salty.

The best definition of boundaries still comes from my friend Kelly Rae Roberts. Kelly Rae was an oncology social worker who followed her dreams and became a prolific, globally recognized artist. After experiences with some of her art students copying her work and selling it, she addressed her art community with a very straightforward blog post on "What's OK and What's Not OK" in terms of using her images. For example, it's okay to be inspired by her work, but not okay to copy it and sell it. This is a simple but profound way to set boundaries. As we say in our organization, *Clear is kind. Unclear is unkind.*

Too often we forget about the "what is okay" part, and that leads to unnecessary disconnection. When people set a boundary with us, we can feel that they're denying us our right to our thinking and feeling. When we explain up front what's okay, we move the focus to where it belongs: This *expression* of your feelings or thinking is the problem.

*It's okay to be pissed. It's not okay to raise your voice and pound on the table.*

*It's okay to change your mind. It's not okay to assume that I'm okay with the changes without talking to me.*

*It's okay to want to be able to do the things your friends are allowed to do. I totally get that. What's not okay is breaking our rules to do them.*

*It's okay to disagree with me, but it's not okay to ridicule my ideas and beliefs.*

# Comparative Suffering

Empathy is not finite, and compassion is not a pizza with eight slices. When you practice empathy and compassion with someone, there is not less of these qualities to go around. There's more. Love is the last thing we need to ration in this world. But fear and scarcity trigger comparison, and even pain and hurt are not immune to being assessed and ranked.

Because COVID unleashed such massive fear and anxiety, we saw comparative suffering everywhere:

*My husband died, and that grief is worse than your grief over missing your daughter's wedding.*

*I'm not allowed to talk about how disappointed I am about my job changing because my friend just found out that his wife has COVID.*

*You're worried about your teenager becoming disconnected and isolated during quarantine when thousands of people in India are dying?*

What we fail to understand is that the family in India doesn't benefit more if you conserve your concern only for them and withhold it from your child who is also suffering.

Yes, perspective is critical. But I'm a firm believer that sharing how we feel—even complaining—is okay as long as we piss and moan with a little perspective. Hurt is hurt, and every time we honor our own struggle and the struggles of others by responding with empathy and compassion, the healing that results affects all of us.

# #8

# Places We Go When We Fall Short

Shame, Self-Compassion, Perfectionism, Guilt, Humiliation, Embarrassment

I came across a quote the other day that read, "Science is not the truth. Science is finding the truth. When science changes its opinion, it didn't lie to you. It learned more." The first thing I thought of was this section of the book.

If you're familiar with any of my work, you know that I've been researching and writing on shame, guilt, humiliation, and embarrassment for more than twenty years. Over these two decades, we've learned more about how these emotions work, and researchers have come up with innovative ways of measuring them, but nothing has fundamentally shifted my thinking on them—until recently. New research on the connection between humiliation and violence has completely changed the way I think about that emotion and reinforced my belief that shame and humiliation will never be effective social justice tools.

We're going to talk about these four terms together because we have the tendency to use them interchangeably, even though the experiences are very different in terms of biology, biography, behavior, backstory, and self-talk. And they lead to radically different outcomes. We're also going to talk about the important role self-compassion plays in moving through shame and how perfectionism is a function of shame.

Let's start with some short definitions and examples to differentiate the four emotions, then we'll dig deeper into each one.

**Shame**—I am bad. The focus is on self, not behavior. The result is feeling flawed and unworthy of love, belonging, and connection. Shame is not a driver of positive change.

You get back a quiz and your grade is F. Your self-talk is *I'm so stupid*.

**Guilt**—I did something bad. The focus is on behavior. Guilt is the discomfort we feel when we evaluate what we've done or failed to do against our values. It can drive positive change and behavior.

You get back a quiz and your grade is F. Your self-talk is *Going to the party instead of studying for this quiz was so stupid* (versus *I'm so stupid*).

**Humiliation**—I've been belittled and put down by someone. This left me feeling unworthy of connection and disgusted with myself. This was unfair and I didn't deserve this. With shame, we believe that we deserve our sense of unworthiness. With humiliation, we don't feel we deserve it.

The student sitting next to you sees the F at the top of your quiz and tells the class, "This idiot can't even pass a quiz in here. He's as stupid as they come." Everyone laughs. You feel dumb and enraged.

**Embarrassment**—I did something that made me uncomfortable, but I know I'm not alone. Everyone does these kinds of things. Embarrassment is fleeting, sometimes funny.

Your teacher is handing out quizzes and you come back from the bathroom with toilet paper stuck to your shoe.

# Shame

> I hated the internal wounds, the words that said I was worthless and unwanted, the teasing, the ridicule that echoed in my ears and shattered my insides into dust. If given the choice, I'd have picked a beating over being shamed.
>
> — ANTWONE QUENTON FISHER, *Finding Fish*

Reading Antwone Fisher's book *Finding Fish* was a *Sliding Doors* moment for me. I had just started researching shame and I was getting pushback from every direction. Everyone thought it was too difficult a topic to study. There were very few research articles on shame twenty years ago, and the first one I found warned that the decision to study shame had been the death of many academic careers. I devoured *Finding Fish* right when it came out. Fisher writes about shame with such haunting detail that it solidified my decision to study this emotion that we all experience and all hate talking about.

Here are my shame 1-2-3s:

1.  We all have it. Shame is universal and one of the most primitive emotions that we experience. The only people who don't experience it are those who lack the capacity for empathy and human connection.

2.  We're all afraid to talk about it. Sometimes we can feel shame when we just say the word "shame." But it's getting easier as more people are talking about it.

3.  The less we talk about it, the more control it has over us. Shame hates being spoken.

When we hear the word "shame," our first thought is either *I have no idea what that means and I don't want to know,* or *I know exactly what that is and I don't want to talk about it.* We can also make up that shame is something that happens to other people, not us. But shame is in all of us. Here are some examples shared by the research participants from our early study on shame:

- Shame is hiding the fact that I'm in recovery.

- Shame is raging at my kids.

- Shame is bankruptcy.

- Shame is getting laid off and having to tell my pregnant wife.

- Shame is my boss calling me an idiot in front of the client.

- Shame is not making partner.

- Shame is my husband leaving me for my next-door neighbor.

- Shame is my partner asking me for a divorce and telling me that she wants children, but not with me.

- Shame is my DUI.

- Shame is infertility.

- Shame is telling my fiancé that my dad lives in France when in fact he's in prison.

- Shame is internet porn.

- Shame is flunking out of school. Twice.

- Shame is hearing my parents fight through the walls and wondering if I'm the only one who feels this afraid.

Connection, along with love and belonging (two expressions of connection), is why we are here, and it is what gives purpose and meaning to our lives. Shame is the fear of disconnection—it's the fear that something we've done or failed to do, an ideal that we've not lived up to, or a goal that we've not accomplished makes us unworthy of connection. *I'm unlovable. I don't belong.*

**Here's the definition of shame that emerged from my research: Shame is the intensely painful feeling or experience of believing that we are flawed and therefore unworthy of love, belonging, and connection.**

Shame thrives on secrecy, silence, and judgment. If you put shame into a petri dish and douse it with these three things, it will grow exponentially into every corner and crevice of our lives.

The antidote to shame is empathy. If we reach out and share our shame experience with someone who responds with empathy, shame dissipates.

Shame needs you to believe that you're alone. Empathy is a hostile environment for shame.

Self-compassion also helps us move through shame, but we need empathy as well for an important reason: Shame is a social emotion. Shame happens between people and it heals between people. Even if I feel it alone, shame is the way I see myself through someone else's eyes. Self-compassion is often the first step to healing shame—we need to be kind to ourselves before we can share our stories with someone else.

As I mentioned in the previous chapter, Kristin Neff's research on self-compassion has been a life changer for me. Neff runs the Center for Mindful Self-Compassion, where she studies how we develop and practice self-compassion. **According to Neff, self-compassion has three elements: self-kindness, common humanity, and mindfulness.** This is how she defines each of these elements:

**Self-kindness vs. self-judgment:** "Self-compassion entails being warm and understanding toward ourselves when we suffer, fail, or feel inadequate, rather than ignoring our pain or flagellating ourselves with self-criticism. Self-compassionate people recognize that being imperfect, failing, and experiencing life difficulties [are] inevitable, so they tend to be gentle with themselves when confronted with painful experiences rather than getting angry when life falls short of set ideals."

**Common humanity vs. isolation:** "Self-compassion involves recognizing that suffering and personal inadequacy is part of the shared human experience—something that we all go through rather than being something that happens to 'me' alone."

**Mindfulness vs. over-identification:** "Mindfulness is a non-judgmental, receptive mind state in which one observes thoughts and feelings as they are, without trying to suppress or deny them. We cannot ignore our pain and feel compassion for it at the same time. At the same time, mindfulness requires that we not be 'over-identified' with thoughts and feelings, so that we are caught up and swept away by negative reactivity."

I highly recommend that you take her self-compassion inventory at www.self-compassion.org. You can learn a lot about your strengths and your areas that need attention. Being a shame researcher for so many years, I'm really good at common humanity. Even though shame says *It's just you!* I know we all struggle. Self-kindness is my growth area for sure. Like most people, I talk to myself in ways that I would never talk to people I love. I try to remind myself—if I wouldn't talk that way to Ellen or Charlie when they make a mistake or drop a ball, I shouldn't talk that way to myself. Self-kindness is both more difficult and more revolutionary than we think.

## The Four Elements of Shame Resilience

Across our research, the participants who could move through shame without sacrificing their values and authenticity shared four practices when overcoming shame. We reverse-engineered how they worked through shame to come up with a process that all of us can use. These steps rarely happen in this order—they just all need to happen for us to develop resilience to shame:

**Recognizing shame and understanding its triggers**. Can you physically recognize when you're in the grip of shame, name it, feel your way through it, and figure out what messages and expectations triggered it? This is why Neff's concept of mindfulness is so important. We can't pretend it's not happening or get swept away (which is easy with shame).

**Practicing critical awareness.** Can you reality-check the messages and expectations that are driving your shame? Are they realistic? Attainable? Are they what you want to be or what you think others need or want from you?

**Reaching out**. Are you owning and sharing your story? We can't experience empathy if we're not connecting.

**Speaking shame.** Are you talking about how you feel and asking for what you need when you feel shame? Silence, secrecy, and judgment fuel shame.

# Shame in Culture

One reason we get so confused about the term "shame" and what it means is that we misuse it all the time. People throw around the word "shameless" when they see someone make a self-serving or unethical decision—they attribute unconscionable behavior to a lack of shame. This is wrong and dangerous. As I write in *Dare to Lead*:

Shame isn't the cure, it's the cause. Don't let what looks like a bloated ego and narcissism fool you into thinking there's a lack of shame. Shame and fear are almost always driving that unethical behavior. We're now seeing that shame often fuels narcissistic behavior. In fact, I define narcissism as the shame-based fear of being ordinary.

Grandiosity and bluster are easy to assign to an overinflated ego. It's tough to get a glimpse of the fear and lack of self-worth that are actually behind the posturing and selfishness because posturing leads to weaponizing hurt and turning it on other people.

The last thing people like that need is more shame. More accountability for their behavior and lack of empathy? Yes. More shame just makes them more dangerous, gives them the opportunity to redirect attention to the shaming behavior, and, weirdly, can drum up support from others who are also looking for a way to discharge their pain and an enemy to blame.

Shame is not a compass for moral behavior. It's much more likely to drive destructive, hurtful, immoral, and self-aggrandizing behavior than it is to heal it. Why? Because where shame exists, empathy is almost always absent. That's what makes shame dangerous. The opposite of experiencing shame is experiencing empathy. The behavior that many of us find so egregious today is more about people being empathyless, not shameless.

Ronda Dearing, our senior director for research, has also studied shame for decades and was one of my early heroes in the field. Her summary of

# "

Where **perfectionism** exists, shame is always lurking.

how empathy and shame work together (or, actually, do not work together) is incredibly helpful:

Empathy is an other-focused emotion. It draws our attention outward, toward the other person's experience. When we are truly practicing empathy, our attention is fully focused on the other person and trying to understand their experience. We only have thoughts of self in order to draw on how our experience can help us understand what the other person is going through.

Shame is an egocentric, self-involved emotion. It draws our focus inward. Our only concern with others when we are feeling shame is to wonder how others are judging us. Shame and empathy are incompatible. When feeling shame, our inward focus overrides our ability to think about another person's experience. We become unable to offer empathy. We are incapable of processing information about the other person, unless that information specifically pertains to their view of us.

# Perfectionism

Shame is the birthplace of perfectionism. **Perfectionism** is not striving to be our best or working toward excellence. Healthy striving is internally driven. Perfectionism is externally driven by a simple but potentially all-consuming question: *What will people think?*

It may seem counterintuitive, but one of the biggest barriers to working toward mastery is perfectionism. In our leadership research, we've learned that achieving mastery requires curiosity and viewing mistakes and failures as opportunities for learning. Perfectionism kills curiosity by telling us that we have to know everything or we risk looking "less than." Perfectionism tells us that our mistakes and failures are personal defects, so we either avoid trying new things or we barely recover every time we inevitably fall short.

"

It may seem counterintuitive, but one of the biggest barriers to working toward mastery is **perfectionism**. In our leadership research, we've learned that achieving mastery requires **curiosity** and viewing mistakes and failures as opportunities for learning. Perfectionism kills curiosity by telling us that we have to know everything or we risk looking 'less than.' Perfectionism tells us that **our mistakes and failures are personal defects**, so we either avoid trying new things or we barely recover every time we inevitably fall short.

Papers by Paul Hewitt and colleagues and Simon Sherry and colleagues provide evidence that people with high levels of perfectionistic traits:

- Are doomed to fail at meeting their own expectations and the expectations that they assume are held by others

- Perceive themselves as consistently falling short of others' expectations

- Behave in ways that result in perceived and actual exclusion and rejection by others

- Feel socially disconnected and have fewer social connections

I write a lot about perfectionism across my books. It's a healthy dose of "Researcher, heal thyself." I often call myself a recovering perfectionist and an aspiring "good-enoughist."

**In *The Gifts of Imperfection,* I explain how perfectionism emerged from our research. The definition that best fit the data is that perfectionism is a self-destructive and addictive belief system that fuels this primary thought: If I look perfect, live perfectly, work perfectly, and do everything perfectly, I can avoid or minimize the painful feelings of shame, judgment, and blame.**

Perfectionism is not self-improvement. Perfectionism is, at its core, about trying to earn approval and acceptance. Most perfectionists were raised being praised for achievement and performance (good grades, good manners, nice appearance, sports prowess, rule following, people pleasing).

Somewhere along the way, we adopt this dangerous and debilitating belief system: I am what I accomplish and how well I accomplish it. Please. Perform. Perfect. Healthy striving is self-focused—*How can I improve?* Perfectionism is other-focused—*What will they think?*

Understanding the difference between healthy striving and perfectionism is critical to laying down the shield and picking up your life. Research shows that perfectionism hampers success. In fact, it often sets you on the

**"**

**Perfectionism** is a self-destructive and addictive belief system that fuels this primary thought: If I look perfect, live perfectly, work perfectly, and do everything perfectly, I can avoid or minimize the painful feelings of **shame, judgment, and blame**.

path to depression, anxiety, addiction, and life paralysis. "Life paralysis" refers to all of the opportunities we miss because we're too afraid to put anything out in the world that could be imperfect. It's also all of the dreams that we don't follow because of our deep fear of failing, making mistakes, and disappointing others. It's terrifying to risk when you're a perfectionist; your self-worth is on the line.

As previously mentioned, perfectionism is a self-destructive and addictive belief system that we use to try to protect ourselves from feelings of shame, judgment, and blame. It is a twenty-ton shield that we lug around thinking it will protect us when in fact it's the thing that's really preventing us from taking flight. Let me explain why I describe perfectionism as being both self-destructive and addictive.

Perfectionism is self-destructive simply because there is no such thing as perfection. Perfection is an unattainable goal. Additionally, perfectionism is more about perception—we want to be perceived as perfect. Again, this is unattainable—there is no way to control perception, regardless of how much time and energy we spend trying.

Perfectionism is addictive, because when we invariably do experience shame, judgment, and blame, we often believe it's because we weren't perfect enough. So rather than questioning the faulty logic of perfectionism, we become even more entrenched in our quest to live, look, and do everything just right.

Feeling shamed, judged, and blamed (and the fear of these feelings) are realities of the human experience. Perfectionism actually increases the odds that we'll experience these painful emotions and often leads to self-blame: *It's my fault. I'm feeling this way because I'm not good enough.*

# Guilt

**Like shame, guilt is an emotion that we experience when we fall short of our own expectations or standards. However, with guilt, our focus is on having done something wrong and on doing something to set things**

**right, like apologizing or changing a behavior.** Remorse, a subset of guilt, is what we feel when we acknowledge that we have harmed another person, we feel bad about it, and we want to atone for our behavior.

While shame is highly correlated with addiction, violence, aggression, depression, eating disorders, and bullying, guilt is negatively correlated with these outcomes. Empathy and guilt work together to create a force that is adaptive and powerful. This is why when we apologize for something we've done, make amends, or change a behavior that doesn't align with our values, guilt—not shame—is most often the driving force.

We feel guilty when we hold up something we've done or failed to do against our values and find they don't match up. It's a psychologically uncomfortable feeling, but one that's helpful. The discomfort of cognitive dissonance is what drives meaningful change. Shame, however, corrodes the very part of us that believes we can change and do better.

# Humiliation

All the cruel and brutal things, even genocide, start with the humiliation of one individual.

— KOFI ANNAN, Ghanaian diplomat and
Nobel Peace Prize recipient

**Based on the research, we can define humiliation as the intensely painful feeling that we've been unjustly degraded, ridiculed, or put down and that our identity has been demeaned or devalued.** Humiliation is most similar to shame in that we feel fundamentally flawed. But the most relevant distinction is that humiliation arises because someone else pointed out our flaws, and we don't feel we deserved it. The entire key to understanding humiliation is that when it happens to us, it feels unjust.

Linda Hartling is the director of a global transdisciplinary group called Human Dignity and Humiliation Studies (they prefer to call themselves nurturers of dignity). Hartling and her colleagues describe humiliation as "unjustified mistreatment that violates one's dignity and diminishes one's sense of worth as a human being."

Until recently, I held the belief that humiliation, though detrimental, was a less dangerous emotional experience than shame. The reasoning behind that thinking (and what emerged from our data) was that we hide our shame because we think we deserve to feel that way. In other words, we buy into the messaging that we're not enough. In contrast, when we feel humiliated, we think that we didn't deserve whatever happened to make us feel that way. In our interviews, participants seemed not to buy into the messaging that they were flawed as much as they did with shame.

A collection of studies changed my mind. In 2003, Susan Harter and colleagues issued a report that examined the media profiles of ten prominent school shooters between 1996 and 1999. Harter and her colleagues reported that "*in every case,* the shooters described how they had been ridiculed, taunted, teased, harassed or bullied by peers (because of their inadequate appearance, social or athletic behavior), spurned by someone in whom they were romantically interested, or put down, in front of other students, by a teacher or school administrator, *all events that led to profound humiliation.*"

That report prompted a series of studies by Jeff Elison and Susan Harter that found links for peer rejection, humiliation, depression, and anger with both suicidal and homicidal ideation. Perhaps more important, their studies suggest that bullying alone does not lead to aggression. Instead, individuals who are bullied become violent specifically when feelings of humiliation accompany the bullying.

This finding has tremendous implications for how we think about bullying and how we help bullying survivors heal. And, given that humiliation is often an attack against a social identity (ethnicity, race, sexual orientation), we must investigate what we are doing in organizational, community, and school cultures to foster safety and what we are doing consciously or unconsciously that gives people permission to belittle others.

And finally, the third article we discovered was by Linda Hartling, who ties together research from several areas to propose a model explaining how humiliation can lead to violence.

Hartling suggests that humiliation can trigger a series of reactions, including social pain, decreased self-awareness, increased self-defeating behavior, and decreased self-regulation, that ultimately lead to violence. Hartling and colleagues state that "humiliation is not only the most underappreciated force in international relations, it may be the *missing link* in the search for root causes of political instability and violent conflict . . . perhaps the most toxic social dynamic of our age."

This connection between humiliation and aggression/violence explains much of what we're seeing today. Amplified by the reach of social media, dehumanizing and humiliating others are becoming increasingly normalized, along with violence. Now, rather than humiliating someone in front of a small group of people, we have the power to eviscerate someone in front of a global audience of strangers.

I know we all have deeply passionate political and cultural beliefs, but shame and humiliation will never be effective social justice tools. They are tools of oppression. I remember reading this quote from Elie Wiesel years ago and it's become a practice for me—even when I'm enraged or afraid: "Never allow anyone to be humiliated in your presence."

# Embarrassment

**Embarrassment is a fleeting feeling of self-conscious discomfort in response to a minor incident that was witnessed by others.** When looking back on embarrassing incidents, we are usually able to see them as kind of funny and something that could have happened to anyone. Researcher Rowland Miller writes, "Embarrassment does not persist for long periods of time, lasting only a few minutes instead of hours or days—a point nicely illustrated by the unique physiological marker of embarrassment, the blush."

When we feel embarrassed, we can feel exposed, flustered, and clumsy, but we tend to respond to our embarrassment in nonthreatening ways like using humor, saying we're sorry, or sometimes just moving on and not even acknowledging it. Those of us who are more sensitive about social norms and being accepted are more susceptible to embarrassment.

Some research suggests that there are three types of events that can trigger embarrassment:

1.  Committing a faux pas or social mistake,

2.  Being the center of attention, and

3.  Being in a sticky social situation.

And, just in case you're wondering, the secondhand embarrassment feeling is real. We absolutely can feel vicarious embarrassment when we see others in embarrassing situations, even complete strangers. If we know the person in the embarrassing situation, it's even worse.

I'll never forget the first time I felt that sensation. I was watching *I Love Lucy* reruns after school, and I'm not sure what crazy thing she was doing, but I thought I was going to die. I remember jumping up from the sofa and turning off the TV during the episode where Lucy and Ethel get jobs working on a conveyor belt at a chocolate factory. They couldn't keep up with the speed of the belt, so they started shoving chocolates in their mouths and down their shirts. I couldn't take it. I went back to watch it when I was writing this—it still gets me. Maybe that's what makes scenes like this one iconic—we don't just watch them, we feel them.

Last, we know from the research that "Embarrassment takes years to develop, and its emergence coincides with the self-conscious ability to understand what others may be thinking of us." If you've raised tweens or teens, or even been in their vicinity, you know that they often spend more time being embarrassed than not. It's constant cringe when we first start seeing ourselves through others' eyes, and it stays that way until we get to midlife and fall apart before we realize it takes just too much energy to try to manage perception.

# #9

# Places We Go
# When We Search
# for Connection

Belonging, Fitting In, Connection,
Disconnection, Insecurity, Invisibility,
Loneliness

# Belonging and Fitting In

We have to belong to ourselves as much as we need to belong to others. Any belonging that asks us to betray ourselves is not true belonging.

Any discussion of **belonging** has to start with acknowledging that love and belonging are irreducible needs for all people. In the absence of love and belonging, there is always suffering. Expanding on Maslow's hierarchy of needs, recent research shows that finding a sense of belonging in close social relationships and with our community is essential to well-being. What makes belonging essential for us is the fact that we are a social species. We can't survive without one another.

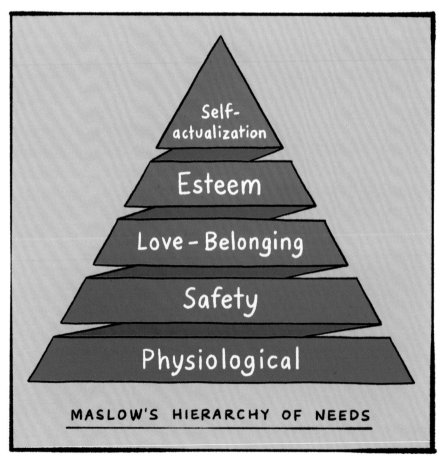

Comic art by **GAVIN AUNG THAN**

154

Although I started my career studying connection, shame, and vulnerability, the topic of belonging always emerged in the data. You can't study the emotions and experiences that define what it means to be human without constantly bumping into belonging—it's just too primal.

In 2017, I published *Braving the Wilderness: The Quest for True Belonging and the Courage to Stand Alone.* It's a book about what it means to belong in this increasingly divisive and disconnected world.

As a grounded theory researcher, my job is to understand what we call "the main concern" of study participants. For *Braving the Wilderness,* I approached the research with these broad questions: When it comes to belonging, what are people trying to achieve or feel? What are they concerned about?

We have to belong to ourselves as much as we need to belong to others. Any **belonging** that asks us to betray ourselves is not true belonging.

> **"**
> True **belonging** is the spiritual practice of believing in and belonging to yourself so deeply that you can share your most **authentic** self with the world and find sacredness in both being a part of something

and standing alone in the wilderness. True belonging doesn't require you to change who you are; it requires you to be who you are.

Below is how I explained the findings that emerged in *Braving the Wilderness:*

> We want to be a part of something—to experience real connection with others—but not at the cost of their authenticity, freedom, or power. Participants further reported feeling surrounded by "us versus them" cultures that create feelings of spiritual disconnection.
>
> When I dug deeper into what they meant by "spiritually disconnected," the research participants described a diminishing sense of shared humanity. Over and over, participants talked about their concern that the only thing that binds us together now is shared fear and disdain, not common humanity, shared trust, respect, or love.
>
> Reluctant to choose between being loyal to a group and being loyal to themselves, but lacking that deeper spiritual connection to shared humanity, they were far more aware of the pressure to "fit in" and conform.

What was counterintuitive for me, as I identified the main concerns, is that a deeper sense of belonging and "connection to a larger humanity gives people more freedom to express their individuality without fear of jeopardizing belonging." *I can be myself when I know that I'm with people who recognize the inextricable, unnamable, spiritual connection that is shared humanity, because belonging is not in jeopardy.*

True belonging doesn't require us to change who we are; it requires us to be who we are.

Our yearning for belonging is so hardwired that we often try to acquire it by any means possible, including trying to fit in and hustling for approval and acceptance. Not only are these efforts hollow substitutes for belonging, but they are the greatest barriers to belonging. When we work to fit in and be accepted, our "belonging" is tenuous. If we do or say something that's true to who we are but outside the expectations or rules of the group, we risk everything. If people don't really know who we are and what we believe or think, there's no true belonging.

# **Love** and **belonging** are irreducible needs for all people. In the absence of these experiences, there is always suffering.

Because we can feel belonging only if we have the courage to share our most authentic selves with people, our sense of belonging can never be greater than our level of self-acceptance.

We can never truly belong if we are betraying ourselves, our ideals, or our values in the process. That is why it's a mistake to think that belonging is passive and simply about joining or "going along" with others. It's not. **Belonging is a practice that requires us to be vulnerable, get uncomfortable, and learn how to be present with people without sacrificing who we are.** When we sacrifice who we are, we not only feel separate from others, but we even feel disconnected from ourselves.

Many years ago, I asked a large group of eighth graders to break into small teams and come up with the differences between "fitting in" and "belonging." I've shared these findings in a couple of my books, and they

"

Because we can feel **belonging** only if we have the courage to share our most authentic selves with people, our sense of belonging can never be greater than our level of **self-acceptance**.

still take my breath away. For this book, I asked Gavin to draw the kids holding their poster-size Post-its, the way I remembered it. It's one thing for me to bullet out their responses; it's something altogether different to see them standing there holding these signs on the stage of an empty auditorium. (See illustration on the next page.)

Clearly, they understand the differences in their bones. For many tweens and teens, belonging or not belonging feels like life or death.

As a child I never felt like I belonged in my family. I felt different as an introvert in a family where introversion was mistaken for weakness and extroversion for confidence. I also felt weird and alone in my small world. Because nothing was normalized, and there were no conversations or TikToks about the unsaid stuff—how emotions can be overwhelming, how bodies work, how relationships can suck, how parents just don't understand, how normal people are lonely—I thought something was wrong with me.

My feelings of not belonging are still something that I have to work on—they can still show up in weird ways when I'm not expecting it. What's so powerful (and hard) is that the more my siblings and I talk about and share our experiences, the more I think everyone in my family felt the same way. A little on the outside of the myth of what we were supposed to be. I have a lot of empathy and compassion for my parents. They came from hardscrabble, working-class families where addiction and mental health issues were rarely addressed and there wasn't enough money to cover them up with shiny things. I can only imagine the pictures of sub-urban perfection that drove their pain as first generation "professionals." And their fury.

As a parent, my goal is to help my children believe in and belong to them-selves, and to know that, no matter what, they always belong at home. That we see them and love them for who they are. The pressure to fit in is real and unrelenting, but if we can create that sense of inextricable con-nection, it's a fierce protector as they navigate belonging. Be here. Be you. Belong.

THE DIFFERENCES BETWEEN **FITTING IN** AND **BELONGING**

**BELONGING** is being somewhere where you want to be, and they want you.

**FITTING IN** is being somewhere where you want to be, but they don't care one way or the other.

Not belonging at school is really hard. But it's <u>NOTHING</u> compared to what it feels like when you don't belong at <u>HOME</u>.

NOT LIVING UP TO YOUR PARENTS' EXPECTATIONS

NOT BEING AS COOL OR POPULAR AS YOUR PARENTS WANT YOU TO BE

"

Be here.

Be you.

Belong.

# Belonging Uncertainty

In research, **belonging uncertainty** is the term sometimes used to describe questioning one's social belongingness. Belonging uncertainty can be high among members of marginalized groups, and this can have real consequences. For example, among underrepresented students at mainstream academic organizations, belonging uncertainty can have a negative impact on motivation and achievement.

As we think about belonging uncertainty, it's important to remember that belonging is not about the number of friends one has in a space. According to researchers Gregory Walton and Shannon T. Brady, "It is a more general inference, drawn from cues, events, experiences, and relationships, about the quality of fit or potential fit between oneself and a setting. It is experienced as a feeling of being accepted, included, respected in, and contributing to a setting, or anticipating the likelihood of developing this feeling."

Paola Sánchez Valdez is our organization's first postgraduate social work fellow. She joined us right after completing her master's degree in social work from Columbia University. She's on the research team for this book and is helping us develop a strategy to bring Dare to Lead training to first generation college students at the University of Texas at Austin. She has shared a lot with me and others about her experiences of belonging uncertainty, and I asked her if she would write something for the book. This is her story:

I was ten years old when my mother confirmed what I knew all along. We were watching the 2006 immigration reform protests unfold on the news when she turned to me and said, "You see those people? They're fighting for us . . . for our dreams." That day I learned I was undocumented, and I wanted nothing more than to be marching with those people and to feel like I finally belonged somewhere.

I always knew I was different. My Ecuadorian features set me apart from the predominately white, rural area which my family had settled in. But even then, I knew my feelings of not belonging stemmed from a more precarious place. It was a place I didn't know how to name or how to describe. I just knew that when my parents kissed me goodbye, it always felt like it could be the last time. I could be separated from them at any moment and be forced to go to a country I didn't know.

Once I got to high school, my feelings of not belonging became even more inescapable. I realized that I didn't have the same opportunities as my friends and peers, such as getting a driver's license, applying to college, or even receiving financial aid. After I lived through fifteen years of being undocumented, the Deferred Action for Childhood Arrivals (DACA) program allowed me to come out of the shadows and pursue my dreams. I was able to apply to the University of Virginia, and I was accepted. Shortly after, I became a U.S. permanent resident—a privilege I do not take lightly, as it's not afforded to many of my family members, friends, and community members.

Even though I was no longer undocumented, the trauma that came from living most of my life in limbo followed me into college. I longed to share my story and to build meaningful connections with others, but my fear of not belonging, coupled with the lack of diversity at my university, prevented me from doing so. After several months of contemplating dropping out, I told my story to one of my friends who confided in me that her family was also undocumented. It was the first time I had shared my experiences and identity with anyone other than my own family.

That night we recounted moments of injustice and bigotry we endured within our conservative towns and drew similarities of feeling that way at our university. We identified a lack of awareness and support for undocumented students and eventually invited others into the conversation. Within a couple of weeks, we met several undocumented students and together created a student advocacy organization to help uplift their voices and concerns at UVA. Years later, this organization has spearheaded actions that have cultivated political and cultural systemic change, not only on campus but also in the surrounding communities and the state of Virginia as a whole.

In many Latin American countries, we have a saying that goes *"ni de aquí, ni de allá,"* meaning "not from here, not from there." I still resonate with this saying even though I've been documented for nearly eight years. I don't know if I'll ever feel like I belong to this country or another, but what I do know is that **I belong to myself.**

The accepting, loving space my friend and I provided each other that night sparked a fire inside me to connect with and advocate alongside others facing structural inequities. It's been the honor of my life to help create brave spaces of belonging for those ready to share their stories. Together we fight to create change within ourselves and our communities because, as my favorite quote says, *"Quisieron enterrarnos, pero no sabían que éramos semillas"* . . . "They wanted to bury us, but they didn't know we were seeds."

## Diversity, Equity, Inclusion, and Belonging

> I don't believe your antiracist work is complete or valid or useful if you haven't engaged with Black humanity.

> — TARANA BURKE, *You Are Your Best Thing*

In our Dare to Lead work, we talk a lot about **belonging** as a critical component of diversity, equity, and inclusion (DEI) work. We actually call it DEIB (to include belonging) in our work, and our organization's position statement is called our Belonging Statement. Why? Because people should feel a strong sense of belonging in an organization and shape the culture through representation, co-creation, influence, and that *inextricable, unnamable, spiritual connection that is shared humanity.* Anything less is not enough.

Aiko Bethea is a Dare to Lead facilitator and expert in DEIB work. She's also a tremendous thought-partner and teacher when it comes to bringing belonging to organizational cultures. If you're interested in the intersection of belonging, leadership, and culture, I recommend listening to the two-part *Dare to Lead* podcast that we did together. It's a great resource for a team to listen to then discuss.

# Connection and Disconnection

One of the interesting things about Grounded Theory research is that, unlike the majority of other research methodologies, we don't start with a review of the existing literature. Barney Glaser and Anselm Strauss developed Grounded Theory in 1967, and, through a very strange turn of events, Barney served as the methodologist on my dissertation committee. I remember him telling me, "How do you know what literature to review before you start? You don't get to decide what this research is about—your participants do. You'll follow them where they go—not the other way around. This is based on their lived experiences, not the researcher's academic pet interests. Trust and follow what emerges from the data."

At first, I thought, "Awesome. Lit reviews are so time-consuming." Well, it turns out that once your theory or hypothesis emerges from the data, you're required to do an entire literature *analysis,* not just a review, to understand how your theory fits with or pushes against what other researchers have found. And because you didn't start by following existing lines of inquiry, grounded theories often support, refute, and challenge in equal measure. *Insert anxious emoji face.*

After my first study on shame and connection, I tiptoed into the literature to see where existing work aligned with what I had found and where it didn't. Early in that process, I found Relational-Cultural Theory (RCT) and the group of researchers and clinicians behind it from the Stone Center at Wellesley. It felt like home. Here was a theory that was also built from lived experience and, as Maureen Walker described it, "depicted culture as more than the scenic backdrop for the unfolding of development; rather, culture is viewed as an active agent in relational processes that shape human possibility."

The RCT theorist Judith Jordan writes, "The need for connection in which growth is a priority is the core motivation in people's lives. In growth-fostering relationships, people are able to bring themselves most fully and authentically into connection." From an evolution perspective connection was about survival, today it's what gives purpose and meaning to our lives. Research shows that "people who have strong connections with others are happier, healthier, and better able to cope with the stresses of everyday life."

**Across my research, I define connection as the energy that exists between people when they feel seen, heard, and valued; when they can give and receive without judgment; and when they derive sustenance and strength from the relationship.**

Connection is in our neurobiology. This is why our experiences of disconnection are so painful and why chronic disconnection leads to social isolation, loneliness, and feelings of powerlessness.

"

**Connection** is the energy that exists between people when they feel **seen, heard, and valued;** when they can give and receive without judgment; and when they derive sustenance and strength from the relationship.

Here's how Judith Jordan explains **disconnection:**

> RCT sees disconnections as normative and inevitable in relation-
> ships; they occur when one person misunderstands, invalidates,
> excludes, humiliates, or injures the other person in some way.
> Acutedisconnections occur frequently in all relationships. If they
> can be addressed and reworked, they are not problematic; in fact,
> they become places of enormous growth.
>
> When an injured person, particularly one who has less power, can
> represent [their] experience of disconnection or pain to the more
> powerful person and be responded to, with interest or concern, the
> less powerful, hurt person has a sense of "mattering," of having an
> effect on the other. This strengthens connection as well as a sense of
> relational competence.

Jordan goes to explain that when disconnection is not addressed, as frequently occurs in unequal power structures, chronic disconnection and
disempowerment arise, and the person "often loses touch with [their] own
feelings and inner experience."

This is such a powerful example of how disconnection from another person can create disconnection within ourselves.

One of the most important learnings to come out of the research for this
book is how to recognize, name, and talk about my feelings of disconnection. I think we underestimate how much disconnection hurts. And it
hurts more than our feelings. It can cause physical pain.

**Disconnection is often equated with social rejection, social exclusion,
and/or social isolation, and these feelings of disconnection actually
share the same neural pathways with feelings of physical pain.** Current
neuroscience research shows that the pain and feelings of disconnection
are often as real as physical pain. And just as healing physical pain requires
describing it, talking about it, and sometimes getting professional help, we
need to do the same thing with emotional pain.

A couple of serious watch-outs when it comes to disconnection. The first comes from researcher Trisha Raque-Bogdan. She writes, "To avoid the pain and vulnerability that may result when their efforts to achieve connection are unsuccessful, individuals may enact their own disconnection strategies, such as hiding parts of themselves or discounting their need for others. They may learn that it is safer to keep their feelings and thoughts to themselves, rather than sharing them in their relationships."

This means that rather than making a bid for connection and having the bid ignored or rejected, we hide out or pretend we don't need anyone. I think most of us have done this—I know I have. And it's a recipe for loneliness and, for me, blame. I can withhold a bid for connection, then blame someone for not responding. It's a lot of scrambling to avoid being hurt. And it doesn't even work.

The second watch-out is about perfectionism. There's actually a "perfectionism social disconnection model," and this research shows that people who are high on the perfectionistic traits scale behave in ways that cause perceived and actual exclusion/rejection by others. In other words, my perfectionism drives me to show up in ways that lead people to push me away. This doesn't surprise me, but it's still painful to think about, because ultimately our perfectionism is about trying to avoid being excluded or rejected.

Even though I've studied some of these topics for years, the process of writing this book led me to make connections and see relationships that have escaped me, such as the symmetry of these findings:

*Authenticity is a requirement for belonging, and fitting in is a threat.*

*Authenticity is a requirement for connection, and perfectionism (a type of fitting in) is a threat.*

# Insecurity

We use the term **insecure** a lot.

*I'm feeling really insecure.*
*They're acting so insecure.*
*He's super insecure.*
*Do you think she just feels insecure?*

We normally use it to refer to self-doubt or a lack of confidence, but there's way more to it.

There are three types of insecurity:

1. **Domain-specific insecurity** occurs when we are insecure about a specific domain or resource in life, for example, food insecurity, financial insecurity, or a lack of physical safety. Combating domain-specific insecurity is about access and resources. Here's an example of how the term *food insecurity* is used in a report by Feeding America:

   *"In early 2020, the novel coronavirus (COVID-19) began to spread across the United States, and one of the results was an economic recession that ended years of declining rates of food insecurity—the lack of access to sufficient food because of limited financial resources."*

2. **Relationship** or **interpersonal insecurity** occurs when we don't feel we have a supportive and trusting relationship. It can happen either in a specific relationship or as an overarching feeling about all of our relationships. It makes us feel uncertain about being loved, trusted, protected, and valued. This kind of insecurity varies based on the relationship partner.

   *I feel really insecure about my relationship with Deepa. Sometimes she seems interested in me, and other times I feel like I'm bugging her.*

3. **General** or **personal insecurity** occurs when we are overly critical of our weaknesses. This may include being overly critical of our body image or our performance at work.

   *I feel really insecure when I have to present to my managers and the leadership team. I'm a terrible speaker.*

According to researchers Alice Huang and Howard Berenbaum, the opposite of personal insecurity is **self-security,** which they define as "the open and nonjudgmental acceptance of one's own weaknesses."

What's really interesting about their research findings is that we can have high self-esteem but still be insecure if we're overly critical of our imperfections. Because our self-esteem is an assessment of who we are and what we've accomplished compared to our values and our goals, even with high self-esteem we can still feel insecure if we're self-critical. That is powerful.

In initial studies, Huang and Berenbaum found that self-security is positively correlated with self-compassion and negatively correlated with shame-proneness, neuroticism, fear of negative evaluation, self-aggrandizement, and relationship conflict. They also found that people who are more secure are more willing to be vulnerable with others. Their findings suggest that if we are comfortable with our own weaknesses (in other words, if we are self-secure), we are more successful at being emotionally close to others and more likely to have healthy relationships.

What strikes me here is how feelings of both personal and interpersonal insecurity might cause us to behave in ways that push others away or to pull away from others, for fear of being rejected. It's similar to what we learned about the relationship between perfectionism and disconnection. Without awareness, our fear of being hurt can push us to show up in ways that increase the certainty that we'll be hurt.

# " Self-security is 'the open and nonjudgmental acceptance of one's own weaknesses.'

—*Alice Huang and Howard Berenbaum*

## Invisibility

Given that we are all here to be seen, known, and loved, invisibility is one of the most painful human experiences.

**I define invisibility as a function of disconnection and dehumanization, where an individual or group's humanity and relevance are unacknowledged, ignored, and/or diminished in value or importance.**

Researchers Rebecca Neel and Bethany Lassetter discuss findings across multiple fields, including psychology and sociology, that addresses invis-

I define invisibility as a function of **disconnection** and **dehumanization,** where an individual or group's humanity and relevance are unacknowledged, ignored, and/or **diminished** in value or importance. Given that we are all here to be seen, known, and loved, invisibility is one of the most painful human experiences.

ibility in terms of stigma and stereotypes. They offer several examples, such as not getting proper credit for spoken or written material, having limited or negative cultural representations of the group you belong to, experiencing outright discrimination, or being viewed as a symbol of your overall group without being recognized as an individual.

Just as there are different types of insecurity, there are different types of invisibility. There's *interpersonal invisibility* (between people), *group invisibility,* and *representational invisibility.* Neel and Lassetter explain, "When a group is invisible, instead of being actively discriminated against and targeted with negative prejudices . . . members of that group are ignored and overlooked. Invisibility may manifest as being passed over for promotions and recognition; not being seen as a viable friend, romantic partner, or teammate; or being passively excluded from social situations."

It's important to understand that invisibility is its own form of stigmatization. Many individuals who are members of marginalized groups find themselves caught in an ever-tightening vise of two types of dehumanization—stereotyping and invisibility.

# Loneliness

I researched loneliness for over a year when I was writing *Braving the Wilderness.* I'm going to recap what I learned with you here, and share some new data. Even before the COVID pandemic, government and public health officials were calling loneliness a significant health threat.

John Cacioppo founded the field of social neuroscience, and he fundamentally changed the way researchers and clinicians understand loneliness. He dedicated his career to scientific inquiry and to helping us understand what it means to be human. He died in 2018, and though I didn't know him, his work has forever shaped my understanding of loneliness.

The information below is adapted from *Braving the Wilderness.*

"

To grow into an adulthood for a social species, including humans, is not to become **autonomous and solitary**, it's to become the one on whom **others can depend.** Whether we know it or not, our brain and biology have been shaped to favor this outcome.

— *John Cacioppo on loneliness*

Cacioppo and his colleague William Patrick defined loneliness as "perceived social isolation." We experience loneliness when we feel disconnected. Maybe we've been pushed to the outside of a group that we value, or maybe we're lacking a sense of true belonging. **At the heart of loneliness is the absence of meaningful social interaction—an intimate relationship, friendships, family gatherings, or even community or work group connections.**

It's important to note that loneliness and being alone are very different things. Being alone or inhabiting solitude can be a powerful and healing thing. As an introvert, I deeply value alone time, and I often feel the loneliest when I'm with other people.

While there remains deep alignment between what I've found in my research and what Cacioppo has found, it wasn't until I processed his work that I fully understood the important role loneliness plays in our lives. He explains that as members of a social species, we don't derive strength from our rugged individualism, but rather from our collective ability to plan, communicate, and work together.

Our neural, hormonal, and genetic makeup support interdependence over independence. He explains, "To grow into an adulthood for a social species, including humans, is not to become autonomous and solitary, it's to become the one on whom others can depend. Whether we know it or not, our brain and biology have been shaped to favor this outcome." Of course we're a social species. That's why connection matters. It's why shame is so painful and debilitating. It's why we're wired for belonging.

Cacioppo explains how the biological machinery of our brains warns us when our ability to thrive and prosper is threatened. Hunger is a warning that our blood sugar is low and we need to eat. Thirst warns us that we need to drink to avoid dehydration. Pain alerts us to potential tissue damage. And loneliness tells us that we need social connection—something as critical to our well-being as food and water. He explains, "Denying you feel lonely makes no more sense than denying you feel hungry."

Yet we do deny our loneliness. As someone who studies shame, I find myself back in territory that I know well. We feel shame around being lonely—as if feeling lonely means there's something wrong with us. We feel shame even when our loneliness is caused by grief, loss, or heartbreak. Cacioppo believes much of the stigma around loneliness comes from how we have defined it and talked about it for years. We used to define **loneliness** as a "gnawing, chronic disease without redeeming features." It was equated with shyness, depression, being a loner or antisocial, or possessing bad social skills. He gives a great example of this by noting how we often use the term "loner" to describe a criminal or bad guy.

Cacioppo explains that loneliness is not just a sad condition—it's a dangerous one. The brains of social species have evolved to respond to the feeling of being pushed to the social perimeter—being on the outside—by going into self-preservation mode. When we feel isolated, disconnected, and lonely, we try to protect ourselves. In that mode, we want to connect, but our brain is attempting to override connection with self-protection. That means less empathy, more defensiveness, more numbing, and less sleeping. Unchecked loneliness fuels continued loneliness by keeping us afraid to reach out.

To combat loneliness, we must first learn how to identify it and to have the courage to see that experience as a warning sign. Our response to that warning sign should be to find connection. That doesn't necessarily mean joining a bunch of groups or checking in with dozens of friends. Numerous studies confirm that it's not the quantity of friends but the quality of a few relationships that actually matters.

If you're anything like me, and you find yourself questioning the idea that starvation and loneliness are equally life-threatening, let me share the study that really brought all of this together for me. In a meta-analysis of studies on loneliness, researchers Julianne Holt-Lunstad, Timothy B. Smith, and J. Bradley Layton found the following: Living with air pollution increases your odds of dying early by 5 percent. Living with obesity, 20 percent. Excessive drinking, 30 percent. And living with loneliness? It increases our odds of dying early by 45 percent.

In early 2020, one of the first guests on *Unlocking Us* was Surgeon General Dr. Vivek Murthy. We talked about his new book, *Together: The Healing Power of Human Connection in a Sometimes Lonely World.*

In a 2017 *Harvard Business Review* article, Dr. Murthy writes, "During my years caring for patients, the most common pathology I saw was not heart disease or diabetes; it was loneliness. The elderly man who came to our hospital every few weeks seeking relief from chronic pain was also looking for human connection: He was lonely. The middle-aged woman battling advanced HIV who had no one to call to inform that she was sick: She was lonely too. I found that loneliness was often in the background of clinical illness, contributing to disease and making it harder for patients to cope and heal."

Dr. Murthy confirms the connection between loneliness and our physical health, explaining that loneliness is associated with a greater risk of cardiovascular disease, dementia, depression, and anxiety. And at work, he states that loneliness "reduces task performance, limits creativity, and impairs other aspects of executive function such as reasoning and decision making."

# #10

# Places We Go When the Heart Is Open

Love, Lovelessness, Heartbreak, Trust, Self-Trust, Betrayal, Defensiveness, Flooding, Hurt

# Love

Everywhere we learn that love is important, and yet we are bombarded by its failure. In the realm of the political, among the religious, in our families, and in our romantic lives, we see little indication that love informs decisions, strengthens our understanding of community, or keeps us together. This bleak picture in no way alters the nature of our longing. We still hope that love will prevail. We still believe in love's promise.

— bell hooks, *All About Love*

Distinguished emotions researcher Barbara Fredrickson describes the umbrella term **love** as including "the preoccupying and strong *desire* for further connection, the powerful *bonds* people hold with a select few and the *intimacy* that grows between them, the *commitments* to loyalty and faithfulness." In Fredrickson's view, love permeates everyday interactions with others (ranging from strangers and acquaintances to friends and spouses), forming the emotional context from which to strengthen relationships.

Interestingly, there is debate among researchers about whether love is an emotion. However, among everyone else, love is clearly thought of as an emotion. In a study conducted by Shaver and colleagues, undergraduates were asked to rate 213 emotion words in terms of whether they would call the word an emotion: (1 = *"I definitely* would not *call this an emotion"* to 4 *"I definitely* would *call this an emotion"*). The word "love" received the highest average rating (3.94) of all the words on the list, edging out the word "hate" (3.90).

As someone who is committed to research that reflects our lived experiences, I find that Shaver's study and Fredrickson's description both align with what my team heard: Love is an emotion that we're capable of feeling in many different contexts—from intimate partner relationships and family bonds to friends and pets.

"

We cultivate **love** when we allow our most **vulnerable** and powerful selves to be deeply seen and known, and when we honor the spiritual connection that grows from that offering with **trust, respect, kindness, and affection.**

Love is not something we give or get; it is something that we nurture and grow, a **connection** that can be cultivated between two people only when it exists within each one of them—we can love others only as much as we love ourselves.

**Shame, blame, disrespect, betrayal,** and the withholding of affection damage the roots from which love grows. Love can survive these injuries only if they're acknowledged, healed, and rare.

"

We need more **real love.** Gritty, dangerous, wild-eyed, justice-seeking love.

It's always a risk to define a term like "love." I personally think it might be best left to the poets, artists, and yacht rock songwriters. However, a definition did emerge from our research, and it's withstood the test of new data:

> We cultivate love when we allow our most vulnerable and powerful selves to be deeply seen and known, and when we honor the spiritual connection that grows from that offering with trust, respect, kindness, and affection.

> Love is not something we give or get; it is something that we nurture and grow, a connection that can be cultivated between two people only when it exists within each one of them—we can love others only as much as we love ourselves.

> Shame, blame, disrespect, betrayal, and the withholding of affection damage the roots from which love grows. Love can survive these injuries only if they're acknowledged, healed, and rare.

I'll confess that I don't think we'll ever be able to fully unravel the mysteries of love, or, to be honest, many of the other emotions we experience. At least I hope not. I think attempting to better understand ourselves and each other is essential. But so is mystery.

# Lovelessness

The quote that opens this section on love is from bell hooks's book *All About Love*. hooks is a professor, social critic, and writer whose work has shaped my life. In fact, I often say that her work is responsible for 90 percent of the stretch marks on my mind. As a first-time university teacher, I carried her book *Teaching to Transgress* with me at all times, and I slept with it next to me on my nightstand. She teaches that the injustice and systemic oppression that we see in the world today stem from a deep, collective **lovelessness** and calls for an ethic of love. It sounds overly simplistic, but when you read her work you understand that a love ethic is a rigorous calling.

hooks writes,

> Refusal to stand up for what you believe in weakens individual morality and ethics as well as those of the culture. No wonder then that we are a nation of people, the majority of whom, across race, class, and gender, claim to be religious, claim to believe in the divine power of love, and yet collectively remain unable to embrace a love ethic and allow it to guide behavior, especially if doing so would mean supporting radical change. Fear of radical changes leads many citizens of our nation to betray their minds and hearts.

I don't want to betray my mind or heart. I want to live by a love ethic. We need more love between us, but also among us. Not rainbow and unicorn love, or commercialized love. We need more real love. Gritty, dangerous, wild-eyed, justice-seeking love.

# Heartbreak

**I researched heartbreak when I was writing *Rising Strong*. I learned that heartbreak is more than just a painful type of disappointment or failure. It hurts in a different way because heartbreak is always connected to love and belonging.**

Joe Reynolds, a retired Episcopal priest, has taught me the most about heartbreak. I shared his essay in *Rising Strong*, but I want to share it here again. I truly don't think we can read it enough.

> Heartbreak is an altogether different thing. Disappointment doesn't grow into heartbreak, nor does failure. Heartbreak comes from the loss of love or the perceived loss of love. My heart can be broken only by someone (or something, like my dog, though a part of me really believes my dog is a person) to whom I have given my heart. There may be expectations, both met and unmet, in a relationship that ends in heartbreak, but disappointment is not the cause of the heartbreak. There may be failures within the relationship—indeed,

there certainly will be, for we are imperfect vessels to hold the love of another person—but the failures didn't cause the heartbreak. Heartbreak is what happens when love is lost.

Heartbreak can come from being rejected by the one you love. The pain is more intense when you thought the other person loved you, but the expectation of returned love isn't necessary for heartbreak. Unrequited love can be heartbreaking.

The death of a loved one is heartbreaking. I didn't expect them to live forever, and death is nobody's fault regardless of smoking, bad diets, no exercise, or whatever. But my heart is broken anyway. A related heartbreak is the death of something unique, maybe even essential, in someone I love. I didn't want my children to stay children all their lives, but at times the loss of innocence was heartbreaking.

**"**

# Heartbreak is what happens when love is lost.

— *Joe Reynolds*

The loss of love doesn't have to be permanent to be heartbreaking. Moving away from a loved one can break your heart. Change in another person I love may be a good thing. It may be significant personal growth, and I may be happy about it and proud of it. It can also change our relationship and break my heart.

The list goes on. There is a plethora of ways in which a heart can be broken . . . The common denominator is the loss of love or the perceived loss of love.

To love with any level of intensity and honesty is to become vulnerable. I used to tell couples getting married that the only thing I could tell them with certainty was that they would hurt each other. To love is to know the loss of love. Heartbreak is unavoidable unless we choose not to love at all. A lot of people do just that.

Every time we love, we risk heartbreak. Despite how lonely heartbreak feels, it's universal. I remember sitting next to a woman in an airport terminal waiting for our plane to board, and she started weeping. She was probably in her early sixties, and she was by herself. When I asked her if she was okay and if I could get her anything, she didn't reply, she just shook her head and looked away. I returned to reading my book until, about twenty minutes later, the woman said, "We had to put our dog down. My heart is broken."

She wasn't looking at me when she said it, she was looking straight ahead. I said, "I'm so sorry," and I squeezed her forearm. We ended up talking until we boarded, and when we deplaned in Houston, she gave me a hug.

That happened about fifteen years ago. I had never had a pet of my own at that point in my life, but having experienced heartbreak in several other contexts, I could connect with the sense of loss and longing that she was feeling. I didn't question her grief, but I remember thinking to myself, *Man, I'm glad I don't have a dog. I don't think a dog would be worth heartbreak.*

Fast-forward to two years ago, when my first dog, Daisy—a rescue bichon—got untreatable cancer after ten healthy and wonderful years with us. The drive home from the vet's office without her was unbearable. That night allfour of us were sobbing in a big heap on the couch. I looked at my

# 66

# The **brokenhearted** are the bravest among us—they **dared to love.**

kids, who were inconsolable, and said, "We loved Daisy so much. This is heartbreak." Then I looked over at Lucy, our second bichon, who was also missing Daisy, and thought, *God, this hurts. And it's totally worth it.* The brokenhearted are the bravest among us—they dared to love.

## Trust

**In *The Thin Book of Trust: An Essential Primer for Building Trust at Work,* Charles Feltman defines trust as "choosing to risk making something you value vulnerable to another person's actions."** He defines **distrust** as a general assessment that "what is important to me is not safe with this person in this situation (or any situation)." These definitions perfectly capture what emerged from our data on trust and mistrust.

Trust is more of a cognitive assessment than an emotion. But, as we all know, conversations about trust can bring up a lot of emotions, especially hurt and defensiveness. It's difficult to talk about trust in our personal or professional relationships, because it's such a big concept. If someone says "I don't trust you," it feels like a general assault on our character.

We've spent the past ten years trying to figure out exactly what constitutes trust. What are the specific behaviors we're talking about when we talk about trust? Seven elements of trust emerged from our data, and we use the acronym BRAVING:

**Boundaries:** You respect my boundaries, and when you're not clear about what's okay and not okay, you ask. You're willing to say no.

**Reliability:** You do what you say you'll do. At work, this means staying aware of your competencies and limitations so you don't overpromise and are able to deliver on commitments and balance competing priorities.

**Accountability:** You own your mistakes, apologize, and make amends.

**Vault:** You don't share information or experiences that are not yours to share. I need to know that my confidences are kept, *and* that you're not sharing with me any information about other people that should be confidential.

**Integrity:** You choose courage over comfort. You choose what is right over what is fun, fast, or easy. And you choose to practice your values rather than simply professing them.

**Nonjudgment:** I can ask for what I need, and you can ask for what you need. We can talk about how we feel without judgment. We can ask each other for help without judgment.

**Generosity:** You extend the most generous interpretation possible to the intentions, words, and actions of others.

When we bring Dare to Lead training into organizations, this is one of the most adopted tools. It gives all of us a framework to get specific about what's working in our trust building and what needs our attention. I can say to someone, *We're working hard on developing trust in our relationship in these areas, and I feel we need to work more on these areas. What's your experience?*

We most often think about trust between people and groups, but we often forget about the importance of self-trust. **Self-trust is normally the first casualty of failure or mistakes. We stop trusting ourselves when we hurt others, get hurt, feel shame, or question our worth.**

I recently celebrated twenty-five years of sobriety, and when I was reflecting on what that's meant in my life, I couldn't stop thinking about self-trust. Returning to the definition from Feltman, I realized that my sobriety has taught me that I can trust myself and my actions when it comes to protecting what I value. There are still occasions when I have to slow down and get intentional so I don't end up distrusting or betraying myself, but I know increased self-trust has been a huge gift of sobriety. Here's how we use the BRAVING tool to think about self-trust:

B—Did I respect my own boundaries? Was I clear about what's okay and what's not okay?

R—Was I reliable? Did I do what I said I was going to do?

A—Did I hold myself accountable?

V—Did I respect the vault and share appropriately?

I—Did I act from my integrity?

N—Did I ask for what I needed? Was I nonjudgmental about needing help?

G—Was I generous toward myself?

# Betrayal

For there to be betrayal, there would have to have been trust first.

— SUZANNE COLLINS, *The Hunger Games*

**Betrayal is so painful because, at its core, it is a violation of trust.** It happens in relationships in which trust is expected and assumed, so when it's violated, we're often shocked, and we can struggle to believe what's happening. It can feel as if the ground beneath us has given way.

Most betrayals happen among spouses, romantic partners, friends, co-workers, and occasionally family members. The most common types of betrayals include extramarital affairs or cheating on a steady dating partner, lying, betraying confidences, and rejecting or abandoning a partner. When betrayal is the result of physical or sexual abuse perpetrated by a trusted partner or family member (such as is the case in domestic violence or child abuse perpetrated by a parent), it is referred to as *betrayal trauma*.

When we're injured by betrayal, we can suffer high levels of anxiety, depression, anger, sadness, jealousy, decreased self-worth, embarrassment, humiliation, shame, and even trauma symptoms. When I read these symptoms, the first thing I thought about was the times I betrayed myself. As we just covered, self-trust is important, and when we violate that, often to make someone else happy or in a bid for acceptance, I think we can feel self-betrayal too.

There have been times in my life when I've said something that I didn't believe, or did something I didn't want to do, in order to avoid feeling left out. The harshest consequence of that for me was dealing with my own betrayal. I've been thinking a lot about Naomi Osaka and Simone Biles pulling out of competitions to protect their mental and emotional well-being. It's inspiring to watch these women choose to disappoint others and endure cheap-seat criticism over their refusal to betray their bodies, minds, and spirits.

There's another type of betrayal called *institutional betrayal*. Researchers explain that this type of betrayal occurs when "an institution causes harm [by action or inaction] to an individual who trusts or depends upon that institution." Factors that contribute to institutional betrayal include strict membership requirements (military training, elite sports); the existence of prestige or power differentials (caregivers versus patients, clergy versus parishioners); and rigid priorities, such as extreme efforts to protect the reputation of the organization.

Perhaps the most devastating organizational betrayal is a cover-up. In *Dare to Lead,* I explain,

> Cover-ups are perpetrated not only by the original actors, but by a culture of complicity and shame. Sometimes individuals are complicit because staying quiet or hiding the truth benefits them and/or doesn't jeopardize their influence or power. Other times, people are complicit because it's the norm—they work in a cover-up culture that uses shame to keep people quiet.
>
> Either way, when the culture of a corporation, nonprofit, university, government, church, sports program, school, or family mandates that it is more important to protect the reputation of that system and those in power than it is to protect the basic human dignity of individuals or communities, you can be certain of the following problems:
>
> Shame is systemic.
>
> Complicity is part of the culture.
>
> Money and power trump ethics.
>
> Accountability is dead.
>
> Control and fear are management tools.
>
> And there's a trail of devastation and pain.

It's possible to heal betrayal, but it's rare because it requires significant courage and vulnerability to hear the pain we've caused without becoming defensive. In our research, we found that the only way back from betrayal is accountability, amends, and action. None of these things are possible without acknowledging the pain and possibly trauma that we have caused someone without rationalizing or making excuses. We're also much better as individuals and as a culture at shaming and blaming than we are at actual accountability.

# Defensiveness

**At its core, defensiveness is a way to protect our ego and a fragile self-esteem.** Our research team member Ellen Alley explains that our self-esteem is considered fragile when our failures, mistakes, and imperfections decrease our self-worth. In our work, the opposite of a fragile self-esteem is *grounded confidence*. With grounded confidence, we accept our imperfections and they don't diminish our self-worth. It makes sense that defensiveness occurs in areas of our lives where we have fragile self-esteem, or across several areas of our lives if the fragility is more general. Any perceived call-out of our weakness is experienced as an attack on our worth, so we fight hard to defend ourselves against it.

In order to try to limit our exposure to information that differs from how we think of ourselves, we get defensive and overjustify, make excuses, minimize, blame, discredit, discount, refute, and reinterpret. Defensiveness blocks us from hearing feedback and evaluating if we want to make meaningful changes in our thinking or behavior based on input from others.

In our Dare to Lead training, we work with participants to figure out what defensiveness looks like for them, what it feels like, and whether there are some situations that are more likely to trigger it than others. To increase self-awareness, we ask folks to think back to a time when they received difficult feedback and try to remember what their bodies were doing, what thoughts were coming up, and what emotions they were feeling. The vast majority of people struggle to remember the exact thoughts and feelings, which makes sense, given that many of us go into fight-or-flight mode in these situations.

However, for the most part, people can remember their physical responses: Folding their arms over their chest, shoving their hands into their pockets, getting tunnel vision, feeling their heart race, looking down, and getting dry mouth are just a few. It's worth thinking about the physical cues that show up for you when experiencing defensiveness and devising a strategy that can help pull you back into the present moment.

When I get defensive, I often get tunnel vision and start planning what I'm going to say instead of listening. But I have found some ways to disarm my defensiveness. My strategy is to subtly open my palms, even if my hands are just hanging by my side or on my lap, and actually say, "I'm sorry. Can you say that again? I really want to understand." It's pretty effective. If I'm having a really hard time, I might say, "I'm sorry. I'm feeling overwhelmed. I'm going to get a glass of water. Can we sit down in ten minutes and start again?"

# Flooding

This seems like the perfect place to talk about the concept of flooding. The body can become overwhelmed when it senses danger, and for a lot of us, a difficult conversation, hard feedback, or an argument is enough to send our body into overdrive. We can feel overwhelmed, attacked, and confused. **According to the Gottman Institute, flooding is "a sensation of feeling psychologically and physically overwhelmed during conflict, making it virtually impossible to have a productive, problem-solving discussion."**

In his book *Why Marriages Succeed or Fail: And How You Can Make Yours Last,* John Gottman explains, "We each have a sort of built-in meter that measures how much negativity accumulates during such interactions. When the level gets too high for you, the needle starts going haywire and flooding begins. Just how readily people become flooded is individual." He also shares that flooding is affected by how much stress you have going on in your life. The more pressure we're under, the more likely we are to be easily flooded.

One of the worst patterns that I brought to my marriage from my family was "Get back in here and fight with me!" Growing up, we didn't take breaks during fights. No one ever said, "This is no longer productive and we should take a time-out before someone gets their feelings hurt." Our strategy was get louder and meaner until you win or someone else is crying. When I first married Steve, in the middle of a heated argument he would say, "Let's stop and take a break." I was like, "What are you talking about?"

At some point, I realized that stopping scared me. Fighting together seemed less painful than hurting alone. Looking back, I just didn't know how to do it. I had never been taught or seen it modeled. Gottman's work helped me understand the mechanics behind "Okay, can we circle back in twenty minutes?" or "Okay, how much time do you need?" Knowing that we're coming back to finish the discussion, and when, reassures me in some way.

This research also helped me realize that it wasn't just Steve who was getting overwhelmed. I get overwhelmed too. The difference is our strategies. He shuts down; I lash out. Disastrous.

Now when I feel flooded, I'm as likely to say "Time-out" as he is. This is a good thing because, according to Gottman, chronic flooding sets us up to dread communicating. Gottman discusses this effect in the context of marriages and partnerships, but I've seen the same thing in organizations. I've interviewed many research participants who experience chronic flooding with their bosses, so much so that every time they're called into the office, they're already on the path to overwhelm.

There's only so much our bodies and nervous systems can stand before they flip the survival switch and stop communicating and start protecting or attacking. Looking back, I've never once regretted calling a time-out at home or work. Not once. I've never experienced a little time and space being a bad thing, but I have plenty of regrets the other way around.

# Hurt

I'm not sure there's a braver sentence in the human catalog of brave sentences than "My feelings are hurt." It's simple, vulnerable, and honest. But we don't say it very often. We get pissed off, or we hurt back, or we internalize the hurt until we believe we deserve it and that something is wrong with us. But rarely do we say "This really hurt my feelings."

**The definition of hurt from a team of researchers led by Anita Vangelisti goes a long way in explaining why acknowledging hurt is so difficult. They write, "Individuals who are hurt experience a combination of sadness at having been emotionally wounded and fear of being vulnerable to harm. When people feel hurt, they have appraised something that someone said or did as causing them emotional pain."**

I've **never once regretted** calling a time-out at home or work. Not once. I've never experienced a little time and space being a bad thing, but I have **plenty of regrets** the other way around.

We all know that it's really scary to put our heart on the line and say, "I feel wounded and sad about what happened yesterday, and I'm afraid to get hurt again." It's deeply vulnerable, but it's also universal. All of us have felt this way. Often. And a lot. It's impossible to be in relationships and avoid ever feeling hurt, just as it's impossible to know love without knowing what it feels like to have a broken heart.

Vangelisti and team explain that hurt happens through social interaction. In fact, hurt feelings are most often caused by people with whom we have close relationships when we feel devalued or rejected by the other person. Most behaviors that result in hurt feelings are not intended to be hurtful; they typically involve actions that are thoughtless, careless, or insensitive. However, "the more intentional an action is perceived [as], the more hurtful it feels."

Our hurt feelings are typically experienced simultaneously with other emotions, such as sadness, anger, anxiety, jealousy, or loneliness. As a result, they don't always feel the same way, as most other emotions do. However, research indicates that even though hurt feelings are a mix of several emotions, they are a distinct emotional experience, not just a combination of other negative emotions. As I was explaining this to my teenage son, all I could come up with is the rainbow snow cone analogy: There's grape, cherry, lime, lemon, orange, and blueberry, but you don't really taste all of those when you eat it. It just tastes like a rainbow snow cone.

Our reactions to hurt feelings can be self-blaming, or we might cry, lash out, or retaliate by trying to hurt the other person, and/or seek out other relationships to find comfort. When reparation doesn't seem possible, hurt feelings can turn into anger or sadness.

One thing that motivates me to be a little braver in how I handle my hurt feelings is research that shows that when we respond to hurt feelings with anger, the other person tends to match our anger with more anger. I can tell you this has happened in my kitchen about 1,365 times. However, when repair seems possible and we share our hurt feelings and try to reconnect without the anger, the other person tends to respond with constructive actions including apologies and amends. I've tried "I'm so pissed off right now because you're a jerk but I'm going to say that my feelings are hurt so you apologize right this second." *It's clearly not what they had in mind.*

One last note about hurt feelings: Researchers Mark Leary and Carrie Springer have interesting thoughts on the language of hurt feelings. Unlike most other emotions, the expression "hurt feelings" lacks obvious synonyms. The words "wounded" and "pained" have similar connotations, but these words are typically not used to describe emotional experience. Also, although many emotions such as sadness or grief can be described as distressing or painful, "hurt feelings" seems to have a more specific connotation than general emotional pain. An example might be grief. If I'm grieving over the loss of someone close to me, I might tell you, "I'm really hurting," but I probably wouldn't say, "Her death hurt my feelings." It's a great reminder of the power of language. When we're expressing emotion, it's important to differentiate "experiencing hurt" from "having hurt feelings."

"

I'm not sure there's a **braver** sentence in the human catalog of brave sentences than **'My feelings are hurt.'** It's **simple, vulnerable, and honest.** But we don't say it very often. We get pissed off, or we hurt back, or we internalize the hurt until we believe we deserve it and that something is wrong with us. But rarely do we say 'This really hurt my feelings.'

# #11

# Places We Go When Life Is Good

Joy, Happiness, Calm, Contentment, Gratitude, Foreboding Joy, Relief, Tranquility

And I wish you joy and happiness. But above all of this,
I wish you love.

— DOLLY PARTON, "I Will Always Love You"

When I hear that line I immediately think of Dolly Parton and I immediately *feel* Whitney Houston. I had the great pleasure of talking to Dolly on the *Unlocking Us* podcast. She was incredible. Can you believe she wrote "I Will Always Love You" and "Jolene" in the same day?

In Dolly's gorgeous book *Songteller,* she tells the story of Kevin Costner's office calling about using "I Will Always Love You" in a movie. Dolly had worked with the person who was doing the music for the film, liked him, and said yes. She writes,

> But that was the last I'd heard of it. Then one day I was driving my Cadillac back home to Brentwood from my office. I had the radio on, and all of a sudden I heard this spoken voice say, "If I should stay . . ." It caught my ear, but I didn't recognize it. Then, when it went into the music, I thought I was going to wreck the car. I have never had such an overwhelming feeling. I had to pull off to the side of the road, because it just got bigger and bigger and better and better. I have never experienced a greater feeling in my life than hearing Whitney Houston sing that song for the first time.

I don't think there's a better wish for someone you care about than joy, happiness, and love. Even in 1973, Dolly clearly knew that joy and happiness are two separate emotions.

We need both, but how we experience them and how they affect us are different.

**Joy** is sudden, unexpected, short-lasting, and high-intensity. It's characterized by a connection with others, or with God, nature, or the universe. Joy expands our thinking and attention, and it fills us with a sense of freedom and abandon.

**Happiness** is stable, longer-lasting, and normally the result of effort. It's lower in intensity than joy, and more self-focused. With happiness, we feel a sense of being in control. Unlike joy, which is more internal, happiness seems more external and circumstantial.

In *The Gifts of Imperfection,* I quote Anne Robertson, a theologian and writer, on the difference between joy and happiness:

> She explains that the Greek word for happiness is *Makarios,* which was used to describe the freedom of the rich from normal cares and worries, or to describe a person who received some form of good fortune, such as money or health. Robertson compares this to the Greek word for joy, which is *chairo.* Chairo was described by the ancient Greeks as the "culmination of being" and the "good mood of the soul." Robertson writes, "Chairo is something, the ancient Greeks tell us, that is found only in God and comes with virtue and wisdom. It isn't a beginner's virtue; it comes as the culmination. They say its opposite is not sadness, but fear."

# Joy

I love thinking of joy as "the good mood of the soul." There is definitely something soulful about joy. **Based on our research, I define joy as an intense feeling of deep spiritual connection, pleasure, and appreciation.**

Researcher Matthew Kuan Johnson explains that people find experiences of joy difficult to articulate. He hypothesizes that the very nature of joy pushes the boundaries of our ability to communicate about lived experience via spoken language. He also suggests that because language can shape lived experience, cultures that have more words to describe the emotion of joy may also experience joy more richly.

Johnson shares that while experiencing joy, we don't *lose ourselves,* we *become more truly ourselves.* He suggests that with joy, colors seem brighter, physical movements feel freer and easier, and smiling happens involuntarily. Some researchers even describe spontaneous weeping as part of the overwhelming experience of joy.

For me personally, one of the greatest lessons I've learned from two decades of research has been understanding the relationship between joy and gratitude.

Researchers describe the relationship between joy and gratitude as an "intriguing upward spiral." I also love this term—such a great antidote to the downward spirals that we always hear about and, unfortunately, sometimes experience.

The intriguing upward spiral goes like this:

Trait gratitude predicts greater future experiences of in-the-moment joy.

Trait joy predicts greater future experiences of in-the-moment gratitude.

And dispositional or situational joy predicts greater future subjective well-being.

It all just spirals up.

In *Daring Greatly,* I tell a story about an outing with Ellen during which I had the privilege of witnessing the expansive and incredible nature of joy and gratitude at play.

This seems like yesterday, but it happened sixteen years ago, when Ellen was in the first grade. We played hooky one afternoon and spent the day at Hermann Park. At one point we were on a paddleboat in the middle of a pond when I realized she had stopped pedaling and was sitting perfectly still in her seat. Her head was tilted back, and her eyes were closed. The sun was shining on her uplifted face, and she had a quiet smile on her face. I was so struck by her beauty and her vulnerability and the joy on her face that I could barely catch my breath.

I watched for a full minute, but when she didn't move, I got a little nervous. "Ellie? Is everything okay, sweetie?"

Her smile widened and she opened her eyes. She looked at me and said, "I'm fine, Mama. I was just making a picture memory."

I had never heard of a picture memory, but I liked the sound of it. "What's that mean?"

"Oh, a picture memory is a picture I take in my mind when I'm really, really happy. I close my eyes and take a picture, so when I'm feeling sad or scared or lonely, I can look at my picture memories."

She used the word "happy," as we often do, but there's no question that I was witnessing joy, that swirl of deep spiritual connection, pleasure, and appreciation.

# Happiness

Let me tell you what does *not* make me happy: the fact that there's really no consensus in the research when it comes to defining happiness. I think this is the case for a couple of reasons. First, even the most prominent happiness researchers describe happiness as an ambiguous word that has been used historically as an overarching term to describe an entire realm of positive emotions. Second, the vast majority of research we have examines happiness as a trait (part of who we are), not a state (something we experience). In fact, in our keyword literature searches, out of approximately fifteen thousand articles on happiness, we found only twelve articles that described their focus as "state happiness." That comes to 0.08 percent of studies.

Looking at happiness as a trait, researchers found that people's "usual" level of happiness is fairly stable and highly based on hereditary factors, and that for most people, the level could be described as being on the happy side of neutral. (*Happy Side of Neutral* is yet another great band name.)

**Looking at the data we've collected, I would define the state of happiness as feeling pleasure often related to the immediate environment or current circumstances.**

We need happy moments and happiness in our lives; however, I'm growing more convinced that the pursuit of happiness may get in the way of deeper, more meaningful experiences like joy and gratitude. I know, from the research and my experiences, that when it comes to parenting, what makes children happy in the moment is not always what leads them to developing deeper joy, grounded confidence, and meaningful connection.

# Calm

**I define calm as creating perspective and mindfulness while managing emotional reactivity.**

When I think about calm people, I think about people who can bring perspective to complicated situations and experience their feelings without reacting to heightened emotions.

For the *Gifts of Imperfection* research, when people described themselves as calm or talked about other people describing them as calm, I asked a lot of questions. Did they think their calmness was a trait or a practice or both? Did maintaining calm feel like work or like a default setting? Did they see calm modeled growing up? Did they remember learning it?

For personal reasons, I've stayed curious about calm over the years, and the themes and patterns I found in the original research continue to emerge.

First, whether calm is a practice or something more inherent, there are behaviors specific to cultivating and maintaining calm that include a lot of self-questioning. The process seems to be centered on breath, perspective taking, and curiosity:

1. *Calm is an intention. Do we want to infect people with more anxiety, or heal ourselves and the people around us with calm?* As the psychologist and writer Harriet Lerner says, "Anxiety is contagious. Intensity and reactivity only breed more of the same. Calm is also contagious. Nothing is more important than getting a grip on your own reactivity."

2. *Do we match the pace of anxiety, or do we slow things down with breath and tone?*

3.  *Do we have all the information we need to make a decision or form a response? What do we need to ask or learn?*

As someone who has to work on calm as a practice rather than a trait, I've shortened this to two quick questions I ask myself when I feel fear, panic, or anxiety rising:

*Do I have enough information to freak out?* The answer is normally no.

*Will freaking out help?* The answer is always no.

# Contentment

> When you are discontent, you always want more, more, more. Your desire can never be satisfied. But when you practice contentment, you can say to yourself, "Oh yes—I already have everything that I really need."
>
> — The 14th DALAI LAMA

**Contentment** is about satisfaction, and that, ironically, is an unsatisfying idea for a lot of people. It just doesn't seem like enough in a world that tells us every minute should be *big* and life should be OMG-level exciting at all times. We've somehow slipped into a way of being where a text that reads: "I'll stop and get milk on the way home" earns a four-emoji reply along with AWESOME!!!! YOU'RE #1! By these standards, contentment feels a little *meh*.

However, if you think about it, we are surrounded by scarcity, and most of us are almost desperate to feel satisfied and to experience the "enoughness" that contentment brings.

**Based on a summary of data we collected and the existing research, I define contentment as the feeling of completeness, appreciation, and "enoughness" that we experience when our needs are satisfied.**

# "

*Do I have enough information to freak out?* The answer is **normally no.**

*Will freaking out help?* The answer is **always no.**

Several researchers categorize all emotions into one of two categories: low arousal and high arousal. Contentment is characterized as a low-arousal positive emotion, along with peace, tranquility, and satisfaction. These are comfy, old-pair-of-jeans emotions.

I don't have any data to back this up, but I bet if you asked people after 2020 how they'd feel about a life that feels content and satisfying, you'd get a lot of takers. Including me.

Contentment is positively correlated with greater life satisfaction and well-being, and preliminary evidence shows that experiences of contentment might reverse the cardiovascular effects of negative emotion.

One piece of research that grabbed me by the shoulders is that on one of the instruments that measures contentment, 71 percent of the variance in life satisfaction is measured by a single item:

"All things considered, how satisfied are you with your life as a whole these days?"

This always leads to the age-old question: If we're not satisfied with our life as a whole, does this mean we need to go get and do the stuff that will make us satisfied so we can be content, or does this mean we stop taking for granted what we have so we can experience real contentment and enoughness?

# Gratitude

Call me a qualitative researcher, but I'm starting to see a trend here. It appears that many of the emotions that are good for us—joy, contentment, and gratitude, to name a few—have *appreciation* in common.

There is overwhelming evidence that gratitude is good for us physically, emotionally, and mentally. There's research that shows that gratitude is correlated with better sleep, increased creativity, decreased entitlement, decreased hostility and aggression, increased decision-making skills, decreased blood pressure—the list goes on. The research is persuasive, and

**"**

**Gratitude** is
an emotion that
reflects our **deep
appreciation** for what
we value, what brings
meaning to our lives,
and what makes us
**feel connected** to
ourselves and others.

I've read countless research articles and books on gratitude, but I still struggled to understand exactly why it helps so much. Until I read this by Robert Emmons.

Emmons is the "world's leading scientific expert on gratitude." He is a professor of psychology at the University of California, Davis, and the founding editor in chief of *The Journal of Positive Psychology*. He writes,

> Research on emotion shows that positive emotions wear off quickly. Our emotional systems like newness. They like novelty. They like change. We adapt to positive life circumstances so that before too long, the new car, the new spouse, the new house—they don't feel so new and exciting anymore.
>
> But gratitude makes us appreciate the value of something, and when we appreciate the value of something, we extract more benefits from it; we're less likely to take it for granted.
>
> In effect, I think gratitude allows us to participate more in life. We notice the positives more, and that magnifies the pleasures you get from life. Instead of adapting to goodness, we celebrate goodness. We spend so much time watching things—movies, computer screens, sports—but with gratitude we become greater participants in our lives as opposed to spectators.

The two lines that resonate with my research are:

"Instead of adapting to goodness, we celebrate goodness."

"We become greater participants in our lives as opposed to spectators."

The phrase "adapting to goodness" reminds me of a quote I've seen all over social media: "Remember the day you prayed for the things you have now." I normally scroll right past the heavy inspirational quotes, but this one got my attention. I think adapting to goodness without feeling gratitude is a function of scarcity. We either want things for the wrong reasons, then feel disappointed when we acquire them, or we just can't accumulate enough to feel whole, so we accumulate and adapt, never valuing or appreciating.

And the line about living our lives versus being spectators simply reminds me of how many people I've interviewed over the past two decades who talked about simply wanting to feel more alive. Is part of the value of practicing gratitude extending the life of the emotions that make us feel most alive?

**There are about as many definitions of gratitude as there are researchers, poets, and writers who examine the emotion in their work. Many of the existing research definitions don't resonate with the way people described their experiences of gratitude to me in interviews or in writing. Here's what emerged from our work: Gratitude is an emotion that reflects our deep appreciation for what we value, what brings meaning to our lives, and what makes us feel connected to ourselves and others.**

While gratitude is an emotion, if we want to experience its full power, we must also make it a practice. Over the past two decades, the research has taught me that, despite the catchy phrase "an attitude of gratitude," gratitude is a practice. It's tangible. An attitude is a way of *thinking;* a practice is a way of *doing, trying, failing, and trying again.*

The research participants that I interviewed over the years described keeping gratitude journals, doing daily gratitude meditations or prayers, creating gratitude art, using gratitude check-ins with their teams at work, even stopping during their stressful, busy days to actually say these words out loud: "I am grateful for . . ." In our house, we go around the table at dinner and take turns sharing one gratitude. It's small, but it's also big. It gives me a window into the lives of the people I love the most. It's celebrating goodness.

Last, I want to share something that recently popped up on social media. I posted something about the importance of gratitude and someone left a comment that said they thought gratitude might be overrated as a cure for depression, trauma, and anxiety. What I would say is that gratitude is not a cure for anything and we need to be wary of any single practice or approach that's sold as fixing or curing complex mental health issues. Gratitude is a practice that can enrich our lives in meaningful ways. In the world of mental health and social emotional learning, the term "cure" feels like snake oil to me.

# Foreboding Joy

When I give talks, people always seem surprised by the finding that joy is the most vulnerable human emotion. Given that I study fear and shame, people are hesitant to believe that something as positive as joy can make us squirm. Then I share what is almost certainly the most surprising finding for most people: **If you're afraid to lean into good news, wonderful moments, and joy—if you find yourself waiting for the other shoe to drop—you are not alone. It's called "foreboding joy," and most of us experience it.**

This is when things get really quiet.

**Foreboding joy** is one of those practically universal experiences that everyone thinks of as something only they do. A few people don't experience it, but most of us do. And when it comes to parents . . . 95 percent of the parents we interviewed experience foreboding joy with their children.

When we lose our tolerance for vulnerability, joy becomes foreboding. No emotion is more frightening than joy, because we believe if we allow ourselves to feel joy, we are inviting disaster. We start dress-rehearsing tragedy in the best moments of our lives in order to stop vulnerability from beating us to the punch. We are terrified of being blindsided by pain, so we practice tragedy and trauma. But there's a huge cost.

When we push away joy, we squander the goodness that we need to build resilience, strength, and courage.

The good news? In our research we found that everyone who showed a deep capacity for joy had one thing in common: They practiced gratitude. In the midst of joy, there's often a quiver, a shudder of vulnerability. Rather than using that as a warning sign to practice imagining the worst-case scenario, the people who lean into joy use the quiver as a reminder to practice gratitude.

# Relief

**The definition that best aligns with our findings is from researchers Ira Roseman and Andreas Evdokas. They describe relief as "feelings of ten-**

**"**

When we lose our tolerance for **vulnerability,** joy becomes foreboding. No emotion is more frightening than **joy,** because we believe if we allow ourselves to feel joy, we are inviting disaster. We start dress-rehearsing **tragedy** in the best moments of our lives in order to stop vulnerability from beating us to the punch. We are terrified of being blindsided by pain, so we practice **tragedy and trauma.** But there's a huge cost.

When we push away joy, we squander the goodness that we need to build resilience, **strength, and courage.**

sion leaving the body and being able to breathe more easily, thoughts of the worst being over and being safe for the moment, resting, and wanting to get on to something else."

When most of us think of how relief feels, we go immediately to a deep exhale and a long, breathy "Whew." Well, it turns out that there's something to that "sigh of relief." Sighing serves as a type of reset button for our body. It not only *signals* relief to our body, but it *enhances* relief, and it reduces muscle tension.

# Tranquility

**Tranquility** may be my new favorite emotion. Why? **Check out the research definition: "Tranquility is associated with the absence of demand" and "no pressure to do anything."**

No demands? No pressures? Sign me up. Or should I say "Take me away."

"Tranquil environments" provide many restorative elements that are needed to counter mental fatigue and attention depletion. Researchers Rachel and Stephen Kaplan found that there are four essential elements of a restorative environment: a sense of getting away, a feeling of immersion, holding attention without effort, and compatibility with one's preferences.

Additional research shows that there are auditory and visual components to tranquil environments, including elements of nature and low levels of noise. Settings that induce high tranquility include fields and forests and large bodies of water; urban settings tend not to induce tranquility.

Like I said. Take me away.

One thing to note: There's a difference between feeling content and feeling tranquil. With contentment, we often have the sense of having completed something; with tranquility, we relish the feeling of doing nothing.

# #12

# Places We Go When We Feel Wronged

---

Anger, Contempt, Disgust, Dehumanization,
Hate, Self-Righteousness

# Anger

**If you look across the research, you learn that anger is an emotion that we feel when something gets in the way of a desired outcome or when we believe there's a violation of the way things should be.** When we feel anger, we believe that someone or something else is to blame for an unfair or unjust situation, and that something can be done to resolve the problem.

Anger is an action emotion—we want to do something when we feel it and when we're on the receiving end of it. Additionally, according to Charles Spielberger, an influential anger researcher, angry feelings can vary in intensity, "from mild irritation or annoyance to fury and rage."

Anger is also a full-contact emotion. Because it activates our nervous system and can hijack our thoughts and behaviors, it can take a real toll on our mental and physical health. Researchers explain that regulating and coping with anger rather than holding on to or expressing chronic anger is crucial for the health of our brain (it reduces psychiatric problems) and other organs in the body. There is also an interesting biological component to anger. A substantial amount of research indicates that our propensity for anger and aggression is partially hereditary, but the specific gene locations have not yet been identified.

## What I've Learned, Unlearned, and Continue to Learn About Anger. Dammit.

I've spent a lot of my career saying that anger is a secondary or "indicator" emotion that often conceals emotions that are harder to recognize, name, or own. According to 91 percent of emotions experts, I'm wrong. Yes, 91 percent of emotions experts believe that anger is a primary emotion. Maybe it's semantics and our differences come down to how we define "primary." Or maybe I've got it (and had it) all wrong. Honestly, there are a lot of debates in the research that I don't think are worth digging into because they don't teach us much, but this debate is worth understanding.

As I mentioned in the introduction, we asked around seventy-five hundred people to identify all of the emotions that they could recognize and name when they're experiencing them. The average was three: glad, sad, and mad—or, as they were more often written, happy, sad, and pissed off. Couple this extremely limited vocabulary with the importance of emotional literacy, and you basically have a crisis. It's this crisis that I'm trying to help address in this book.

Over the past two decades, when research participants talked about being angry, the story never stopped there. Their narratives of anger unfolded into stories of betrayal, fear, grief, injustice, shame, vulnerability, and other emotions. Ultimately the combination of data showing how limited emotional vocabularies can be with our experiences of interviewing people about anger and watching them consistently reveal other emotions behind the anger led me to challenge the idea that anger is a primary emotion.

The more data we collected, including interviews with more than fifteen hundred therapists and counselors, the more certain I became that anger is a secondary or "indicator" emotion that can mask or make us unaware of other feelings that are out of reach in terms of language, or that are much more difficult to talk about than anger. We live in a world where it's much easier to say "I'm so pissed off" than "I feel so betrayed and hurt." It's even easier to say "I'm angry with myself" than "I'm disappointed with how I showed up."

Clinicians and educators use many tools to help clients and students uncover the emotions that show up as anger. I think these are especially helpful:

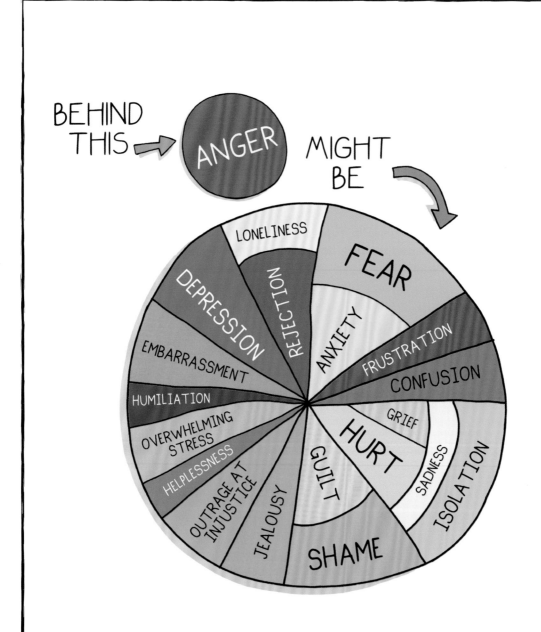

©2000 Creative Therapy Associates, Inc., Cincinnati, Ohio

Even if you look at the list of eighty-seven emotions and experiences in this book, more than twenty of them are likely to present as anger or with anger. Feeling increasingly confident that anger is a secondary or indicator emotion, I was left with some big questions to answer: In the face of injustice, can we just be enraged, furious, angry? Does it have to be masking or indicating something, or can we just be mad? The answer to both of these questions is yes, and . . .

As a former union organizer and lifelong activist, I think anger is often the most compassionate response to experiencing or witnessing injustice. It can be a powerful catalyst for change that doesn't need to be explained or justified. And I still think that behind the anger is a tempest of pain, grief, betrayal, disappointment, and other emotions.

In *Braving the Wilderness,* I write about pain, hate, and anger—especially as they pertain to social justice issues. I'm going to share an excerpt with you here:

> Sometimes owning our pain and bearing witness to struggle means getting angry. When we deny ourselves the right to be angry, we deny our pain. There are a lot of coded shame messages in the rhetoric of "Why so hostile?" "Don't get hysterical," "I'm sensing so much anger!" and "Don't take it so personally." All of these responses are normally code for *Your emotion or opinion is making me uncomfortable* or *Suck it up and stay quiet.*
>
> One response to this is "Get angry and stay angry!" I haven't seen that advice borne out in the research. What I've found is that, yes, we all have the right and need to feel and own our anger. It's an important human experience. *And* it's critical to recognize that maintaining any level of rage, anger, or contempt (that favorite concoction of a little anger and a little disgust) over a long period of time is not sustainable.
>
> Anger is a catalyst. Holding on to it will make us exhausted and sick. Internalizing anger will take away our joy and spirit; externalizing anger will make us less effective in our attempts to create change and forge connection. It's an emotion that we need to transform into something life-giving: courage, love, change, compassion, justice.
>
> Or sometimes anger can mask a far more difficult emotion like grief, regret, or shame, and we need to use it to dig into what we're really feeling. Either way, anger is a powerful catalyst but a life-sucking companion.

So, do I think anger is a primary emotion or not? I don't know. There are so many competing lists of "primary emotions," I don't know if it matters whether anger belongs on one of those lists. Here are the three things I *do* know from the work I've done over the past twenty-plus years:

**"**

**Anger** is a catalyst. Holding on to it will make us **exhausted and sick.** Internalizing anger will take away our joy and spirit; externalizing anger will make us less effective in our attempts to create change and forge connection. It's an emotion that we need to transform into something life-giving: **courage, love, change, compassion, justice.**

1. Anger often masks emotions that are more difficult to name and/or more difficult to own.

2. Just as an indicator light in our car tells us to pull over and check things out, anger is a very effective emotional indicator light that tells us to pull over and check things out.

3. Anger, in response to experiencing or witnessing injustice, pain, and struggle, can be a powerful catalyst for change. But, by definition, a catalyst *sparks* change, it's not *the* change.

## Contempt

> When someone is angry at you, you've still got traction with them, but when they display contempt, you've been dismissed.
>
> — PAMELA MEYER

When I hear the word "contempt," I immediately think of two of my favorite researchers, John and Julie Gottman. John is known across the globe for more than forty years of research on marital stability and divorce prediction. He is the author or co-author of more than two hundred published academic articles and more than forty books. Julie is a highly respected clinical psychologist and expert on marriage, domestic violence, gay and lesbian adoption, same-sex marriage, and parenting issues who co-designed the national clinical training program in Gottman Method Couples Therapy.

Why do I think of them when I think of contempt? Because John describes contempt as "perhaps the most corrosive force in marriage," and his research on marriage has identified contemptuous communication as a strong predictor of divorce. In fact, through a series of studies conducted in their lab, where they observed thousands of couples, John Gottman and his research partner were able to predict with over 90 percent accuracy which couples would eventually divorce.

**Contempt** is one of the most damaging of the four negative communication patterns that predict divorce. The other three are criticism, defensiveness, and stonewalling. These took on the name of the Four Horsemen of the Apocalypse—a term that originates from Christian mythology.

In his book *Why Marriages Succeed or Fail,* John Gottman writes, "What separates *contempt* from criticism is the *intention to insult* and *psychologically abuse* your partner. With your words and body language, you're lobbing insults right into the heart of your partner's sense of self. Fueling these contemptuous actions are negative thoughts about the partner—he or she is stupid, disgusting, incompetent, a fool. In direct or subtle fashion, that message gets across along with the criticism."

We can feel and show contempt toward individuals or groups. In either instance, being on the receiving end of contempt is often painful because

# The Four Horsemen
## and How to Stop Them With Their Antidotes

### Criticism
Verbally attacking or blaming your partner's character.

*"Why do you always make us late?!"*

### Gentle Start-Up
State how you feel about the situation, and what you need.

*"I feel frustrated about being late. I need to be on time."*

### Defensiveness
Victimizing yourself to ward off a perceived attack or to reverse the blame.

*"Come on, you know I have a hard time getting up in the morning!"*

### Take Responsibility
Accept your partner's perspective and offer an apology for any wrongdoing.

*"I'm sorry for running late. I know how important it is for you to be on time."*

### Contempt
Attacking your partner's sense of self with insulting or abusive language that communicates superiority.

*"I learned how to tell time when I was five. When are you ever gonna learn?"*

### Describe Your Own Feelings and Needs
Express your positive needs instead of your partner's flaws.

*"It's important to me to be punctual. Please help me with that."*

### Stonewalling
Withdrawing from interaction to avoid conflict and convey disapproval, distance, and separation.

*Thinking: "I can't take this anymore. I gotta get out of here."*

### Self-Soothing
Ask for a break using a signal or word that you both agree on. Spend the break doing a calming activity on your own.

*"Timeout. I need a break. I'm going to go for a walk, and we can talk again in 30 minutes."*

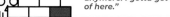

it's shaming and belittling. Over the past five years, contempt between political and ideological groups has been at an all-time high. Think about the political climate today as you read this description from an article on the Gottmans' website:

> When you communicate with contempt, the results can be cruel. Treating others with disrespect and mocking them with sarcasm and condescension are forms of contempt. So are hostile humor, name-calling, mimicking, and body language such as eye-rolling and sneering. In whatever form, contempt is poisonous to a relationship because it conveys disgust and superiority, especially moral, ethical, or characterological. **Contempt, simply put, says, "I'm better than you. And you are lesser than me."**

Contempt results in distancing, ignoring, or excluding the contemptible person—they are not considered worthy of one's time or energy. This attitude seems partially attributable to the key distinguishing feature between contempt and anger, namely that contempt results when there is the perception that the contemptible person is incapable of change. But also, a person feeling contempt often wants or needs to feel better about themselves, and they do so by diminishing the person who is the object of their contempt. It's no wonder that "research has shown that the contemptuous person is likely to experience feelings of low self-esteem, inadequacy, and shame."

In a March 2019 *New York Times* opinion piece entitled "Our Culture of Contempt," Arthur C. Brooks writes,

> Political scientists have found that our nation is more polarized than it has been at any time since the Civil War. One in six Americans has stopped talking to a family member or close friend because of the 2016 election. Millions of people organize their social lives and their news exposure along ideological lines to avoid people with opposing viewpoints. What's our problem?

> A 2014 article in *The Proceedings of the National Academy of Sciences* on "motive attribution asymmetry"—the assumption that

your ideology is based in love, while your opponent's is based in hate—suggests an answer. The researchers found that the average Republican and the average Democrat today suffer from a level of motive attribution asymmetry that is comparable with that of Palestinians and Israelis. Each side thinks it is driven by benevolence, while the other is evil and motivated by hatred—and is therefore an enemy with whom one cannot negotiate or compromise.

People often say that our problem in America today is incivility or intolerance. This is incorrect. Motive attribution asymmetry leads to something far worse: contempt, which is a noxious brew of anger and disgust. And not just contempt for other people's ideas, but also for other people. In the words of the philosopher Arthur Schopenhauer, contempt is "the unsullied conviction of the worthlessness of another."

Brooks goes on to say,

Contempt makes political compromise and progress impossible. It also makes us unhappy as people. According to the American Psychological Association, the feeling of rejection, so often experienced after being treated with contempt, increases anxiety, depression and sadness. It also damages the contemptuous person by stimulating two stress hormones, cortisol and adrenaline. In ways both public and personal, contempt causes us deep harm.

Brooks's solution is not that we need to disagree less, but we need to learn how to disagree better—without contempt or cruelty. It's really not far off from the Gottmans' approach of teaching us how to replace negative communication patterns with new skills that convey respect and appreciation.

# Disgust

❏ I might be willing to try eating monkey meat, under some circumstances.

❏ It bothers me to hear someone clear a throat full of mucus.

❏ If I see someone vomit, it makes me sick to my stomach.

❏ It would not upset me at all to watch a person with a glass eye take the eye out of the socket.

❏ Even if I was hungry, I would not drink a bowl of my favorite soup if it had been stirred by a used but thoroughly washed flyswatter.

Gross. I know. Welcome to disgust.

These are five items from the Disgust Scale—Revised (DS-R), a valid and reliable measure of disgust developed by a team of researchers in the mid-1990s and revised in 2007. Jonathan Haidt, the lead researcher on the team that created the scale, is a social psychologist and writer who is the Thomas Cooley Professor of Ethical Leadership at the New York University Stern School of Business. Haidt poses a critical question:

> Disgust is a fascinating emotion. Its elicitors are a puzzle: it makes sense that we are disgusted by things that can contaminate our food, but why does this food-related emotion extend itself so deeply into our social world, so that people feel disgusted by certain ethnic groups (or by racism), by homosexuality (or by homophobia), and by a variety of social and moral violations that don't involve anything physically contaminating?

## Understanding Disgust

**With contempt, we look down on the other person and we want to exclude or ignore them. With disgust, inferiority is not the issue, the feeling is more physical—we want to avoid being "poisoned" (either literally or figuratively).** The poisoning thing is real. Researchers believe that "The experience of disgust encourages individuals to distance themselves from the emotion eliciting source, thereby limiting contact and exposure to the potentially infectious or toxic target." I love that Steven Pinker refers to disgust as "intuitive microbiology."

**According to emotions research pioneer Paul Ekman, disgust "arises as a feeling of aversion towards something offensive. We can feel disgusted**

by something we perceive with our physical senses (sight, smell, touch, sound, taste), by the actions or appearances of people, and even by ideas." Ekman found that "disgust contains a range of states with varying intensities" from mild dislike and aversion to repugnance, revolution, and intense loathing. "All states of disgust are triggered by the feeling that something is aversive, repulsive and/or toxic."

Ekman, who has made invaluable contributions to the study of emotions, especially in identifying the relationships between emotions and facial expressions, explains that when we feel disgust, we often wrinkle our nose, choke or gag, cover our mouth or nose while hunching over (as if we might vomit), recoil or back away, and say "yuck" or "ew."

Circling back to the question posed by Jonathan Haidt: How does an emotion that is hardwired to protect us from actual toxins and poisons become something that we feel toward other people? Researchers explain that *core disgust* is thought to protect the body from ingestion of contaminants, while disgust in an interpersonal context is thought to "protect" us from unseemly behavior or contamination of the soul.

But it's not just unseemly behavior that makes us feel disgust toward other people. We've taken an emotion that keeps us safe from the stuff that can make us sick and turned it into an emotion that can be weaponized against people who make us sick, simply because we either disagree with them or they are different from us. One example of this is the dangerous relationship between disgust and dehumanization. Researchers Maria Miceli and Cristiano Castelfranchi found that reactions of disgust can rapidly lead to dehumanizing, othering, and marginalizing individuals or groups of people.

This element of dehumanization seems to be one of the characteristics that distinguishes disgust from contempt. They write, "The disrespect involved in disgust implies that *human dignity is perceived as alienable.* The person is responsible for the bad action [they have] done, but the very effect of that action is dehumanizing: by performing it, one has *responsibly degraded oneself to sub-human.*"

They go on to explain how "moral disgust is even more dangerous because of its dehumanizing implications. Disgusting people, if no longer viewed as

"

With disgust, we've taken an emotion that keeps us safe from the stuff that can make us **sick** and turned it into an emotion that can be **weaponized** against people who make us sick.

persons, can suffer much more than 'othering' and marginalization." Once we dehumanize people, violence and cruelty toward them become easier to perpetrate because the parts of us that are hardwired to not hurt other people turn off—in our minds, we've stripped them of their humanity.

Another difference that makes disgust more dangerous is that once a target is viewed with disgust, this judgment seems to be permanent; evaluations of disgust seem to indicate a reprehensible moral character that is immutable and unforgivable. At least with anger, an apology or reparation has the potential to reverse the damage done.

# Dehumanization

**Dehumanization** continues to be one of the greatest threats to humanity. If we're going to save ourselves and one another, we need to understand what it is and how it works. I've adapted what I wrote about the dehumanization process in *Braving the Wilderness* and am including it here as a primer. After researching and writing on disgust, I made connections that I've missed in the past. So, while adapted from *Braving the Wilderness,* the section includes some new thoughts.

> David Livingstone Smith, the author of *Less Than Human,* explains that dehumanization is a response to conflicting motives. We want to harm a group of people, but it goes against our wiring as members of a social species to actually harm, kill, torture, or degrade other humans. Smith explains that very deep and natural inhibitions prevent us from treating other people like animals, game, or dangerous predators. He writes, "Dehumanization is a way of subverting those inhibitions."
>
> Dehumanization is a process. I think Michelle Maiese, a professor in the philosophy department at Emmanuel College, lays it out in a way that makes sense, so I'll use some of her work here to walk us through it. **Maiese defines dehumanization as "the psychological process of demonizing the enemy, making them seem less than**

**human and hence not worthy of humane treatment."** Dehumanizing often starts with creating an *enemy image*. As we take sides, lose trust, and get angrier and angrier, we not only solidify an idea of our enemy, but also start to lose our ability to listen, communicate, and practice even a modicum of empathy.

Once we see people on "the other side" of a conflict as morally inferior and even dangerous, the conflict starts being framed as good versus evil. Maiese writes, "Once the parties have framed the conflict in this way, their positions become more rigid. In some cases, zero-sum thinking develops as parties come to believe that they must either secure their own victory, or face defeat. New goals to punish or destroy the opponent arise, and in some cases more militant leadership comes into power."

Dehumanization has fueled innumerable acts of violence, human rights violations, war crimes, and genocides. It makes slavery, torture, and human trafficking possible. Dehumanizing others is the process by which we become accepting of violations against human nature, the human spirit, and, for many of us, violations against the central tenets of our faith.

How does this happen? Maiese explains that most of us believe that people's basic human rights should not be violated—that crimes like murder, rape, and torture are wrong. Successful dehumanizing, however, creates *moral exclusion*. Groups targeted based on their identity—gender, ideology, skin color, ethnicity, religion, age—are depicted as "less than" or criminal or even evil. The targeted group eventually falls out of the scope of who is naturally protected by our moral code. This is moral exclusion, and dehumanization is at its core.

Dehumanizing always starts with language, often followed by images. We see this throughout history. During the Holocaust, Nazis described Jews as *Untermenschen*—subhuman. They called Jews rats and depicted them as disease-carrying rodents in everything from military pamphlets to children's books. Hutus involved in the Rwanda genocide called Tutsis cockroaches. Indigenous people are

"

Language matters. It's the raw material of story, it changes how we feel about ourselves and others, and it's a portal to **connection.**

With the same amount of power, language can also be used to strip people of their **dignity** and humanity. With awareness about how dehumanization works, comes the responsibility to call out dangerous language when we recognize it.

often referred to as savages. Serbs called Bosnians aliens. Slave owners throughout history considered slaves subhuman animals.

What really struck me as I was rereading this and looking at new research on dehumanization is that the language we use to dehumanize is effective because it actually taps into "core disgust"—we reduce people to the types of things that make us physically recoil as we do from cockroaches, rats, and "infestations." We reduce people into the things that make us grossed out.

One of the arguments of this book is that language matters. It's the raw material of story, it changes how we feel about ourselves and others, and it's a portal to connection. With the same amount of power, language can also be used to strip people of their dignity and humanity. With awareness about how dehumanization works comes the responsibility to call out dangerous language when we recognize it.

# Hate

Hatred will always motivate people for destructive action.

— AGNETA FISCHER, ERAN HALPERIN,
DAPHNA CANETTI, AND ALBA JASINI, "Why We Hate"

**According to researcher Robert Sternberg, hate is a combination of various negative emotions including repulsion, disgust, anger, fear, and contempt.** We feel hate toward individuals or groups that we believe are intentionally malicious and unlikely to change. What's interesting is that we can develop hate toward people we do not know personally simply based on their affiliation with a group or ideology that doesn't align with our beliefs.

Research shows that a lack of direct contact with such individuals can actually *strengthen* hate. This confirms my belief that people are harder to hate close up, and easier to hate when we're behind our ideological bunker and they're behind theirs.

What's really fascinating is that hate is actually fueled by our need for connection. I call this *common enemy intimacy*. I may not know anything about you, but we hate the same people and that creates a counterfeit bond and a sense of belonging. I say "counterfeit" because the bond and belonging are not real, they hinge on my agreeing with you and not challenging the ideas that connect us. That's not true belonging.

Sternberg found that hate moves from place to place on a "current," and it needs this current to grow and travel. He explains that "those currents are provided by cynical leaders who capitalize on people's insecurities to bolster their own power." He writes, "When instigators seek to gain traction for their leadership by spreading hate, they often attract observer(s) who do nothing or who, over time, move from being observers to being participant/observers to being active participants." Sternberg also states that "the more the leaders whip up powerful stories, even ones of hate, the more people follow them."

We know from the research that hate crime victims "generally have not done anything specific: They are terrorized for who they are, not for what they have done." For me, this immediately brings to mind all of the innocent trans people—particularly Black women—who have been targeted, beaten, and killed, not because of anything they've done, but because of who they are.

In an interview with *The Daily Beast,* the actress and activist Laverne Cox talks about the documentary *Disclosure,* which addresses the dehumanization of trans people. She explains, "This is what our film tries to grapple with, this paradox of visibility. That we're potentially more targeted because we're more visible. And so then the need for justice, the need for real justice and understanding and hearts and minds to be changed so that the existence of a trans person doesn't [cause] someone to react in a way that that trans person might lose their life."

The research that I found the most devastating explained that the "goal of hate is not merely to hurt, but to ultimately eliminate or destroy the target, either mentally (humiliating, treasuring feelings of revenge), socially (excluding, ignoring), or physically (killing, torturing), which may be accompanied by the goal to let the wrongdoer suffer."

If this isn't enough to make me return to the days when I had toddlers and banned the word "hate" from my vocabulary, I don't know what is.

Hate crimes are meant to terrorize more than a single person; the goal is to embed fear so deeply in the heart of a community that fear becomes a crushing way of life for everyone who shares that identity. There is no simple way to stop hate, however, Sternberg explains:

> It is not clear that there is any magic bullet for curing hate. But any mechanism that helps one understand things from others' points of view—*love, critical thinking, wisdom, engagement with members of target groups*—at least makes hate less likely, because it is harder to hate people if you understand that in many respects they are not all so different from you.

# Self-Righteousness

> The self-righteous scream judgments against others to hide the noise of skeletons dancing in their own closets.
>
> — JOHN MARK GREEN

I can tell you exactly what I was wearing and where I was sitting twenty-five years ago when someone in an AA meeting said, "Part of my sobriety is letting go of self-righteousness. It's really hard because it feels so good. Like a pig rolling in shit."

I remember thinking, *Oh, God. I'm not sure exactly what that means, but I think I roll around in that shit too.*

From that day forward, I started thinking of self-righteousness as a threat to my self-respect, my well-being, and my sobriety. Unfortunately, it's virtually impossible to add it to the abstinence list—it's not as binary as having or not having a Bud Light or a cigarette—but I definitely see it as a slippery behavior that necessitates some self-reflection. And possibly amends.

**According to researchers, "Self-righteousness is the conviction that one's beliefs and behaviors are the most correct."** People who exhibit self-righteousness see things as black and white—they tend to be closed-minded, inflexible, intolerant of ambiguity, and less likely to consider others' opinions.

It is important to realize that **self-righteousness** is different from **righteousness**. In the case of righteousness, we are appropriately reacting to a true injustice, we are *trying to do the right thing*. When feeling self-righteous, we feel morally superior to others and are *trying to convince ourselves or others* that we are doing the right thing. Moral outrage in response to injustice can be classified as righteous anger when motivated by a "true" concern about injustice, whereas when moral outrage is self-enhancing, it is self-righteous anger.

I wish I had understood all this better back then—especially the difference between self-righteousness and righteousness. I always thought about self-righteousness in terms of "terminal uniqueness"—a term from the recovery movement that means you think you're different from everyone else. You're the exception, your addiction struggle is the exception, your story is the exception, and so on. I didn't know what I know now, I just told myself that I needed more humility and less thinking I was better than, more right, and always the exception. I had to stop assuming that people who disagreed with me didn't care about people or issues as much as I did. It's funny how thinking "I'm better than" can slip into "I'm worthless" in mere seconds. Letting go of the first slowly releases us from the second.

Given the political climate today, it's important to understand that moral outrage is self-enhancing and related to self-righteous anger. I've had to be super conscientious about the moral outrage and instead focus on doing the next right thing. If there's anything that looks and feels like a pig rolling in shit these days, it's performative moral outrage, especially on social media.

# #13

# Places We Go to Self-Assess

Pride, Hubris, Humility

Unless you want to be swept away in a sea of inspirational Pinterest quotes, don't google "pride and humility." From Bible verses to the worst 1980s corporate motivational posters, everyone seems to have an opinion about the importance of humility and the dangerous nature of pride. You don't see too many inspirational quotes about hubris, but if you search political news articles from 2016 to 2020, you'll be swallowed whole.

But here's the thing. Most of the quotes have it wrong. Let's break it down.

**Pride is a feeling of pleasure or celebration related to our accomplishments or efforts.**

**Hubris is an inflated sense of one's own innate abilities that is tied more to the need for dominance than to actual accomplishments.**

**Humility is openness to new learning combined with a balanced and accurate assessment of our contributions, including our strengths, imperfections, and opportunities for growth.** We really get this wrong. More to come.

# Pride

**Pride is a feeling of pleasure or celebration related to our accomplishments or efforts.**

Many researchers distinguish hubris from pride by referring to the pride we experience when we've accomplished something as *authentic pride*. Authentic pride typically has a positive connotation and descriptors that include words like "accomplishment," "mastery," "triumph," "confidence," and "self-worth." It is positively associated with self-esteem and negatively associated with shame-proneness.

Researchers Lisa Williams and Joel Davies explain that we don't just feel pride about our own accomplishments, there is a "family of pride experiences." I can feel proud of myself, proud of you, proud of us.

If you take in the research across the board, authentic pride, or feeling good about what we accomplish, is a healthy thing. However, Ronda Dearing from our research team points out, "There's another common way that we sometimes use the word 'pride' that doesn't quite fit with the research or with my experience. People commonly say things like 'Pride got in the way,' for example when someone fresh out of college turns down a job that they feel overqualified for. Or we might say 'He was too proud to accept help,' for example when a single dad is struggling financially and turns down his parents' offer of a temporary loan."

After rumbling on this use, we agreed that context and story are necessary to figure out what's driving these behaviors. It could be anything—hubris, fear, shame, defensiveness. The learning here is to stay curious when we see or experience these behaviors. They don't fit with authentic pride and there's probably more to the story.

# Hubris

**Hubris is an inflated sense of one's own innate abilities that is tied more to the need for dominance than to actual accomplishments.** It is negatively correlated with self-esteem and positively correlated with narcissism and shame-proneness. In simpler terms, the higher the hubris, the lower the self-esteem, and the higher the hubris, the higher the narcissism and shame-proneness.

Dominance, which is a type of status that is coerced through aggression or intimidation, plays a significant role in hubris. Researchers write, "Hubristic pride may have evolved to motivate behaviors, thoughts, and feelings oriented toward attaining dominance, whereas authentic pride may have evolved to motivate behaviors, thoughts, and feelings oriented toward attaining prestige." I'm not crazy about the word "prestige"—it sounds arrogant. But it's helpful to know that in the research, prestige status is earned—prestige-based leaders are admired for their skills or knowledge, as distinct from dominance status, which is obtained by force.

To those of us observing hubris, it looks and feels terrible. However, to the person experiencing hubris, it feels good. They puff up and feel blustery and superior. Furthermore, the person experiencing hubris doesn't really care what we think. Researchers found that hubris can increase levels of dominance, and, interestingly, dominance "does not require respect or social acceptance." So when you watch someone do something out of sheer hubris and you think to yourself, *Don't they see how badly this is being received?*—remember, it doesn't need to be received well for them to feel good about it.

As I mentioned earlier, hubris is positively correlated with narcissism. In *Daring Greatly,* I write about how everything from Facebook and influencer culture to the increasingly insane behavior of politicians has pushed the term "narcissism" into the zeitgeist. While it's penetrated social consciousness enough that most people correctly associate it with a pattern of behaviors that include grandiosity, a pervasive need for admiration, and a lack of empathy, almost no one understands how every level of severity in this diagnosis is underpinned by shame.

Narcissism is shame-based. In fact, **I define narcissism as the shame-based fear of being ordinary.**

# " Narcissism is the shame-based fear of being ordinary.

Read this next paragraph slowly. Then reread it. It's mind-blowing.

Research led by Jessica Tracy found that "For the narcissist, positive views of the self are too essential to leave to the whim of actual accomplishments, for they are what prevent the individual from succumbing to shame and low self-esteem. Instead, narcissists come to experience a globalized 'hubristic' pride, characterized by feelings of arrogance and egotism, which is distinct from the more achievement-based and pro-social 'authentic' pride."

Hubris sounds like an almost foolproof way to assert yourself in the world—no accomplishments, no respect, no social acceptance needed. You would, however, have to hone your bullying skills and be open to being seen as an asshole. The price (in addition to the aforementioned downsides) is that folks with trait hubristic pride are more likely to experience chronic anxiety, engage in aggression and hostility, and struggle with intimate partner relationships and general social support.

What does hubris actually look like? Researchers say that it mirrors the physical patterns of dominance display—the head has a downward (rather than upward) tilt, with a widened stance, and less smiling. Not hard to picture.

# Humility

I'm ending this section with humility to give you something more uplifting. While the origin of the word "hubris" is Greek and was used to describe a pride and ambition so great that they offend the gods and lead to one's downfall, "humility" comes from the Latin word *humilitas,* meaning groundedness. Humility is quieter but more genuine and ultimately more powerful than hubris. And—as with pride—we've got a lot of it wrong.

**Humility is openness to new learning combined with a balanced and accurate assessment of our contributions, including our strengths, imperfections, and opportunities for growth.**

I can sum up humility with one sentence that emerged from the research that informed *Dare to Lead: I'm here to get it right, not to be right.*

What humility isn't: downplaying yourself or your accomplishments, which according to researchers is modesty, not humility. It's also not low self-esteem or meekness or letting people walk all over you.

The emotion of humility involves understanding our contributions in context, in relation to both the contributions of others and our own place in the universe. It's different from pride in that when we feel pride, we focus entirely on the positive aspects of a specific accomplishment (which can still be healthy and productive).

The term "*intellectual humility*" refers specifically to a willingness to consider information that doesn't fit with our current thinking. People who demonstrate intellectual humility don't lack confidence or conviction. They may hold strong views, but they are also open to hearing other points of view. They are curious and willing to adjust their beliefs when faced with new or conflicting information. Humility allows us to admit when we are wrong—we realize that getting it right is more important than needing to "prove" that we are right.

As we leave this section, hopefully we can also leave behind the ideas that hubris is just a benign form of supersized pride, that pride is bad for us, and that humility is weakness. Pride can be good for us, hubris is dangerous, and humility is key to grounded confidence and healthy relationships.

"

I'm here
to get it right,

**not to be right.**

# Cultivating Meaningful Connection

## Theory

It is a capital mistake to theorize before one has data. Insensibly one begins to twist facts to suit theories, instead of theories to suit facts.

— ARTHUR CONAN DOYLE,

"A Scandal in Bohemia"

I'll never forget the day when Dr. Paul Raffoul, my epistemology professor, drew the circle of science on the board. It was my first class in the social work doctoral program at the University of Houston, and seeing that circle on the board felt like a moment from a Dan Brown book. It was the PhD student's first clue to finding the inner sanctum. Dr. Raffoul was

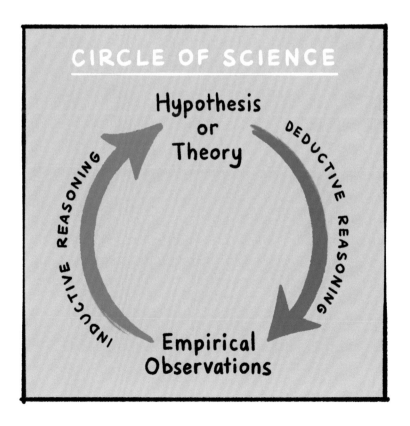

one of the few faculty members that I continued to address as "Dr." even after I was hired as a tenure-track assistant professor and we became colleagues. He always wore a suit and tie with a coordinating U of H baseball cap, and he always had a twinkle in his eye when he talked about that circle. It's like he was thinking, *You have no idea what I'm talking about right now, oh, but you will. All will be revealed.*

As a grounded theory researcher, I work up from the bottom of that circle, following an inductive approach and generating theories from mostly qualitative data. I'll occasionally use quantitative methods for something, but I love language, words, and story. The theories that I develop are then often tested using deductive and quantitative methods. Some old-school deductive folks argue that their approach is the most valuable, but today there's a widely held belief that we need both. We should not test and build on theories that are just conjecture—especially when it comes to hypothesizing about underrepresented groups while knowing very little about their stories and lived experiences. Having an empirically based theory adds to the rigor of science. The value is in the full circle. (PS: I think the circle of science would be way more popular if we had an Elton John song like "The Circle of Life.")

The word "theory" is not as complicated as it sounds. We all have theories. For example, you probably have a theory about the traffic patterns by your house, or the reason one team at work is always late delivering projects, or why your parents get to the airport six hours before their flight departs. We theorize all day long.

**I think the best definition is from behavioral scientist Fred Kerlinger (another great teaching from Dr. Raffoul's course). Kerlinger defines theory as: "A set of interrelated constructs (concepts), definitions, and propositions that present a systematic view of phenomena specifying relations among variables, with the purpose of explaining and predicting the phenomena."**

If you break down your theory about the traffic patterns in your neighborhood, it will more than likely include propositions and concepts that come together to paint a picture of what's going on (for example, the number of cars at the high rise down the street, the line getting out of the grocery store, the need for a light at a busy intersection, the new school zone, etc.). Theorizing is part of meaning-making—it's how we explain the relationships between different variables.

The only difference between our everyday theories about how things work and the inductive research I do is that my theories are based on observations or data that we methodically collect and analyze. We observe the traffic, count the cars, pull data from the city, time the lights, review accident reports, interview neighbors, and generate a theory or a hypothesis: If we do this, then . . . Or, these changes will have a positive effect on . . .

Once the theory is out in the world, my research colleagues may come behind me and test that theory deductively by temporarily setting up stop signs or traffic lights and analyzing the outcome. Part of the beauty of the circle of science is its iterative nature—researchers test and retest, from the bottom up and from the top down. The findings evolve and our level of understanding keeps getting closer and closer to "truth." It may seem as if the findings are changing or the initial findings were wrong. But often it is the case that new data has given us a more accurate understanding of the data that came before. This, my friends, is the circle of science. (By the way, I'm totally asking Elton John and Brandi Carlile to do a duet on this. TikTok, we're coming for you.)

## Near Enemies

Now that I've forced you through a primer on theory building, I'm going to share a new theory with you that's the culmination of my work since the beginning—and I do mean the very start. My dissertation is actually on connection. This new work is a theory on cultivating meaningful connection.

While this new theory draws heavily on all my previous work, there was something missing—a piece that I couldn't quite figure out until I started this research. That elusive piece was rediscovering the Buddhist concept of **near enemies**. Studying near enemies took me down the research rabbit hole, and the more I read, the more I realized that for years I've underestimated this concept's power and contribution to explaining human behavior.

I explained it in Chapter Seven where we talk about pity being the near enemy of compassion, but before we get to the new theory, I want to dig deeper. Several writers and researchers whose work I admire and turn to often, including Kristin Neff, Chris Germer, and Jack Kornfield, write about near enemies. To get our heads and hearts around this concept, I thought I'd share a different definition and a couple of examples.

In an incredibly timely and powerful article, "The Near and Far Enemies of Fierce Compassion," Chris Germer writes, "Near enemies are states that appear *similar* to the desired quality but actually undermine it. Far enemies are the *opposite* of what we are trying to achieve. For example, a near enemy of loving-kindness is sentimentality—similar but different. A far enemy of loving-kindness is ill will—the opposite of loving-kindness. Similarly, a near enemy of compassion is pity and a far enemy is cruelty."

Without the language of near and far enemies, and without the tools of emotional granularity and self-awareness, the difference between how we want to show up and the near enemies of these practices feels nuanced. But this type of nuance predicts the difference between wholeheartedness and brokenheartedness.

Jack Kornfield explains that near enemies may seem like the qualities that we believe are important, and may even be mistaken for them, but they are different and often undermine our practices. He writes, "The near enemies depict how spirituality can be misunderstood or misused to separate us from life."

When I read that last sentence, I had to break it down and reread it about twenty times:

**"The near enemies depict how spirituality can be misunderstood or misused to separate us from life."**

I define spirituality as the deeply held belief that we are inextricably connected to each other by something greater than ourselves. I have friends who are atheists who every day practice inextricable connection—they hurt when others hurt and they know that none of us are free until all of us are free. I have friends who talk endlessly about their religion and wear scripture on their T-shirts, yet demonstrate no connection to anyone's suffering but their own and maybe that of the people in their immediate circle. I make this point because we're not talking about religion here. We're talking about the irrepressible human spirit.

When I look at Kornfield's sentence and think about my twenty-plus years of research on connection, my translation is:

**On the surface, the near enemies of emotions or experiences might look and even feel like connection, but ultimately they drive us to be disconnected from ourselves and from each other. Without awareness, near enemies become the practices that fuel separation, rather than practices that reinforce the inextricable connection of all people.**

This is huge.

To really get this concept in our bones, I want to share two more examples with you from Jack Kornfield.

On love, he writes;

> The near enemy of love is attachment. Attachment masquerades as love. It says, "I will love this person (because I need something from them)." Or, "I'll love you if you'll love me back. I'll love you, but only if you will be the way I want." This isn't the fullness of love. Instead there is attachment—there is clinging and fear. True love allows, honors, and appreciates; attachment grasps, demands, needs, and aims to possess.

On equanimity, he writes:

> The near enemy of equanimity is indifference or callousness. We may appear serene if we say, "I'm not attached. It doesn't matter what happens anyway, because it's all transitory." We feel a certain peaceful relief because we withdraw from experience and from the energies of life. But indifference is based on fear. True equanimity is not a withdrawal; it is a balanced engagement with all aspects of life.

It is opening to the whole of life with composure and ease of mind, accepting the beautiful and terrifying nature of all things.

I needed the concept of near enemies because when it comes to cultivating meaningful connection, the far enemies—the real opposites—are not what get in the way most of the time. They're easy to recognize—we don't get tricked into believing that everything is okay; they are up front with their disconnection. It's the near enemies of connection—the imposters that can look and feel like cultivating closeness—that sabotage relationships and leave us feeling alone and in pain. And because they're so stealthy, we often internalize the pain and think that something is wrong with us. Near enemies can feel like manipulation and even gaslighting. Of course the far enemies destroy connection too—but you see them coming.

## A Grounded Theory on Cultivating Meaningful Connection

Cultivating meaningful connection is a daring and vulnerable practice that requires **grounded confidence, the courage to walk alongside others,** and **story stewardship.** I'm not going to walk you through every element of the theory—most are self-explanatory now that we have the language—but I do want to give you an overview and introduce you to some new concepts. As we talk about the theory, you'll see that each of the three major categories that support cultivating meaningful connection has its own near and far enemies, as does each of the skill sets that support those categories.

### Developing Grounded Confidence

I first introduced the term **grounded confidence** in *Dare to Lead.* The core learning in *Dare to Lead* is that it's not fear that gets in the way of courage, it's armor—how we self-protect when we feel uncertain or fearful. Our armoring behaviors keep us from showing up in ways that are aligned with our values. As we learn to recognize and remove our armor, we replace it with grounded confidence. The concept was in its infancy when I wrote about it several years ago. It only included three properties: the abilities to rumble with vulnerability, stay curious, and practice new skills. What you see now is a much fuller concept with more properties. And my guess is that we'll continue to work on this for years to come.

# A Grounded Theory on
### CULTIVATING MEANINGFUL CONNECTION

by Brené Brown

Developing
**Grounded Confidence**

Practicing
**the Courage to Walk Alongside**

Practicing
**Story Stewardship**

**CONNECTION** is the energy that exists between people when they feel seen, heard, and valued; when they can give and receive without judgment; and when they derive sustenance and strength from the relationship.

# SKILL SET 1 FOR CULTIVATING MEANINGFUL CONNECTION

| SKILL SETS FOR CULTIVATING MEANINGFUL CONNECTION | NEAR ENEMIES | FAR ENEMIES |
|---|---|---|
| Developing **GROUNDED CONFIDENCE** (LEARNING & IMPROVING) | **KNOWING AND PROVING** | **PROTECTING FRAGILE SELF-WORTH** |
| **Knowing and applying the language of human experience and emotion** | Shaping emotion and experience to fit what we know | Acting out, shutting down, or giving up |
| **Practicing courage** | Not owning our hurt, pain, and fear. "Everything is fine." | Choosing armor or comfort over courage |
| **Rumbling with vulnerability** | Performing and/or avoiding vulnerability | Shutting down or acting out in vulnerability |
| **Staying curious** | Challenging & criticizing more than exploring and contributing | Showing indifference, disinterest, defensiveness |
| **Practicing humility** | Confusing modesty and insecurity with humility | Hustling and hubris |
| **Committing to mastery and practice** | Self-protecting with perfectionism | Getting stuck in fear and shame |
| **Feeling embodied and connected to self** | Thinking and acting our emotions without feeling them | Feeling disembodied and disconnected from ourselves |

Comic art by GAVIN AUNG THAN

# SKILL SET 2 FOR CULTIVATING MEANINGFUL CONNECTION

| SKILL SETS FOR CULTIVATING MEANINGFUL CONNECTION | NEAR ENEMIES | FAR ENEMIES |
|---|---|---|
| Practicing **THE COURAGE TO WALK ALONGSIDE** | **CONTROLLING THE PATH** | **WALKING AWAY** |
| **Knowing and applying the language of human experience and emotion** | Shaping emotion and experience to fit what we know | Acting out, shutting down, or giving up |
| **Committing to be other-focused** | Performing concern while trying to control or distance | Defaulting to self-protecting and self-focused |
| **Practicing compassion** | Showing pity and comparing suffering | Cruelty and/or creating distance, separation, disconnection, and treating others like they're invisible |
| **Practicing empathy** | Defaulting to sympathy and other empathy misses | Creating distance, separation, disconnection, and treating others like they're invisible |

NOTES

| SKILL SETS FOR CULTIVATING MEANINGFUL CONNECTION | NEAR ENEMIES | FAR ENEMIES |
|---|---|---|
| Practicing THE COURAGE TO WALK ALONGSIDE | CONTROLLING THE PATH | WALKING AWAY |
| **Practicing non-judgment** | Performing non-judgment but judging, comparing, blaming, and distancing | Judging |
| **Sharing "power with" and "power to"** | "Helping" by trying to control people, perceptions, or outcomes | Leveraging power over |
| **Being relational** | Being transactional; connecting for gain, fitting in, or control | Disengaging and disconnecting |
| **Setting and respecting boundaries** | Becoming enmeshed or creating distance | Being enmeshed or building walls |

NOTES

# SKILL SET 3 FOR CULTIVATING MEANINGFUL CONNECTION

| SKILL SETS FOR CULTIVATING MEANINGFUL CONNECTION | NEAR ENEMIES | FAR ENEMIES |
|---|---|---|
| Practicing **STORY STEWARDSHIP** (HONORING STORY AS SACRED) | **PERFORMING CONNECTION WHILE DRIVING DISCONNECTION** | NOT VALUING STORY <br> **DAMAGING TRUST & SELF-TRUST** |
| **Knowing and applying the language of human experience and emotion** | Shaping emotion and experience to fit what we know | Acting out, shutting down, or giving up |
| **Rumbling with story – listening, discovering, and staying curious** | Creating separation by knowing, advice-giving, and problem solving | Showing indifference, disinterest, dismissing, or diminishing |
| **Building narrative trust – believing, acknowledging, and affirming** | Disconnecting through: <br><br> Narrative takeover <br><br> Narrative tap-out <br><br> (including performative affirmation) | Fueling narrative distrust <br><br> Diminishing the humanity of others and ourselves |

NOTES

Developing grounded confidence is driven by a commitment to learning and improving. Its near enemy is knowing and proving. In our culture, we're quick to mistake knowing and proving for confidence, when they're actually a function of low self-worth. Fragile self-worth is the far enemy of grounded confidence. A fragile self-worth drives us to self-protect at all costs.

The last skill under this category is feeling embodied and connected to self. We don't talk enough about the importance of embodiment and what happens to us when we're disconnected from our physical selves. In his book *The Body Keeps the Score*, trauma researcher Bessel van der Kolk writes, "Trauma victims cannot recover until they become familiar with and befriend the sensations in their bodies. Being frightened means that you live in a body that is always on guard. Angry people live in angry bodies. The bodies of child-abuse victims are tense and defensive until they find a way to relax and feel safe. In order to change, people need to become aware of their sensations and the way that their bodies interact with the world around them. Physical self-awareness is the first step in releasing the tyranny of the past."

Van der Kolk goes on to explain that, "The mind needs to be reeducated to feel physical sensations, and the body needs to be helped to tolerate and enjoy the comforts of touch. Individuals who lack emotional awareness are able, with practice, to connect their physical sensations to psychological events. Then they can slowly reconnect with themselves."

Grounded confidence is driven by learning and curiosity—even about our own bodies. For many of us, myself included, it's easier to live in our heads and be completely disconnected from our bodies. But there's a cost. Insomnia, injuries, exhaustion, depression, anxiety—the body has powerful ways to get our attention.

Prentis Hemphill is a writer, an embodiment facilitator, a political organizer, and a therapist. They are the founder and director of the Embodiment Institute and the Black Embodiment Initiative. I've learned so much from Prentis about embodiment—I think their definitions will breathe some life into these words that you see on the model:

Prentis defines embodiment as "the awareness of our body's sensations, habits, and the beliefs that inform them. Embodiment requires the ability to feel and allow the body's emotions. This embodied awareness is necessary to realign what we do with what we believe."

They define disembodiment as "an unawareness, repression or denial of our sensations and emotions, and/or privileging our thinking over our feeling. Disembodiment often leads to an incongruence between the actions we take in the world and the beliefs that we hold."

This piece about values misalignment makes sense because for me, the best indicator light around being out of values is my body. I can't quite describe it, but I feel out of sorts—like you feel when you catch every red light on a long downtown street. My body is out of flow.

Prentis writes, "The habits that become embodied in us are the ones that we practice the most often. And, whether we are aware of it or not, we are always practicing something. When we are disembodied or disconnected from our own feelings and sensations, it's easy to become habituated to practices that we don't believe in or value."

We become what we do—even when those things are outside of who we want to be. Our bodies are our teachers and the messengers who call our attention to what we're absorbing and becoming. This is why we have to learn how to listen, and this is why grounded confidence requires embodiment.

## Practicing the Courage to Walk Alongside

The second major category is **practicing the courage to walk alongside**. One of the great challenges in grounded theory is naming categories and properties in a way that accurately reflects the data and resonates with people's lived experiences. For this category, I found myself asking: What does it mean to be other-focused, to use language in the service of connecting, to be compassionate, empathic, and nonjudgmental?

As soon as I started thinking about this question, I was transported back to my dissertation. The name of the theory that emerged from my dissertation is "Acompañar," which means "to accompany" in Spanish. My dissertation is a study on how helping professionals build and maintain connection with the people they serve. The approach that best reflected what I learned from that data was the "accompaniment" movement—an organizing and social justice approach that comes out of liberation theology activism in Latin America. The work is a commitment to be *with* people—not pushing them from behind or leading from the front, but walking with them in solidarity.

Being other-focused, using language in the service of connecting, practicing compassion, empathy, and nonjudgment, aren't fully in line with all of the tenets of accompaniment, but are fully consistent with practicing the courage to walk alongside.

The near enemy of walking alongside is *controlling the path*. Sometimes it can look and feel like someone is with us, but really they're trying to control either us or the outcome. I think most of us do this more than we'd like to admit. For example, my child comes home and is upset because they got in trouble at school. They were talking while the teacher was talking and they were told that their behavior was disrespectful. I'm trying to be with them in this experience, but I quickly find myself worried about what the teacher will think of my child and, worse, what will they think of me as a parent. So, now, rather than being with my child, I'm trying to control how this is going to go. Forget about asking what happened or checking in to see what they're feeling. *I want to be with you in this* turns into, *You need to email your teacher and apologize right this minute. What were you thinking?*

I once heard Anne Lamott say, "Help is the sunny side of control." Yes and yikes. All of us who were raised taking care of other people and trying to manage environments can default to wanting to control the path, regardless of our great intentions. Especially when "it's in everyone's best interest." The question is always, *Whose best interest are you protecting?* Walking alongside is other-focused. Control is self-focused. *Insert stressed emoji with flat, panicked grin.*

We also see *controlling the path* in larger cultural contexts. For example, politicians who see people suffering and rather than actually walking alongside them, make people *feel* like they're understood and they're not alone, while actually leveraging and exploiting their emotion for political gain and influence. *I see your struggles and your pain. You don't deserve it. Here's who's to blame and here's how I can help you and make them pay.* This near enemy is so seductive that it is often as dangerous as the far enemy: walking away.

Power is another element of walking alongside, and it's not one we talk about often enough. I think it's because we have a weird, negative reaction to the word "power," even though everyone will tell you that powerlessness is one of the most painful human experiences. **My favorite definition of power comes from Martin Luther King, Jr. In a 1968 speech given to striking sanitation workers in Memphis, Reverend King defined power as the ability to achieve purpose and effect change**. The definition does not make the nature of power inherently good or bad, which aligns with what I've learned in my work. What makes power dangerous is how it's used.

**Power over** is dangerous because it's using disproportional influence to achieve gain, even when that diminishes the agency and/or dignity of others.

In their publication *Making Change Happen: Power,* Just Associates, a global interdisciplinary network of activists, organizers, educators, and scholars, defines three variations of power within the context of social justice and activism. They are equally helpful when we think about walking alongside people.

**Power with** is **"based on mutual support, solidarity, collaboration and recognition and respect for differences."**

**Power to** is **"based on the belief that each individual has the power to make a difference."**

**Power within is defined by an ability to recognize differences and respect others, grounded in a strong foundation of self-worth and self-knowledge.** When we operate from a place of power within, we feel comfortable challenging assumptions and long-held beliefs, pushing against the status quo, and asking if there aren't other ways to achieve the highest common good.

**Walking away,** the far enemy of walking alongside, includes both discounting and dominating behaviors such as ignoring, dismissing, power over, and building walls (literally and figuratively). If you combine the entire column of near enemy and far enemy from this category, you'll get an interesting tool for assessing politics. The combination of control and power-over masquerading as connection is especially destructive.

## Practicing Story Stewardship

I'm going to start this section by acknowledging that I've been wrong about something for years. For two decades, I've said, "We need to understand emotion so we can recognize it in ourselves and others." Without exaggeration, I've said this thousands of times and I've heard it from other researchers at least that much. Well, let me go on the record right now: I no longer believe that we can recognize emotion in other people, regardless of how well we understand human emotion and experience or how much language we have.

Why have I stopped believing that we can recognize emotion in other people? Two reasons:

1. Too many emotions and experiences present the exact same way. There's no way to know through observation if your tears come from grief, despair, hopelessness, or resentment, just to name a few. Absolutely no way.

2. While research shows that there are some universal facial expressions for a small number of emotions, how we express what we're feeling and experiencing can be as unique as we are.

So how do we know what other people are feeling? We ask them. It's only then that we are able to connect with the grounded confidence to engage and the courage to walk alongside. When they tell us what they're feeling, what happened, what they fear or desire, we listen and we become trusted stewards of their stories.

**Story stewardship means honoring the sacred nature of story—the ones we share and the ones we hear—and knowing that we've been entrusted**

**with something valuable or that we have something valuable that we should treat with respect and care.** We are good stewards of the stories we tell by trusting them to people who have earned the right to hear them, and telling them only when we are ready. We are good stewards of the stories we hear by listening, being curious, affirming, and believing people when they tell us how they experienced something.

The near enemy of practicing story stewardship is performing connection while driving disconnection. Performative connection means that we're acting interested or invested, but there's more going on under the surface that's really driving disconnection and separation. The issues that most of us struggle with are being the knower, advice-giving, and problem-solving. Problem-solving is tough because some people do want help. The best story stewardship in these moments is just to say, "I'm grateful that you're sharing this with me. What does support look like? I can listen and be with you, I can help problem-solve, or whatever else you need. You tell me."

The greatest threat to story stewardship is the two near enemies of building narrative trust: **narrative takeover** and **narrative tap-out**. Rather than building trust by acknowledging, affirming, and believing, we shut people down when we experience discomfort or disinterest, or when we take over the narrative and make it about us or our perception of what happened. There are examples of both of these in the graphic comic strip that Gavin developed for us, which you'll find in a few pages.

Narrative tap-outs can range from subtle disinterest to complete shutdowns. If we had thought bubbles they'd say "This is too uncomfortable" or "I don't care enough about you to care about this" or "I can't take this on right now." If the reason we're tapping out is the latter, it's so much better to say that than to diminish someone's story.

It sounds weird, but we can tap out of sharing our own stories too. Often this is about a lack of grounded confidence that our stories matter or a lack of self-trust about when and how we share them. Tapping out of stewarding someone's story can feel like betrayal, and tapping out of sharing our own story feels like betraying ourselves.

Narrative takeover is a huge problem in our world. It impacts one-on-one conversations and cultural conversations. Rather than being good stewards of a story, we hijack the story and center ourselves. That centering takes many different shapes, including shifting the focus to us, questioning or not believing what someone is sharing because it's different than our lived experience, or diminishing the importance of an experience because it makes us feel uncomfortable or, worse, complicit.

When we reject the truth of someone's story—the ultimate failure of story stewardship—it's often because we've stealthily centered ourselves in their story, and the narrative takeover is about protecting our ego, behavior, or privilege. The less diverse our lived experiences, the more likely we are to find ourselves struggling with narrative takeover or narrative tap-out.

A cultural example of narrative takeover is the Black Lives Matter movement. This is a life-affirming accountability movement to call attention to the violence being perpetrated against Black people. But rather than listening, learning, and believing the stories of injustice, systemic racism, and pain, groups of white people centered themselves with "all lives matter" and "blue lives matter." There was never a narrative of "white lives and police lives don't matter" in this movement. This was an attempt to, once again, decenter Black lives and take over the narrative.

Like empathy, story stewardship is not walking in someone else's shoes, it's being curious and building narrative trust as they tell you about the experience of being in their own shoes. It's about believing people when they tell you what an experience meant to them. The far enemy of narrative trust is fueling narrative distrust and diminishing the humanity of others and ourselves. Why ourselves? Because when we are reckless with people's stories, we diminish our own humanity.

The following comic is based on a role play that Aiko Bethea and I did on the *Dare to Lead* podcast.

# CULTIVATING MEANINGFUL CONNECTION

Comic art by GAVIN AUNG THAN

"I KNOW THAT, OF COURSE, **NOBODY IN THE ROOM LOOKS LIKE ME.** BUT EVEN AS I WAS MAKING THE PRESENTATION, NO ONE ASKED ME THE QUESTIONS. THEY LOOKED OVER AT BRAD INSTEAD OF ME. AFTERWARDS WHEN PEOPLE SAID, '**GOOD JOB,**' THEY WERE SAYING IT INTO THE SPACE AND TO EACH OTHER. **SO I WAS REALLY DEFLATED.**"

Comic art by GAVIN AUNG THAN

Comic art by GAVIN AUNG THAN

CULTIVATING MEANINGFUL CONNECTION

I THINK INVISIBILITY IS ONE OF THE MOST *PAINFUL* EXPERIENCES I'VE EVER HAD IN MY LIFE.

MY GUT IS, WE NEED TO ADDRESS THIS, BUT I WANT YOU TO THINK ABOUT WHAT SUPPORT *LOOKS LIKE FOR YOU* AND HOW WE CAN DO THIS *TOGETHER.* MORE IMPORTANTLY, HOW I CAN *SUPPORT YOU DOING IT.*

AND THAT SUPPORT CAN LOOK LIKE WHATEVER YOU NEED IT TO LOOK. *I'M SORRY THAT HAPPENED.* I KNOW HOW GOOD THAT WORK WAS, AND I KNOW HOW HARD YOU WORKED TO PUT THAT TOGETHER.

I FEEL *SEEN* AND *HEARD.* I DON'T FEEL DISEMPOWERED, BUT IT TOOK *TIME* AND TOOK HER TO BE *INTROSPECTIVE.*

BUILDING NARRATIVE TRUST MEANT CENTERING HER EXPERIENCE *OVER MY DISCOMFORT,* AND BEING THE LEARNER, *NOT* THE KNOWER. WE BOTH HAD TO BE *VULNERABLE AND BRAVE.*

Comic art by GAVIN AUNG THAN

# Language and Meaningful Connection

As you review the model, you'll see that *knowing and applying the language of human experience and emotion* is a key property of all of the major categories that support meaningful connection. That's how we ended up here, together, sharing this book. When this emerged from the data, I thought, "Damn. I can't write a book on meaningful connection without including some kind of glossary or compendium of emotion and experience words." It was and remains weirdly shocking to me that access to and application of language are central to grounded confidence, walking alongside one another, and story stewardship. I wouldn't have been surprised to see language emerge as core to one of these, but that it's central to all three speaks to its power.

As you can see in the graphic, the near enemy of knowing and applying language is shaping emotion and experience to fit what we know. We take nuanced experiences like despair or hopelessness and force them into whatever language we have—maybe sadness or anger. But this leaves us far less capable of sharing what we're experiencing, getting help, or moving through our experiences productively. It's a near enemy because we may be talking about our feelings or sharing them, but we can't get to healing because we're limited by our language. The far enemy is acting out, shutting down, or giving up. No access to language means we're in pain, we feel alone, and we can't articulate what's happening. In the introduction, I gave an example of trying to tell a doctor about an excruciating pain in your shoulder while your mouth is taped and your hands are tied behind your back. The limits of not being able to explain result in an unbearable level of frustration.

## Atlas of the Heart

While I experienced a lot of tough moments growing up, there were also countless gifts. It sometimes feels like it has to be one or the other, but as we learned in this work, both things can be true and often are true. One of the most valuable gifts in my life was from my mom. She taught us to never look away from pain. The lesson was simple and clear:

> Don't look away. Don't look down.
> Don't pretend not to see hurt.

Look people in the eye.
Even when their pain is overwhelming.
And when you're hurting and in pain, find the people who can
    look you in the eye.

We need to know we're not alone—especially when we're hurting.

Even in my fifties, I find myself wrestling with the same questions that left me confused as a kid: Why do we cause each other so much pain, and why do we turn away from hurt when the only way to the other side of struggle is through it? I don't know why it's so hard to understand—I've been known to run from vulnerability like someone is chasing me. Granted, not very often anymore. It just takes so much more energy and creates so much more emotional churn than having a seat and asking hurt or uncertainty to pull up a chair.

Doing this research and writing this book has taught me that our emotions and experiences are layers of biology, biography, behavior, and backstory. Every single day, our feelings and experiences show up in our bodies, they're shaped by where we come from and how we were raised, they drive how we show up, and each feeling has its own unique backstory. Understanding these emotions and experiences is our life's work. The more we learn, the deeper we can continue to explore.

I've also learned something that has changed how I move through my life on a daily basis: Our connection with others can only be as deep as our connection with ourselves. If I don't know and understand who I am and what I need, want, and believe, I can't share myself with you. I need to be connected to myself, in my own body, and learning what makes me work. This is how I start to develop the grounded confidence I need to move through the world and cultivate meaningful connection with others. Before this work, I didn't give enough importance to spending time and energy connecting to myself. I made that optional if I had anything left after connecting with others. It wasn't working—and now I know why.

In this life, we will know and bear witness to incredible sorrow and anguish, and we will experience breathless love and joy. There will be boring days and exciting moments, low-grade disappointment and seething anger, wonder and confusion. The wild and ever-changing nature of emotions and experiences leaves our hearts stretch-marked and strong, worn and willing.

My hope is that we find that solid ground within us, that shore that offers safe harbor when we're feeling untethered and adrift. The more confident we are about being able to navigate to that place, the more daring our adventures, and the more connected we are to ourselves and each other. The real gift of learning language, practicing this work, and cultivating meaningful connection is being able to go anywhere without the fear of getting lost. Even when we have no idea where we are or where we're going, with the right map, we can find our way back to our heart and to our truest self.

# Gratitude

There is absolutely no way you'd be holding this book in your hands if it weren't for a huge team of people who worked tirelessly to make it happen. The research, the art and design, the planning, the new website, the editing and production, the launch plans, the contracts—it's a miracle and I'm grateful beyond words.

**The Brené Brown Education and Research Group Team**: To Ellen Alley, Suzanne Barrall, Bethany Bloomer, Cookie Boeker, Ronda Dearing, Lauren Emmerson, Kristin Enyart, Margarita Flores, Lauren Smith Ford, Barrett Guillen, Stacy Hollister, Zehra Javed, Charles Kiley, Bryan Longoria, Murdoch Mackinnon, Laura Mayes, Elizabeth Newell, Tati Reznick, Gabi Rodriguez, Ashley Brown Ruiz, Teresa Sample, Nayda Sanchez, Paola Sánchez Valdez, Kathryn Schultz, Tara Seetharam, Anne Stoeber, Donna Van Worthe, Karen Walrond, and Genia Williams. You are the OG awkward, brave, and kind army! I couldn't do it without you and I wouldn't want to. Thank you for making this work possible.

To the research team of Ronda, Ellen, and Paola: Thank you for the greatness and the grind. Ronda, thank you for always having my back. And my eighty-seven emotions and experiences.

**The Random House Team:** To my editor, Ben Greenberg: It's a really good thing that you're so funny and smart and cuss a lot and have great taste in music and eat tacos. Otherwise we'd spend all of our time together crying. You are the very best.

To the Random House team of Barbara Bachman, Maria Braeckel, Catherine Bucaria, Gina Centrello, Susan Corcoran, Nancy Delia, Benjamin Dreyer, Karen Dziekonski, Lisa Feuer, Barbara Fillon, Melissa Folds, Ayelet Gruenspecht, Loren Noveck, Joe Perez, Tom Perry, Sandra Sjursen, Kaeli Subberwal, Andy Ward, Stacey Witcraft, and Theresa Zoro: Thank you for making Random House feel like home. I know how much work it takes to make a book like this happen—I'm grateful.

**The William Morris Endeavor Team**: To Suzanne Gluck, Tracy Fisher, Caitlin Mahony, and the entire team at William Morris Endeavor: Thank you and let's keep changing the world! After we rest.

**The Global Prairie Team:** To Mike and Wendy Hauser—you're family. Thank you for always showing up, being brave, and believing in beauty and excellence in all things.

To Jennifer Barr, Heather Davis, Erica Gonzales, Ashley Lane, and Gina Lanzalaco: You put your heart into this work and I'm grateful. It looks like love.

**To Gavin Aung Than:** I sent you an email that said, "I love your art, will you please help me with this book?" You said YES! and I've been blown away ever since. Thank you so much for breathing life into these words.

**The Home Team:** Love and thanks to Deanne Rogers and David Robinson; Chuck Brown; Jacobina Alley; Corky and Jack Crisci; Ashley and Amaya Ruiz; Barrett, Frankie, and Gabi Guillen; Jason and Layla Brown; Jen, David, Larkin, and Pierce Alley; Shif and Negash Berhanu; Margarita Flores; and Lucy Verni.

To Ashley and Barrett: #youdontknowme #doyourwork #STFD

To Steve, Ellen, and Charlie: You are the breathless love and joy that I write about.

To Lucy: You are the weird Ewok who fills me with wonder. And love.

# Notes

## INTRODUCTION

xiv    ***Leave it to Beaver***    Joe Connelly and Bob Mosher (creators and producers). *Leave It to Beaver,* aired 1957–63.

xv    ***The Exorcist***    William Friedkin (director), *The Exorcist* (Burbank, CA: Warner Bros., 1973).

xv    ***Sybil***    Daniel Petrie (director), *Sybil* (New York: National Broadcasting Company, 1976).

xv    ***Carrie***    Brian De Palma (director), *Carrie* (Beverly Hills, CA: United Artists, 1976).

xxi    **"The limits of my language"**    Ludwig Wittgenstein. *Tractatus Logico-Philosophicus* (London: Kegan Paul, Trench, Trubner & Co., 1922), 74 (page number from 2010 Project Gutenberg eBook version).

xxii    **we have compelling research**    Kristen A. Lindquist, Ajay B. Satpute, and Maria Gendron, "Does Language Do More than Communicate Emotion?" *Current Directions in Psychological Science* 24, no. 2 (2015):99–108. doi: 10.1177/0963721414553440.

xxii    **Language speeds and strengthens**    Ibid.

xxii    **"Learning to label emotions"**    Susan David, *Emotional Agility: Get Unstuck, Embrace Change, and Thrive in Work and Life* (New York: Avery, 2016), 85.

xxii    **"do much, much better at managing"**    Ibid.

xxii    **greater emotion regulation**    Lisa Feldman Barrett, James Gross, Tamlin Conner Christensen, and Michael Benvenuto, "Knowing What You're Feeling and Knowing What to Do About It: Mapping the Relation between Emotion Differentiation and Emotion Regulation," *Cognition and Emotion* 15, no. 6 (2001):713–24. doi: 10.1080/02699930143000239.

xxii    **psychosocial well-being**    Yasemin Erbas, Eva Ceulemans, Madeline Lee Pe, Peter Koval, and Peter Kuppens, "Negative Emotion Differentiation: Its Personality and Well-being Correlates and a Comparison of Different Assessment Methods," *Cognition and Emotion* 28, no. 7 (2014):1196–1213. doi: 10.1080/02699931.2013.875890.

xxii    **emotions "signal rewards and dangers"**    David, *Emotional Agility,* 85.

xxii    **our emotions help us make sense**    As summarized by Yasemin Erbas, Eva Ceulemans, Elisabeth S. Blanke, Laura Sels, Agneta Fischer, and Peter Kuppens, "Emotion Differentiation Dissected: Between-Category, Within-Category, and Integral Emotion Differentiation, and Their Relation to Well-being," *Cognition and Emotion* 33, no. 2 (2019):258–71. doi: 10.1080/02699931.2018.1465894; Yasemin Erbas, Laura Sels, Eva Ceulemans, and Peter Kuppens, "Feeling Me, Feeling You: The Relation between Emotion Differentiation and Empathic Accuracy," *Social Psychological and Personality Science* 7, no. 3 (2016):240–47. doi: 10.1177/1948550616633504.

xxiii    **"As human beings"**    Eduardo Bericat, "The Sociology of Emotions: Four Decades of Progress," *Current Sociology* 64, no. 3 (2016):491–513, 491. doi: 10.1177/0011392115588355.

xxiii    **"It's been said that there are"**    As related to interviewer Julie Beck in Julie Beck, "Hard Feelings: Science's Struggle to Define Emotions," *Atlantic,* February 24, 2015.

xxiv    **Some researchers place all emotions**    As described in Lisa A. Cavanaugh, Deborah J. MacInnis, and Allen M. Weiss, "Perceptual Dimensions Differentiate Emotions," *Cognition and Emotion* 30, no. 8 (2016):1430–45. doi: 10.1080/02699931.2015.1070119.

xxiv    **Individual-specific reactions**    Beck, "Hard Feelings."

xxiv    **"The only thing certain"**    Ibid.

xxiv    **"broad areas of agreement"**    Paul Ekman, "What Scientists Who Study Emotion Agree About," *Perspectives on Psychological Science* 11, no. 1 (2016):31–34, 33. doi: 10.1177/1745691615596992.

xxiv **universal voice and facial expression signals** Ekman, "What Scientists Who Study Emotion Agree About."

xxiv **Ekman believes there is clear evidence** Paul Ekman and Daniel Cordaro, "What Is Meant by Calling Emotions Basic," *Emotion Review* 3, no. 4 (2011):364–70. doi: 10.1177/1754073911410740.

xxv **at least twenty-seven or twenty-eight emotions** Alan S. Cowen and Dacher Keltner, "Self-Report Captures 27 Distinct Categories of Emotion Bridged by Continuous Gradients," *PNAS, Proceedings of the National Academy of Sciences of the United States of America* 114, no. 38 (2017):E7900–E7909. doi: 10.1073/pnas.1702247114; Alan S. Cowen and Dacher Keltner, "What the Face Displays: Mapping 28 Emotions Conveyed by Naturalistic Expression," *American Psychologist* 75, no. 3 (2020):349–64. doi: 10.1037/amp0000488 10.1037/amp0000488.supp.

xxviii **including his book *Sprawlball*** Kirk Goldsberry, *Sprawlball: A Visual Tour of the New Era of the NBA* (New York: Houghton Mifflin Harcourt, 2019).

## #1 PLACES WE GO WHEN THINGS ARE UNCERTAIN OR TOO MUCH

5 **We feel stressed when** Sheldon Cohen, Tom Kamarck, and Robin Mermelstein, "A Global Measure of Perceived Stress," *Journal of Health and Social Behavior* 24, no. 4 (1983):385–96.

5 **Stressful situations cause both** Nida Ali, Jonas P. Nitschke, Cory Cooperman, and Jens C. Pruessner, "Suppressing the Endocrine and Autonomic Stress Systems Does Not Impact the Emotional Stress Experience after Psychosocial Stress," *Psychoneuroendocrinology* 78 (2017):125–30. doi: 10.1016/j.psyneuen.2017.01.015.

6 **In fact, chronic exposure** Bruce S. McEwen, "Stressed or Stressed Out: What Is the Difference?," *Journal of Psychiatry & Neuroscience* 30, no. 5 (2005):315–18.

6 **High levels of perceived stress** Sheldon Cohen and Denise Janicki-Deverts, "Who's Stressed? Distributions of Psychological Stress in the United States in Probability Samples from 1983, 2006, and 2009," *Journal of Applied Social Psychology* 42, no. 6 (2012):1320–34. doi: 10.1111/j.1559-1816.2012.00900.x.

7 **"that our lives are somehow"** Jon Kabat-Zinn, "Overwhelmed," *Mindfulness* 10, no. 6 (2019):1188–89, 1188. doi: 10.1007/s12671-019-01150-6.

7 **When I read that Kabat-Zinn** Ibid.

7 **In fact, researcher Carol Gohm** Carol L. Gohm, "Mood Regulation and Emotional Intelligence: Individual Differences," *Journal of Personality and Social Psychology* 84, no. 3 (2003):594–607. doi: 10.1037/0022-3514.84.3.594.

8 **There's a frightening scene** Mel Stuart (director), *Willy Wonka & the Chocolate Factory* (Burbank, CA: Wolper Productions, 1971).

8 **"There's no earthly way"** Lyrics were modified from the original book version for the movie. Ibid. and Roald Dahl, *Charlie and the Chocolate Factory* (New York: Puffin Books, 1964).

9 **"you are afraid of surrender"** Elizabeth Gilbert (@Elizabeth_gilbert_writer), Instagram post, July 12, 2020.

9 **"an emotion characterized by feelings"** American Psychological Association, "Anxiety," *Psychology Topics*.

10 **"A trait is considered"** The Oxford Review, "The Difference between a State and a Trait," *The Oxford Review of Encyclopaedia of Terms*.

10 **"However, working out"** Ibid.

10 **"generalized anxiety disorder is a condition"** Johns Hopkins Medicine, "What Is Generalized Anxiety Disorder?," *Health*.

10 **Approximately one-third** Borwin Bandelow and Sophie Michaelis, "Epidemiology of Anxiety Disorders in the 21st Century," *Dialogues in Clinical Neuroscience* 17, no. 3 (2015):327–35; Ronald C. Kessler, Maria Petukhova, Nancy A. Sampson, Alan M. Zaslavsky, and Hans-Ullrich Wittchen, "Twelve-Month and Lifetime Prevalence and Lifetime Morbid Risk of Anxiety and Mood Disorders in the United States," *International Journal of Methods in Psychiatric Research* 21, no. 3 (2012):169–84. doi: 10.1002/mpr.1359; Ayelet Meron Ruscio, Lauren S. Hallion, Carmen C. W. Lim, Sergio Aguilar-Gaxiola, Ali Al-Hamzawi, Jordi Alonso, Laura Helena Andrade, et al., "Cross-Sectional Comparison of the Epidemiology of DSM-5 Generalized Anxiety Disorder across the Globe," *JAMA Psychiatry* 74, no. 5 (2017):465–75. doi: 10.1001/jamapsychiatry.2017.0056.

11 **An intolerance for uncertainty** Siqi Chen, Nisha Yao, and Mingyi Qian, "The Influence of Uncertainty and Intolerance of Uncertainty on Anxiety," *Journal of Behavior Therapy and Experimental Psychiatry* 61 (2018):60–65. doi: 10.1016/j.jbtep.2018.06.005; Kevin S. LaBar, "Fear and Anxiety," in *Handbook of Emotions*, edited by Lisa Feldman Barrett, Michael Lewis, and Jeannette M. Haviland-Jones (New York: Guilford Press, 2016), 751–73.

11 **Our anxiety often leads to** David H. Barlow, "Unraveling the Mysteries of Anxiety and Its Disorders from the Perspective of Emotion Theory," *American Psychologist* 55, no. 11 (2000):1247–1263. doi: 0.1037/0003-066X.55.11.1247.

11 **What really got me** Sam Cartwright-Hatton and Adrian Wells, "Beliefs About Worry and Intrusions: The Meta-Cognitions Questionnaire and Its Correlates," *Journal of Anxiety Disorders* 11, no. 3 (1997):279–96. doi: 10.1016/S0887-6185(97)00011-X.

11  **"It is not fear that stops"**  Harriet Lerner, *The Dance of Fear: Rising Above Anxiety, Fear, and Shame to Be Your Best and Bravest Self* (New York: HarperCollins, 2004), 206–07.

12  **Even though excitement**  Chan Jean Lee and Eduardo B. Andrade, "Fear, Excitement, and Financial Risk-Taking," *Cognition and Emotion* 29, no. 1 (2014):178–87. doi: 10.1080/02699931.2014.898611.

12  **Researchers found that labeling**  Alison Wood Brooks, "Get Excited: Reappraising Pre-Performance Anxiety as Excitement," *Journal of Experimental Psychology: General* 143, no. 3 (2014):1144–58. doi: 10.1037/a0035325.

12  **Dread occurs frequently**  Christine R. Harris, "Feelings of Dread and Intertemporal Choice," *Journal of Behavioral Decision Making* 25, no. 1 (2012):13–28. doi: 10.1002/bdm.709.

12  **Because dread makes an anticipated**  Giles W. Story, Ivaylo Vlaev, Ben Seymour, Joel S. Winston, Ara Darzi, and Raymond J. Dolan, "Dread and the Disvalue of Future Pain," *PLOS Computational Biology* 9, no. 11 (2013.):1–18. doi: 10.1371/journal.pcbi.1003335.

12  **For anxiety and dread, the threat**  Sean Wake, Jolie Wormwood, and Ajay B. Satpute, "The Influence of Fear on Risk Taking: A Meta-Analysis," *Cognition and Emotion* 34, no. 6 (2020):1143–59. doi: 10.1080/02699931.2020.1731428.

12  **Fear arises when we need**  Barlow, "Unraveling the Mysteries."

13  **social pain and physical pain**  Naomi I. Eisenberger, "The Pain of Social Disconnection: Examining the Shared Neural Underpinnings of Physical and Social Pain," *Nature Reviews Neuroscience* 13, no. 6 (2012):421–34. doi: 10.1038/nrn3231.

13  **"Throughout evolutionary history, anxiety"**  Lerner, *Dance of Fear,* 49–50.

## #2 PLACES WE GO WHEN WE COMPARE

18  **"comparing the self with others"**  Jerry Suls, René Martin, and Ladd Wheeler, "Social Comparison: Why, with Whom, and with What Effect?" *Current Directions in Psychological Science* 1, no. 5 (2002):159–63, 159.

20  **I've collected data**  Brené Brown, *The Gifts of Imperfection: Let Go of Who You Think You're Supposed to Be and Embrace Who You Are* (Center City, MN: Hazelden Publishing, 2010).

20  **"When we engage in upward social comparison"**  Alicia Nortje, "Social Comparison: An Unavoidable Upward or Downward Spiral," PositivePsychology.com, March 31, 2021.

21  **"Social comparisons can make us"**  Frank Fujita, "The Frequency of Social Comparison and Its Relation to Subjective Well-Being," in *The Science of Subjective Well-Being*, edited by Michael Eid and Randy J. Larsen (New York: Guilford Press, 2008), 254.

21  **"From this perspective, when"**  Ibid., 241.

21  **Whenever I find myself in comparison**  Brené Brown (host), "Brené with Scott Sonenshein on Stretching and Chasing," September 9, 2020, *Unlocking Us,* podcast.

21  **Scott Sonenshein about his wonderful book**  Scott Sonenshein, *Stretch: Unlock the Power of Less—and Achieve More Than You Ever Imagined* (New York: HarperCollins, 2017).

24  **"Reverence is a cardinal virtue"**  Amy L. Ai, Paul Wink, Terry Lynn Gall, Michele Dillon, and Terrence N. Tice, "Assessing Reverence in Contexts: A Positive Emotion Related to Psychological Functioning," *Journal of Humanistic Psychology* 57, no. 1 (2017):64–97, 65. doi: 10.1177/0022167815586657.

26  **"Envy typically involves *two* people"**  Richard H. Smith and Sung Hee Kim, "Comprehending Envy," *Psychological Bulletin* 133, no. 1 (2007):46–64, 47, emphasis added. doi: 10.1037/0033-2909.133.1.46.

26  **recalled episodes of envy**  Katrin Rentzsch and James J. Gross, "Who Turns Green with Envy? Conceptual and Empirical Perspectives on Dispositional Envy," *European Journal of Personality* 29, no. 5 (2015):530–47.

28  **"The core form of jealousy"**  Mingi Chung and Christine R. Harris, "Jealousy as a Specific Emotion: The Dynamic Functional Model," *Emotion Review* 10, no. 4 (2018):272–87, 273. doi: 10.1177/1754073918795257.

28  **We mostly think of jealousy**  David DeSteno, Piercarlo Valdesolo, and Monica Y. Bartlett, "Jealousy and the Threatened Self: Getting to the Heart of the Green-Eyed Monster," *Journal of Personality and Social Psychology* 91, no. 4 (2006):626–41. doi: 10.1037/0022-3514.91.4.626.

28  **In children, jealousy most often**  Meghan K. Loeser, Shawn D. Whiteman, and Susan M. McHale, "Siblings' Perceptions of Differential Treatment, Fairness, and Jealousy and Adolescent Adjustment: A Moderated Indirect Effects Model," *Journal of Child and Family Studies* 25, no. 8 (2016):2405–14. doi: 10.1007/s10826-016-0429-2.

28  **While jealousy is frequently**  Laura K. Guerrero and Peter A. Andersen, "The Dark Side of Jealousy and Envy: Desire, Delusion, Desperation, and Destructive Communication," in *The Dark Side of Close Relationships*, edited by Brian H. Spitzberg and William R. Cupach (Mahwah, NJ: Lawrence Erlbaum Associates Publishers, 1998), 33–70.

28  **high levels of jealousy are directly related**  Heather M. Foran and K. Daniel O'Leary, "Problem Drinking, Jealousy, and Anger Control: Variables Predicting Physical Aggression against a Partner," *Journal of Family Violence* 23, no. 3 (2008):141–48. doi: 10.1007/s10896-007-9136-5.

28    **frequent experiences of jealousy**   Meagan J. Brem, Ryan C. Shorey, Emily F. Rothman, Jeff R. Temple, and Gregory L. Stuart, "Trait Jealousy Moderates the Relationship between Alcohol Problems and Intimate Partner Violence among Men in Batterer Intervention Programs," *Violence Against Women* 24, no. 10 (2018):1132–48. doi: 10.1177/1077801218781948.

28    **It's normal to feel**   Laura K. Guerrero, Annegret F. Hannawa, and Elizabeth A. Babin, "The Communicative Responses to Jealousy Scale: Revision, Empirical Validation, and Associations with Relational Satisfaction," *Communication Methods and Measures* 5, no. 3 (2011):223–49. doi: 10.1080/19312458.2011.596993; Laura K. Guerrero, "Jealousy and Relational Satisfaction: Actor Effects, Partner Effects, and the Mediating Role of Destructive Communicative Responses to Jealousy," *Western Journal of Communication* 78, no. 5 (2014):586–611. doi: 10.1080/10570314.2014.935468; Peter Salovey and Judith Rodin, "The Heart of Jealousy," *Psychology Today* (September 1995), 22–29.

28    **"Jealousy in romance is"**   Maya Angelou, *Wouldn't Take Nothing for My Journey Now* (New York: Random House, 1993), 129.

29    **more satisfied in their romantic relationships**   D.P.H. Barelds and P. Barelds-Dijkstra, "Relations between Different Types of Jealousy and Self and Partner Perceptions of Relationship Quality," *Clinical Psychology & Psychotherapy* 14, no. 3 (2007):176–88. doi: 10.1002/cpp.532.

30    *unwanted identity* **is the most powerful elicitor**   Tamara J. Ferguson, Heidi L. Eyre, and Michael Ashbaker, "Unwanted Identities: A Key Variable in Shame-Anger Links and Gender Differences in Shame," *Sex Roles* 42, no. 3–4 (2000), 133–157.

30    **"I've got a personal question"**   Brené Brown (host), "Dr. Marc Brackett and Brené on 'Permission to Feel'" April 14, 2020, *Unlocking Us,* podcast.

31    **I was alone at the movie theater**   Jodie Foster (director), *Home for the Holidays* (New York: Egg Pictures, 1995).

33    **"epicaricacy" captures the same meaning**   Ciaran J. Breen, "Another Word for Schadenfreude," *The Irish Times,* January 4, 2010.

33    **"It is an old German word"**   Ben Cohen, "Schadenfreude Is in the Zeitgeist, but Is There an Opposite Term? Word for Taking Pain in Another's Pleasure Is 'Gluckschmerz,' or Is It?" *Wall Street Journal,* June 12, 2015.

34    **"schadenfreude-free zone"**   Bill Wrubel (writer) and Bill Lawrence, Jason Sudeikis, Brendan Hunt, and Joe Kelly (creators), *Ted Lasso,* Season 1, Episode 6, "Two Aces," September 4, 2020, Apple TV+.

35    **Schadenfreude involves counter-empathy**   Kathryn F. Jankowski and Hidehiko Takahashi, "Cognitive Neuroscience of Social Emotions and Implications for Psychopathology: Examining Embarrassment, Guilt, Envy, and Schadenfreude," *Psychiatry and Clinical Neurosciences* 68, no. 5 (2014):319–36. doi: 10.1111/pcn.12182.

35    **Schadenfreude has trait-like properties**   Laura C. Crysel and Gregory D. Webster, "Schadenfreude and the Spread of Political Misfortune," *PLoS ONE* 13, no. 9 (2018).

36    **"an emotion typically born out of inferiority"**   Richard H. Smith and Wilco W. van Dijk, "Schadenfreude and Gluckschmerz," *Emotion Review* 10, no. 4 (2018):293–304, 294. doi: 10.1177/1754073918765657.

36    **"When others report success to us"**   Catherine Chambliss, "The Role of Freudenfreude and Schadenfreude in Depression," *World Journal of Psychiatry and Mental Health Research* 2, no. 1 (2018):1–2, 1.

37    **1. Shoy: intentionally**   Ibid., 2.

37    **a leadership lesson I learned**   Abby Wambach, *Wolfpack: How to Come Together, Unleash Our Power, and Change the Game* (New York: Celadon Books, 2019).

37    **"You will not always be the goal scorer"**   Ibid., 56.

## #3 PLACES WE GO WHEN THINGS DON'T GO AS PLANNED

40    **Boredom is the uncomfortable state**   John D. Eastwood, Alexandra Frischen, Mark J. Fenske, and Daniel Smilek, "The Unengaged Mind: Defining Boredom in Terms of Attention," *Perspectives on Psychological Science* 7, no. 5 (2012):482–95. doi: 10.1177/1745691612456044.

40    **What's unique about boredom**   Edwin A. J. van Hooft and Madelon L. M. van Hooff, "The State of Boredom: Frustrating or Depressing?" *Motivation and Emotion* 42, no. 6 (2018):931–46. doi: 10.1007/s11031-018-9710-6.

40    **simple, boring tasks or mundane activities**   Sandi Mann and Rebekah Cadman, "Does Being Bored Make Us More Creative?" *Creativity Research Journal* 26, no. 2 (2014):165–73.

41    *Wicked* **soundtrack**   Stephen Schwartz, *Wicked: A New Musical* (cast album) (New York: Decca Broadway, 2003).

41    **"Boredom is your imagination"**   Sherry Turkle (@Sturkle), "Boredom Is Your Imagination Calling to You," Twitter post, October 31, 2015.

43    **For** *Rising Strong*   Brené Brown, *Rising Strong: The Reckoning. The Rumble. The Revolution* (New York: Random House, 2015).

43 **disappointment is one of the most frequently** Ulrich Schimmack and Ed Diener, "Affect Intensity: Separating Intensity and Frequency in Repeatedly Measured Affect," *Journal of Personality and Social Psychology* 73, no. 6 (1997):1313–29. doi: 10.1037/0022-3514.73.6.1313.

44 **we come away from the experience of disappointment** Eliane Sommerfeld, "The Experience of Disappointment in the Context of Interpersonal Relations: An Exploration Using a Mixed Method Approach," *Current Psychology: A Journal for Diverse Perspectives on Diverse Psychological Issues* 38, no. 6 (2019):1476–89. doi: 10.1007/s12144-017-9703-8.

44 **Here's a story that I shared** Brown, *Rising Strong.*

46 **the power of "painting done"** Brené Brown, *Dare to Lead: Brave Work. Tough Conversations. Whole Hearts.* (New York: Random House, 2018).

46 **unchecked and unexpressed expectations** Brown, *Rising Strong.*

50 **one way to minimize disappointment** Kate Sweeny and James A. Shepperd, "The Costs of Optimism and the Benefits of Pessimism," *Emotion* 10, no. 5 (2010):750–53. doi: 10.1037/a0019016.

50 **When I was researching *Daring Greatly*** Brené Brown, *Daring Greatly: How the Courage to Be Vulnerable Transforms the Way We Live, Love, Parent, and Lead* (New York: Gotham Books, 2012).

50 **Japanese animated film *Spirited Away*** Hayao Miyazaki (director), *Spirited Away* (Tokyo: Studio Ghibli, 2001).

52 **we tend to regret bad outcomes** Marcel Zeelenberg, Wilco W. van Dijk, Antony S. R. Manstead, and Joop van der Pligt, "On Bad Decisions and Disconfirmed Expectancies: The Psychology of Regret and Disappointment," *Cognition and Emotion* 14, no. 4 (2000):521–41. doi: 10.1080/026999300402781.

52 **one of the most powerful lines about regret** Brown, *Rising Strong.*

52 **"So here's something I know"** Joel Lovell, "George Saunders's Advice to Graduates," *New York Times,* July 31, 2013.

52 **a meta-analysis (a study of studies)** Neal J. Roese and Amy Summerville, "What We Regret Most, and Why," *Personality and Social Psychology Bulletin* 31, no. 9 (2005):1273–85. doi: 10.1177/0146167205274693.

53 **One reason we may avoid regret** Hannah Faye Chua, Richard Gonzalez, Stephan F. Taylor, Robert C. Welsh, and Israel Liberzon, "Decision-Related Loss: Regret and Disappointment," *NeuroImage* 47, no. 4 (2009):2031–40. doi: 10.1016/j.neuroimage.2009.06.006.

53 **When I was writing** Brown, *Rising Strong.*

53 **the image was from the film** Rawson Marshall Thurber (director), *We're the Millers* (Burbank, CA: New Line Cinema through Warner Bros. Pictures, 2013).

## #4 PLACES WE GO WHEN IT'S BEYOND US

58 **"If I had influence"** Rachel Carson, *The Sense of Wonder: A Celebration of Nature for Parents and Children* (New York: HarperCollins, 1956).

58 **"Wonder inspires the wish to understand"** Ulrich Weger and Johannes Wagemann, "Towards a Conceptual Clarification of Awe and Wonder: A First Person Phenomenological Enquiry," *Current Psychology: A Journal for Diverse Perspectives on Diverse Psychological Issues* 40, no. 3 (2021):1386–1401, 1393. doi: 10.1007/s12144-018-0057-7.

58 **"to provide a stage"** Ibid., 1387.

59 **"leads people to cooperate"** Dacher Keltner, "Why Do We Feel Awe?" *Greater Good Magazine: Science-Based Insights for a Meaningful Life,* May 10, 2016.

59 **causes them "to fully appreciate"** Jennifer E. Stellar, Amie Gordon, Craig L. Anderson, Paul K. Piff, Galen D. McNeil, and Dacher Keltner, "Awe and Humility," *Journal of Personality and Social Psychology* 114, no. 2 (2018):258–69. doi: 10.1037/pspi0000109, 266.

59 **"awe-inducing events may be"** Dacher Keltner and Jonathan Haidt, "Approaching Awe, a Moral, Spiritual, and Aesthetic Emotion," *Cognition and Emotion* 17, no. 2 (2003):297–314, 312. doi: 10.1080/02699930302297.

62 **"I need time for my confusion"** Adam Grant, *Think Again: The Power of Knowing What You Don't Know.* (New York: Viking, 2021), 199.

62 ***optimal confusion*** This term was coined by D'Mello and colleagues in the following article: Sidney D'Mello, Blair Lehman, Reinhard Pekrun, and Art Graesser, "Confusion Can Be Beneficial for Learning," *Learning and Instruction* 29 (2014): 153–70. doi: 10.1016/j.learninstruc.2012.05.003.

62 **it's categorized as an *epistemic emotion*** Elisabeth Vogl, Reinhard Pekrun, Kou Murayama, and Kristina Loderer, "Surprised–Curious–Confused: Epistemic Emotions and Knowledge Exploration," *Emotion* 20, no. 4 (2020):625–41. doi: 10.1037/emo0000578 10.1037/emo0000578.supp.

62 **we need to stop and think** D'Mello, "Confusion Can Be Beneficial."

62    **"To be effective, learning needs"**    Mary Slaughter and David Rock, "No Pain, No Brain Gain: Why Learning Demands (a Little) Discomfort," *Fast Company,* April 30, 2018 (emphasis added).

63    **too much confusion can lead to frustration**    Sidney D'Mello and Art Graesser, "Confusion and Its Dynamics During Device Comprehension with Breakdown Scenarios," *Acta Psychologica* 151 (2014):106–16. doi: 10.1016/j .actpsy.2014.06.005.

63    **Learning strategies most often used**    Ivana Di Leo, Krista R. Muis, Cara A. Singh, and Cynthia Psaradellis, "Curiosity . . . Confusion? Frustration! The Role and Sequencing of Emotions During Mathematics Problem Solving," *Contemporary Educational Psychology* 58 (2019):121–37. doi: 10.1016/j.cedpsych.2019.03.001.

63    **research on curiosity**    Brené Brown, R*ising Strong: The Reckoning. The Rumble. The Revolution* (New York: Random House, 2015); Brené Brown, *Dare to Lead: Brave Work. Tough Conversations. Whole Hearts.* (New York: Random House, 2018).

64    **the "information gap" perspective**    George Loewenstein, "The Psychology of Curiosity: A Review and Reinterpretation," *Psychological Bulletin* 116, no. 1 (1994):75–98. doi: 10.1037/0033-2909.116.1.75.

64    **"To induce curiosity"**    Ibid., 94.

66    **"The important thing is not to stop questioning"**    William Miller, "Death of a Genius: His Fourth Dimension, Time, Overtakes Einstein," *Life,* May 2, 1955, 61–64, 64.

66    **my team and I define surprise**    Sascha Topolinski and Fritz Strack, "Corrugator Activity Confirms Immediate Negative Affect in Surprise," *Frontiers in Psychology* 6 February 6, 2015:134.

66    **"a bridge between cognition and emotion"**    Barbara Mellers, Katrina Fincher, Caitlin Drummond, and Michelle Bigony, "Surprise: A Belief or an Emotion?" in *Progress in Brain Research*, edited by V. S. Chandrasekhar Pammi and Narayanan Srinivasan (Amsterdam: Elsevier, 2013), 3–19, 3.

66    **In addition to being a short bridge**    Ibid.

67    **surprising news is more likely to be shared**    Jeffrey Loewenstein, "Surprise, Recipes for Surprise, and Social Influence," *Topics in Cognitive Science* 11, no. 1 (2019):178–93. doi: 10.1111/tops.12312.

## #5 PLACES WE GO WHEN THINGS AREN'T WHAT THEY SEEM

70    **his latest book, *Think Again***    Adam Grant, *Think Again: The Power of Knowing What You Don't Know.* (New York: Viking, 2021).

70    **"As consumers of information"**    Ibid., 171.

72    **amusement is connected to humor**    Belinda Campos, Michelle N. Shiota, Dacher Keltner, Gian C. Gonzaga, and Jennifer L. Goetz, "What Is Shared, What Is Different? Core Relational Themes and Expressive Displays of Eight Positive Emotions," *Cognition and Emotion* 27, no. 1 (2013):37–52. doi: 10.1080/02699931.2012.683852.

73    **"pleasurable, relaxed excitation"**    Willibald Ruch, "Amusement," in *The Oxford Companion to Emotion and the Affective Sciences*, edited by David Sander and Klaus R. Scherer (Oxford: Oxford University Press, 2009), 27.

73    **When we feel amusement**    Campos, "What Is Shared, What Is Different?"

73    **breaks involving amusement**    David Cheng and Lu Wang, "Examining the Energizing Effects of Humor: The Influence of Humor on Persistence Behavior," *Journal of Business and Psychology* 30, no. 4 (2015):759–72. doi: 10.1007/s10869-014-9396-z.

74    **"The bittersweet side of appreciating"**    Marc Parent, *Believing It All: What My Children Taught Me About Trout Fishing, Jelly Toast, and Life* (Boston, MA: Little, Brown and Company, 2002).

76    **It's not the same as ambivalence**    Jeff T. Larsen, "Holes in the Case for Mixed Emotions," *Emotion Review* 9, no. 2 (2017):118–23. doi: 10.1177/1754073916639662.

76    **multiple emotions . . . may be rapidly vacillating**    Anthony G. Vaccaro, Jonas T. Kaplan, and Antonio Damasio, "Bittersweet: The Neuroscience of Ambivalent Affect," *Perspectives on Psychological Science* 15, no. 5 (2020):1187–99. doi: 10.1177/1745691620927708.

76    **It's possible that feeling bittersweet**    Ibid.

76    **mixed emotion is not present in very young children**    Ibid.

76    **"There's nothing wrong with celebrating"**    Stephanie Coontz, "Beware Social Nostalgia," *New York Times,* May 18, 2013.

77    **"In the late 1600s,"**    Adrienne Matei,"Nostalgia's Unexpected Etymology Explains Why It Can Feel So Painful," *Quartz*, October 22, 2017.

77    **cures for nostalgia**    Ibid. Article can be accessed at qz.com/1108120/nostalgias-unexpected-etymology-explains -why-it-can-feel-so-painful/.

77    **Nostalgia was considered a medical disease**    Tim Wildschut, Constantine Sedikides, Jamie Arndt, and Clay

Routledge, "Nostalgia: Content, Triggers, Functions," *Journal of Personality and Social Psychology* 91, no. 5 (2006):975–93. doi: 10.1037/0022-3514.91.5.975.

77    **Today, researchers describe *nostalgia***   Constantine Sedikides, Tim Wildschut, Jamie Arndt, and Clay Routledge, "Nostalgia: Past, Present, and Future," *Current Directions in Psychological Science* 17, no. 5 (2008):304–07. doi: 10.1111/j.1467-8721.2008.00595.x.

77    **putting ourselves at the center of a story**   Wildschut, "Nostalgia: Content, Triggers, Functions."

77    **"navigate successfully the vicissitudes"**   Sedikides, "Nostalgia: Past, Present, and Future," 307.

78    **fascinating research from Sandra Garrido**   Sandra Garrido, "The Influence of Personality and Coping Style on the Affective Outcomes of Nostalgia: Is Nostalgia a Healthy Coping Mechanism or Rumination?" *Personality and Individual Differences* 120 (2018):259–64. doi: 10.1016/j.paid.2016.07.021.

78    **"involuntary focus on negative and pessimistic thoughts"**   Ibid., 260.

78    **"highly adaptive"**   Ibid.

79    **worry is focused on the future**   Colette R. Hirsch and Andrew Mathews, "A Cognitive Model of Pathological Worry," *Behaviour Research and Therapy* 50, no. 10 (2012):636–46. doi: 10.1016/j.brat.2012.06.007.

79    **rumination is a strong predictor of depression**   Mark A. Whisman, Alta du Pont, and Peter Butterworth, "Longitudinal Associations between Rumination and Depressive Symptoms in a Probability Sample of Adults," *Journal of Affective Disorders* 260 (2020):680–86. doi: 10.1016/j.jad.2019.09.035.

79    **more likely to pay attention to negative things**   Kelly Yu-Hsin Liao and Meifen Wei, "Intolerance of Uncertainty, Depression, and Anxiety: The Moderating and Mediating Roles of Rumination," *Journal of Clinical Psychology* 67, no. 12 (2011):1220–39. doi: 10.1002/jclp.20846.

79    **it's important to reality-check**   Coontz, "Beware Social Nostalgia."

79    **My favorite book on cognitive dissonance**   Carol Tavris and Elliot Aronson, *Mistakes Were Made (but Not by Me): Why We Justify Foolish Beliefs, Bad Decisions, and Hurtful Acts*, 3rd ed. (New York: Houghton Mifflin Harcourt, 2020).

79    **"engage in all kinds of cognitive gymnastics"**   Elliot Aronson, "Dissonance, Hypocrisy, and the Self-Concept," in *Cognitive Dissonance: Reexamining a Pivotal Theory in Psychology,* 2nd ed., edited by Eddie Harmon-Jones (Washington, DC: American Psychological Association, 2019), 144.

80    **"For Leon Festinger"**   Tavris, *Mistakes Were Made,* v.

80    **"Many of her followers quit their jobs"**   Ibid., 16.

80    **"the believers who had not made"**   Ibid., 16–17.

80    **"those who had given away their possessions"**   Ibid., 17.

80    **"whatever they could to get others"**   Ibid.

81    **"The engine that drives self-justification"**   Ibid., 17–18.

81    **"The greater the magnitude"**   Eddie Harmon-Jones and Judson Mills, "An Introduction to Cognitive Dissonance Theory and an Overview of Current Perspectives on the Theory," in *Cognitive Dissonance: Reexamining a Pivotal Theory in Psychology,* 2nd ed., edited by Eddie Harmon-Jones (Washington, DC: American Psychological Association, 2019), 3.

82    **"Intelligence is traditionally viewed as"**   Grant, *Think Again,* 2.

82    **"The paradox is one of our most valuable"**   Carl G. Jung, "Psychology and Alchemy," in *The Collected Works of C. G. Jung*, edited and translated by Gerhard Adler and R.F.C. Hull. (Princeton, NJ: Princeton University Press, 1980), 15–16.

84    **"False dichotomies"**   Jim Collins and Bill Lazier, *BE (Beyond Entrepreneurship) 2.0: Turning Your Business into an Enduring Great Company*. 2nd Kindle ed. (New York: Portfolio, 2020), 158.

85    **rejecting paradox can result in conflict**   Chris Changwha Chung and Paul W. Beamish, "The Trap of Continual Ownership Change in International Equity Joint Ventures," *Organization Science* 21, no. 5 (2010):995–1015. doi: 10.1287/orsc.1090.0489; Diether Gebert, Sabine Boerner, and Eric Kearney, "Fostering Team Innovation: Why Is It Important to Combine Opposing Action Strategies?" *Organization Science* 21, no. 3 (2010):593–608. doi: 10.1287/orsc.1090.0485; Jonathan Schad, Marianne W. Lewis, Sebastian Raisch, and Wendy K. Smith, "Paradox Research in Management Science: Looking Back to Move Forward," *The Academy of Management Annals* 10, no. 1 (2016):5–64. doi: 10.1080/19416520.2016.1162422.

85    **Irony and sarcasm are forms of communication**   Ruth Filik, Alexandra Țurcan, Christina Ralph-Nearman, and Alain Pitiot, "What Is the Difference between Irony and Sarcasm? An fMRI Study," *Cortex: A Journal Devoted to the Study of the Nervous System and Behavior* 115 (2019):112–22, 113. doi: 10.1016/j.cortex.2019.01.025; Melanie Glenwright and Penny M. Pexman, "Development of Children's Ability to Distinguish Sarcasm and Verbal Irony," *Journal of Child Language* 37, no. 2 (2010):429–51. doi: 10.1017/S0305000909009520.

85    **talking to someone you don't know well**   Ruth Filik, Alexandra Țurcan, Dominic Thompson, Nicole Harvey,

Harriet Davies, and Amelia Turner, "Sarcasm and Emoticons: Comprehension and Emotional Impact," *Quarterly Journal of Experimental Psychology* 69, no. 11 (2016):2130–46. doi: 10.1080/17470218.2015.1106566; Glenwright, "Development of Children's Ability"; Penny M. Pexman and Meghan T. Zvaigzne, "Does Irony Go Better with Friends?" *Metaphor and Symbol* 19, no. 2 (2004):143–63. doi: 10.1207/s15327868ms1902_3.

86    **"the successful comprehension of irony"**    Filik, "What Is the Difference," 113.

86    **Research on intent behind delivery**    Maggie Toplak and Albert N. Katz, "On the Uses of Sarcastic Irony," *Journal of Pragmatics* 32, no. 10 (2000):1467–88. doi: 10.1016/S0378-2166(99)00101-0.

86    **"children do not seem to distinguish"**    Filik, "What Is the Difference," 114.

86    **"Although middle-school-age children"**    Melanie Glenwright, Brent Tapley, Jacqueline K. S. Rano, and Penny M. Pexman, "Developing Appreciation for Sarcasm and Sarcastic Gossip: It Depends on Perspective," *Journal of Speech, Language, and Hearing Research* 60, no. 11 (2017):3295–3309, 3307. doi: 10.1044/2017_JSLHR-L-17-0058.

86    **When I read that these behaviors**    Julia Jorgensen, "The Functions of Sarcastic Irony in Speech," *Journal of Pragmatics* 26, no. 5 (1996):613–34. doi: 10.1016/0378-2166(95)00067-4.

## #6 PLACES WE GO WHEN WE'RE HURTING

90    **"Anguish . . . It's one of those words"**    Ranata Suzuki, "Anguish," *A Life Half Lived*, December 13, 2014.

90    **This painting by August**    August Friedrich Albrecht Schenck, *Anguish*, 1876/1880 (Melbourne, Australia: National Gallery of Victoria).

90    **one of the NGV's most popular works**    Google Arts & Culture, "Anguish: August Friedrich Schenck 1876/1880."

96    *Dark Elegy*    Suse Ellen Lowenstein, *Dark Elegy*, 1989 (Montauk, NY).

96    **"On December 21, 1988"**    Suse Ellen Lowenstein, email message to author, June 2021.

97    **"trilogy of goals, pathways, and agency"**    C. R. Snyder, ed., *Handbook of Hope: Theory, Measures, and Applications* (San Diego: Academic Press, 2000.)

101    **According to Snyder**    Ibid.

101    **Hopelessness arises**    Richard T. Liu, Evan M. Kleiman, Bridget A. Nestor, and Shayna M. Cheek, "The Hopelessness Theory of Depression: A Quarter-Century in Review," *Clinical Psychology: Science and Practice* 22, no. 4 (2015):345–65. doi: 10.1111/cpsp.12125.

102    **Let's look back at C. R. Snyder's work**    Snyder, *Handbook of Hope*.

102    **In more than thirty years of research**    Aaron T. Beck, Robert A. Steer, Maria Kovacs, and Betsy Garrison, "Hopelessness and Eventual Suicide: A 10-Year Prospective Study of Patients Hospitalized with Suicidal Ideation," *The American Journal of Psychiatry* 142, no. 5 (1985):559–563. doi: 10.1176/ajp.142.5.559; Sören Kliem, Anna Lohmann, Thomas Mößle, and Elmar Brähler, "Psychometric Properties and Measurement Invariance of the Beck Hopelessness Scale (BHS: Results from a German Representative Population Sample," *BMC Psychiatry* 18 no. 110 (2018): 1–11. doi.org/10.1186/s12888-018-1646-6.

102    **"the belief that tomorrow will be just like today"**    Rob Bell, "Despair Is a Spiritual Condition," part of Oprah Winfrey's "The Life You Want" Weekend Tour, 2014.

103    **We all fear pain and struggle**    Alexis M. May and E. David Klonsky, "Assessing Motivations for Suicide Attempts: Development and Psychometric Properties of the Inventory of Motivations for Suicide Attempts," *Suicide and Life-Threatening Behavior* 43, no. 5 (2013):532–46; Jessica D. Ribeiro, Xieyining Huang, Kathryn R. Fox, and Joseph C. Franklin, "Depression and Hopelessness as Risk Factors for Suicide Ideation, Attempts and Death: Meta-Analysis of Longitudinal Studies," *The British Journal of Psychiatry* 212, no. 5 (2018):279–86. doi: 10.1192/bjp.2018.27.

103    **Martin Seligman's research**    Martin E. P. Seligman, *Learned Optimism* (New York: Knopf, 1991).

104    **I posted a question on Instagram**    Brené Brown, "Thanks So Much . . ," post on Instagram, Facebook, LinkedIn, Twitter, June 28, 2021.

104    **The films that came up**    Roberto Benigni (director), *Life Is Beautiful (La Vita È Bella)* (Rome, Italy: Melampo Cinematografica, Cecchi Gori Group, 1997); James L. Brooks (director), *Terms of Endearment* (Los Angeles: Paramount Pictures, 1983); Garry Marshall (director), *Beaches* (United States: All Girl Productions, Silver Screen Partners IV, Touchstone Pictures, 1988); Wayne Wang (director), *The Joy Luck Club* (Burbank, CA: Hollywood Pictures, 1993); Steven Spielberg (director), *The Color Purple* (United States: Amblin Entertainment, The Guber-Peters Company, Warner Bros., 1985); Herbert Ross (director), *Steel Magnolias* (United States: TriStar Pictures, Rastar Films, 1989); Ang Lee (director), *Brokeback Mountain* (United States, Canada: Focus Features, River Road Entertainment, Alberta Film Entertainment, Good Machine, 2005); Richard LaGravenese (director), *P.S. I Love You* (United States: Alcon Entertainment, Grosvenor Park Productions, Wendy Finerman Productions, 2007); Pete Docter and Ronnie Del Carmen (directors), *Inside Out* (Burbank, CA: Pixar Animation Studios, Walt Disney

Pictures, 2015); Pete Docter and Bob Peterson (directors), *Up* (Burbank, CA: Pixar Animation Studios, Walt Disney Pictures, 2009).

106   **I was caught off guard in fourth grade**   Norman Tokar (director), *Where the Red Fern Grows* (United States: Doty-Dayton Productions, 1974); Robert Stevenson (director), *Old Yeller* (Burbank, CA: Walt Disney Productions, 1957).

106   **Sadness and depression are not the same thing**   American Psychiatric Association, *Diagnostic and Statistical Manual of Mental Disorders*, 5th ed. (Washington, DC: American Psychiatric Association, 2013).

108   **"Though much has been made"**   Joseph P. Forgas, "Four Ways Sadness May Be Good for You," *Greater Good Science Center,* June 4, 2014.

108   **"Evolutionary theory suggests that"**   Ibid.

108   **Additionally, some scholars have speculated**   Matthew C. Keller and Randolph M. Nesse, "The Evolutionary Significance of Depressive Symptoms: Different Adverse Situations Lead to Different Depressive Symptom Patterns," *Journal of Personality and Social Psychology* 91, no. 2 (2006):316–30. doi: 10.1037/0022-3514.91.2.316.

108   **investigated the sad-film paradox**   Julian Hanich, Valentin Wagner, Mira Shah, Thomas Jacobsen, and Winfried Menninghaus, "Why We Like to Watch Sad Films. The Pleasure of Being Moved in Aesthetic Experiences," *Psychology of Aesthetics, Creativity, and the Arts* 8, no. 2 (2014):130–43. doi: 10.1037/a0035690 10.1037/a0035690 .supp.

108   **"highly significant positive correlation"**   Ibid., 130.

108   **Sadness leads to feeling moved**   Jonna K. Vuoskoski and Tuomas Eerola, "The Pleasure Evoked by Sad Music Is Mediated by Feelings of Being Moved," *Frontiers in Psychology* 8 (2017).

110   **"Hence sadness primarily functions as a contributor"**   Hanich, "Why We Like to Watch Sad Films," 130.

110   **"Grief does not obey your plans"**   Elizabeth Gilbert (@Elizabeth_gilbert_writer), "Grief Does Not Obey," Instagram post, June 6, 2018.

110   *"A central process in grieving"*   Robert A. Neimeyer, "Meaning Reconstruction in Bereavement: Development of a Research Program," *Death Studies* 43, no. 2 (2019):79–91, 80. doi: 10.1080/07481187.2018.1456620.

111   **"When a person adapts to a loss"**   The Center for Complicated Grief, "Complicated Grief Public Overview."

111   **"Each person's grief is as unique as their fingerprint"**   Brené Brown (host), "David Kessler and Brené on Grief and Finding Meaning," March 31, 2020, *Unlocking Us,* podcast.

111   **"Most people who struggle with complicating loss"**   Neimeyer, "Meaning Reconstruction in Bereavement," 84.

113   **Acute grief occurs**   The Center for Complicated Grief, "Complicated Grief Public Overview."

113   **"is not openly acknowledged"**   Tashel Bordere, "Disenfranchisement and Ambiguity in the Face of Loss: The Suffocated Grief of Sexual Assault Survivors," *Family Relations: An Interdisciplinary Journal of Applied Family Studies* 66, no. 1 (2017):29–45, 31. doi: 10.1111/fare.12231.

113   **As an illustrative example**   Ibid.

## #7 PLACES WE GO WITH OTHERS

118   **"virtuous response"**   Shane Sinclair, Susan McClement, Shelley Raffin-Bouchal, Tom Hack, Neil Hagen, Shelagh McConnell, and Harvey Chochinov, "Compassion in Health Care: An Empirical Model," *Journal of Pain and Symptom Management* 51 (2016):193–203, 195. doi: 10.1016/j.jpainsymman.2015.10.009.

118   **"When we practice"**   Pima Chödrön, *The Places That Scare You: A Guide to Fearlessness in Difficult Times* (Boston: Shambhala Publications, 2001).

119   **"'Near enemy' is a useful Buddhist concept"**   Kristin Neff, *Fierce Self-Compassion: How Women Can Harness Kindness to Speak up, Claim Their Power and Thrive.* (New York: HarperCollins, 2021), 38.

120   **"The near enemy of compassion"**   Jack Kornfield, *Bringing Home the Dharma: Awakening Right Where You Are* (Boston: Shambhala Publications, 2011), 103.

120   **Pity involves four elements**   Victor Florian, Mario Mikulincer, and Gilad Hirschberger, "The Anatomy of a Problematic Emotion—the Conceptualization and Measurement of the Experience of Pity," *Imagination, Cognition and Personality* 19, no. 1 (1999.):3–25. doi: 10.2190/4JG9-M79P-HJYK-AQNE.

120   **"Another enemy of compassion"**   Kornfield, *Bringing Home the Dharma,* 103.

120   **empathy helps interpersonal decision making**   Peter Paul Zurek and Herbert Scheithauer, "Towards a More Precise Conceptualization of Empathy: An Integrative Review of Literature on Definitions, Associated Functions, and Developmental Trajectories," *International Journal of Developmental Science* 11, no. 3-4 (2017):57–68. doi: 10.3233/DEV-16224.

121   **at least two elements to empathy**   Ibid.

122   **Theresa Wiseman's Attributes of Empathy**   Theresa Wiseman, "A Concept Analysis of Empathy," *Journal of Advanced Nursing* 23, no. 6 (1996):1162–67. doi: 10.1046/j.1365-2648.1996.12213.x.

122    **Practicing mindfulness**    Kristin Neff, "Self-Compassion: An Alternative Conceptualization of a Healthy Attitude toward Oneself," *Self & Identity* 2, no. 2 (2003):85–101. doi: 10.1080/15298860390129863.

122    **empathy is a skill set**    Jamil Zaki, "Using Empathy to Use People: Emotional Intelligence and Manipulation," *Scientific American,* November 7, 2013.

124    **cancer patients on the receiving end**    Shane Sinclair, Kate Beamer, Thomas F. Hack, Susan McClement, Shelley Raffin Bouchal, Harvey M. Chochinov, and Neil A. Hagen, "Sympathy, Empathy, and Compassion: A Grounded Theory Study of Palliative Care Patients' Understandings, Experiences, and Preferences," *Palliative Medicine* 31, no. 5 (2017):437–47. doi: 10.1177/0269216316663499.

124    **one of my favorite films**    Lulu Wang (director), *The Farewell* (New York: A24, 2019).

124    **tweeted, "Let's be clear"**    Lulu Wang (@thumbelulu), "Let's Be Clear," Twitter post, March 1, 2019.

125    **compassion fatigue occurs**    Olga Klimecki and Tania Singer, "Empathic Distress Fatigue Rather Than Compassion Fatigue? Integrating Findings from Empathy Research in Psychology and Social Neuroscience," in *Pathological Altruism,* edited by Barbara Oakley, Ariel Knafo, Guruprasad Madhavan, and David Sloan Wilson (New York: Oxford University Press, 2012), 369–83.

126    **Empathy Misses**    Brené Brown, *The Gifts of Imperfection: Let Go of Who You Think You're Supposed to Be and Embrace Who You Are* (Center City, MN: Hazelden Publishing, 2010), 15–18.

128    **"The heart of compassion"** Ibid., 16–17

129    **"Boundaries are the distance at which I can love"**    Prentis Hemphill, "Boundaries Are the Distance," Instagram post, April 5, 2021.

130    **a very straightforward blog post**    Kelly Rae Roberts. "What Is and Is Not Okay," *Kelly Rae Roberts: Welcome to My Blog,* March 22, 2009.

## #8 PLACES WE GO WHEN WE FALL SHORT

134    **"Science is not the truth"**    Original source of quote unknown.

134    **the connection between humiliation and violence**    J. Elison and S. Harter, "Humiliation: Causes, Correlates, and Consequences," in *The Self-Conscious Emotions: Theory and Research*, edited by Jessica L. Tracy, Richard W. Robins, and June P. Tangney (New York: Guilford Press, 2007), 310–29; Susan Harter, Sabina M. Low, and Nancy R. Whitesell, "What Have We Learned from Columbine," *Journal of School Violence* 2, no. 3 (2003):3–26. doi: 10.1300/J202v02n03_02; L. M. Hartling, E. Lindner, U. Spalthoff, and M. Britton, "Humiliation: A Nuclear Bomb of Emotions?" *Psicología Política* 46 (2013):55–67, 62.

135    **"I hated the internal wounds"**    Antwone Quenton Fisher, *Finding Fish: A Memoir* (New York: HarperCollins, 2001), 11–12.

135    **Reading Antwone Fisher's book**    Ibid.

135    **was a *Sliding Doors* moment**    Peter Howitt (director), *Sliding Doors* (United States/United Kingdom: Miramax Films/Paramount Pictures, 1998).

135    **The first one I found warned**    Thomas J. Scheff, "Shame in Self and Society," *Symbolic Interaction* 26, no. 2 (2003):239–62. doi: 10.1525/si.2003.26.2.239.

138    **"Self-compassion entails being warm"**    Kristin Neff, "What is Self-Compassion?," Self-Compassion (website).

138    **"Self-compassion involves recognizing"**    Ibid.

138    **"Mindfulness is a non-judgmental"**    Ibid.

140    **"Shame isn't the cure, it's the cause"**    Brené Brown, *Dare to Lead: Brave Work. Tough Conversations. Whole Hearts.* (New York: Random House, 2018), 129.

144    **people with high levels of perfectionistic traits**    Paul L. Hewitt, Gordon L. Flett, Samuel F. Mikail, David Kealy, and Lisa C. Zhang, "Perfectionism in the Therapeutic Context: The Perfectionism Social Disconnection Model," in *The Psychology of Perfectionism: Theory, Research, Applications,* edited by Joachim Stoeber (New York: Routledge/Taylor & Francis Group, 2018), 306–29; Simon B. Sherry, Anna L. MacKinnon, Kristin-Lee Fossum, Martin M. Antony, Sherry H. Stewart, Dayna L. Sherry, Logan J. Nealis, and Aislin R. Mushquash, "Perfectionism, Discrepancies, and Depression: Testing the Perfectionism Social Disconnection Model in a Short-Term, Four-Wave Longitudinal Study," *Personality and Individual Differences* 54, no. 6 (2013):692–97. doi: 10.1016/j.paid.2012.11.017.

144    **perfectionism is a self-destructive**    Brené Brown, *The Gifts of Imperfection: Let Go of Who You Think You're Supposed to Be and Embrace Who You Are* (Center City, MN: Hazelden Publishing, 2010), 76.

146    **with guilt, our focus**    Michael Lewis, "Self-Conscious Emotions: Embarrassment, Pride, Shame, Guilt, and Hubris," in *Handbook of Emotions,* edited by Lisa Feldman Barrett, Michael Lewis, and J. M. Haviland-Jones (New York: Guilford Press, 2016), 792–814.

147    **Remorse, a subset of guilt**    June P. Tangney, Jeff Stuewig, and Logaina Hafez, "Shame, Guilt, and Remorse:

Implications for Offender Populations," *Journal of Forensic Psychiatry & Psychology* 22, no. 5 (2011):706–23. doi: 10.1080/14789949.2011.617541.

147  **shame is highly correlated**  Kerry Nicole Beduna and Kristin Marie Perrone-McGovern, "Recalled Childhood Bullying Victimization and Shame in Adulthood: The Influence of Attachment Security, Self-Compassion, and Emotion Regulation," *Traumatology* 25, no. 1 (2019):21–32. doi: 10.1037/trm0000162; Ronda L. Dearing, Jeff Stuewig, and June P. Tangney, "On the Importance of Distinguishing Shame from Guilt: Relations to Problematic Alcohol and Drug Use," *Addictive Behaviors* 30, no. 7 (2005):1392–1404. doi: 10.1016/j.addbeh.2005.02.002; June Price Tangney, Jeff Stuewig, and Debra J. Mashek, "Moral Emotions and Moral Behavior," *Annual Review of Psychology* 58 (2007):345–72. doi: 10.1146/annurev.psych.56.091103.070145.

147  **Empathy and guilt work together**  June P. Tangney and Ronda L. Dearing, *Shame and Guilt* (New York: Guilford Press, 2002).

147  **"All the cruel and brutal things"**  Rita Coburn Whack (executive producer), "Kofi Annan," *Maya Angelou's Black History Month Special 2013: "Telling Our Stories,"* September 9, 2013.

147  **Linda Hartling is the director**  Human Dignity and Humiliation Studies, *Who We Are* (website).

148  **"unjustified mistreatment"**  Hartling, "Humiliation: A Nuclear Bomb of Emotions?," 62.

148  **"in every case"**  Harter, "What Have We Learned from Columbine," 13, emphasis added.

148  **That report prompted a series of studies**  Elison, "Humiliation: Causes, Correlates, and Consequences."

149  **"humiliation is not only"**  Hartling, "Humiliation: A Nuclear Bomb of Emotions?," 56.

149  **"Never allow anyone to be humiliated"**  Ariel Burger, *Witness: Lessons from Elie Wiesel's Classroom* (New York: Houghton Mifflin Harcourt, 2018), 26.

149  **"Embarrassment does not persist"**  Rowland S. Miller, "Embarrassment and Social Anxiety Disorder: Fraternal Twins or Distant Cousins?" in *Social Anxiety: Clinical, Developmental, and Social Perspectives.,* 3rd ed., edited by Stefan G. Hofmann and Patricia M. DiBartolo (San Diego, CA: Elsevier Academic Press, 2014), 118.

149  **When we feel embarrassed**  Rowland S. Miller, "Is Embarrassment a Blessing or a Curse?" in *The Self-Conscious Emotions: Theory and Research*, edited by Jessica L. Tracy, Richard W. Robins, and June P. Tangney (New York: Oxford University Press, 2007); Miller, "Embarrassment and Social Anxiety Disorder."

150  **three types of events**  John Sabini, Michael Siepmann, Julia Stein, and Marcia Meyerowitz, "Who Is Embarrassed by What?" *Cognition and Emotion* 14, no. 2 (2000):213–40. doi: 10.1080/026999300378941.

150  **We absolutely can feel vicarious embarrassment**  Martin Melchers, Sebastian Markett, Christian Montag, Peter Trautner, Bernd Weber, Bernd Lachmann, Pauline Buss, et al., "Reality TV and Vicarious Embarrassment: An fMRI Study," *NeuroImage* 109 (2015):109–17. doi: 10.1016/j.neuroimage.2015.01.022; Laura Müller-Pinzler, Lena Rademacher, Frieder M. Paulus, and Sören Krach, "When Your Friends Make You Cringe: Social Closeness Modulates Vicarious Embarrassment-Related Neural Activity," *Social Cognitive & Affective Neuroscience* 11, no. 3 (2015):466–75. doi: 10.1093/scan/nsv130.

150  **I was watching *I Love Lucy* reruns**  Jess Oppenheimer, Madelyn Davis, and Bob Carroll, Jr. (writers), *I Love Lucy*, aired 1951–57.

150  **during the episode where Lucy and Ethel**  Jess Oppenheimer, Madelyn Davis, and Bob Carroll, Jr. (writers), *I Love Lucy*, Season 2, Episode 1, "Job Switching," directed by William Asher, September 15, 1952.

150  **"Embarrassment takes years to develop"**  Miller, "Embarrassment and Social Anxiety Disorder," 128.

## #9 PLACES WE GO WHEN WE SEARCH FOR CONNECTION

154  **Maslow's hierarchy of needs**  Abraham H. Maslow, "A Theory of Human Motivation," *Psychological Review* 50, no. 4 (1943):370–96. doi: 10.1037/h0054346.

154  **finding a sense of belonging**  Brooke Massey, Alice Vo Edwards, and Laura Musikanski, "Life Satisfaction, Affect, and Belonging in Older Adults," *Applied Research in Quality of Life* 16 (2021): 1205–19. doi: 10.1007/s11482 -019-09804-2.

155  **I published *Braving the Wilderness***  Brené Brown, *Braving the Wilderness: The Quest for True Belonging and the Courage to Stand Alone* (New York: Random House, 2017).

158  **"We want to be a part"**  Modified slightly from original version. Ibid., 33.

158  **"connection to a larger humanity"**  Ibid.

165  **among underrepresented students**  Gregory M. Walton and Geoffrey L. Cohen, "A Question of Belonging: Race, Social Fit, and Achievement," *Journal of Personality and Social Psychology* 92, no. 1 (2007):82–96. doi: 10.1037/0022-3514.92.1.82.

165  **"It is a more general inference"**  Gregory M. Walton and Shannon T. Brady, "The Many Questions of Belonging," in *Handbook of Competence and Motivation: Theory and Application.,* 2nd ed., edited by Andrew J. Elliot, Carol S. Dweck, and David S. Yeager (New York: Guilford Press, 2017), 272.

168 **"I don't believe your antiracist work is complete"**  Tarana Burke and Brené Brown, eds. *You Are Your Best Thing: Vulnerability, Shame Resilience, and the Black Experience* (New York: Random House, 2021), xviii.

168 **two-part *Dare to Lead* podcast**  Brené Brown (host), "Brené with Aiko Bethea on Inclusivity at Work: The Heart of Hard Conversations (Part 1)," November 9, 2020, *Dare to Lead,* podcast; Brené Brown (host), "Brené with Aiko Bethea on Creating Transformative Cultures (Part 2)," February 8, 2021, *Dare to Lead,* podcast.

168 **developed Grounded Theory in 1967**  Barney G. Glaser and Anselm L. Strauss, *The Discovery of Grounded Theory: Strategies for Qualitative Research* (Chicago: Aldine, 1967).

169 **"depicted culture as more than the scenic backdrop"**  Maureen Walker, "Critical Thinking: Challenging Developmental Myths, Stigmas, and Stereotypes," in *Diversity and Development: Critical Contexts That Shape Our Lives and Relationships,* edited by Dana Comstock (Belmont, CA: Brooks Cole, 2005), 48.

169 **"The need for connection"**  Judith V. Jordan, *Relational–Cultural Therapy,* 2nd ed. (Washington, DC: American Psychological Association, 2018), 30.

169 **"people who have strong connections"**  Roy F. Baumeister and Mark R. Leary, "The Need to Belong: Desire for Interpersonal Attachments as a Fundamental Human Motivation," *Psychological Bulletin* 117, no. 3 (1995):497–529, 510. doi: 10.1037/0033-2909.117.3.497.

171 **"RCT sees disconnections"**  Judith V. Jordan, "Theory," in *Relational–Cultural Therapy,* 2nd ed. (Washington, DC: American Psychological Association, 2018), 30–31.

171 **"often loses touch"**  Ibid., 31.

171 **the pain and feelings of disconnection**  Naomi I. Eisenberger, "The Pain of Social Disconnection: Examining the Shared Neural Underpinnings of Physical and Social Pain," *Nature Reviews Neuroscience* 13, no. 6 (2012):421–34. doi: 10.1038/nrn3231.

172 **"To avoid the pain and vulnerability"**  Trisha L. Raque-Bogdan, "Relational Cultural Theory and Cancer: Addressing the Social Well-Being of a Growing Population," *Practice Innovations* 4, no. 2 (2019):99–111, 102. doi: 10.1037/pri0000087.

172 **a "perfectionism social disconnection model"**  Paul L. Hewitt, Gordon L. Flett, Samuel F. Mikail, David Kealy, and Lisa C. Zhang, "Perfectionism in the Therapeutic Context: The Perfectionism Social Disconnection Model," in *The Psychology of Perfectionism: Theory, Research, Applications,* edited by Joachim Stoeber (New York: Routledge/Taylor & Francis Group, 2018).

173 **Domain-specific insecurity**  Wenjie Yuan and Lei Wang, "Optimism and Attributional Style Impact on the Relationship between General Insecurity and Mental Health," *Personality and Individual Differences* 101 (2016):312–17. doi: 10.1016/j.paid.2016.06.005.

173 **"In early 2020, the novel coronavirus"**  Monica Hake, Adam Dewey, Emily Engelhard, Mark Strayer, Sena Dawes, Tom Summerfelt, and Craig Gunderson, *The Impact of the Coronavirus on Food Insecurity in 2020 & 2021* (Chicago, IL: Feeding America, 2021), italics added.

173 **Relationship or interpersonal insecurity**  Edward P. Lemay, Jr., and Margaret S. Clark, " 'Walking on Eggshells': How Expressing Relationship Insecurities Perpetuates Them," *Journal of Personality and Social Psychology* 95, no. 2 (2008):420–41. doi: 10.1037/0022-3514.95.2.420; Jingyi Lu, Yi Zhang, and Jiayi Liu, "Interpersonal Insecurity and Risk-Taking Propensity Across Domains and Around the Globe," *Evolutionary Psychology* 16, no. 3 (2018). doi: 10.1177/1474704918795520; Hong Zhang, Darius K. S. Chan, Fei Teng, and Denghao Zhang, "Sense of Interpersonal Security and Preference for Harsh Actions against Others: The Role of Dehumanization," *Journal of Experimental Social Psychology* 56 (2015):165–71. doi: 10.1016/j.jesp.2014.09.014.

174 **General or personal insecurity**  Nathaniel S. Eckland, Alice B. Huang, and Howard Berenbaum, "Empathic Accuracy: Associations with Prosocial Behavior and Self-Insecurity," *Emotion* 20, no. 7 (2020): 1306–10. doi: 10.1037/emo0000622 10.1037/emo0000622.supp.

174 **"the open and nonjudgmental"**  Alice B. Huang and Howard Berenbaum, "Accepting Our Weaknesses and Enjoying Better Relationships: An Initial Examination of Self-Security," *Personality and Individual Differences* 106 (2017):64–70, 64. doi: 10.1016/j.paid.2016.10.031.

174 **In initial studies, Huang**  Huang, "Accepting Our Weaknesses."

175 **Rebecca Neel and Bethany Lassetter**  Rebecca Neel and Bethany Lassetter, "The Stigma of Perceived Irrelevance: An Affordance-Management Theory of Interpersonal Invisibility," *Psychological Review* 126, no. 5 (2019):634–59. doi: 10.1037/rev0000143.

177 **"When a group is invisible,"**  Ibid., 634.

177 **I researched loneliness**  Brown, *Braving the Wilderness.*

177 **The information below**  Ibid., 52–55.

179 **"perceived social isolation"**  John T. Cacioppo and William Patrick, *Loneliness: Human Nature and the Need for Social Connection* (New York: Norton, 2008).

179    **"To grow into an adulthood"**    John T. Cacioppo, "The Lethality of Loneliness," TEDxDesMoines, September 9, 2013.

179    **Cacioppo explains how the biological machinery**    Ibid.

179    **"Denying you feel lonely"**    Hafner quotes Cacioppo in her article. Katie Hafner, "Researchers Confront an Epidemic of Loneliness," *New York Times,* September 5, 2016.

180    **"gnawing, chronic disease"**    Cacioppo attributes this definition to a 1973 book by Robert Weiss entitled *Loneliness: The Experience of Emotional and Social Isolation*. John T. Cacioppo, Stephanie Cacioppo, and Dorret I. Boomsma, "Evolutionary Mechanisms for Loneliness," *Cognition and Emotion* 28, no. 1 (2014):3–21, 3. doi: 10.1080/02699931.2013.837379.

180    **loneliness is not just a sad condition**    Cacioppo, "Evolutionary Mechanisms for Loneliness."

180    **In a meta-analysis of studies on loneliness**    Julianne Holt-Lunstad, Timothy B. Smith, and J. Bradley Layton, "Social Relationships and Mortality Risk: A Meta-Analytic Review," *PLoS Medicine* 7, no. 7 (2010):1–20. doi: 10.1371/journal.pmed.1000316.

180    **one of the first guests**    Brené Brown (host), "Dr. Vivek Murthy and Brené on Loneliness and Connection," April 21, 2020, *Unlocking Us,* podcast.

180    **We talked about his new book**    Vivek Murthy, *Together: The Healing Power of Human Connection in a Sometimes Lonely World* (HarperCollins: New York, 2020).

181    **"During my years caring for patients"**    Vivek Murthy, "Work and the Loneliness Epidemic: Reducing Isolation at Work Is Good for Business," *Harvard Business Review*, September 26, 2017, 2–3 (reprint version).

181    **"reduces task performance"**    Murthy, "Work and the Loneliness Epidemic," 3.

## #10 PLACES WE GO WHEN THE HEART IS OPEN

184    **"Everywhere we learn that love"**    bell hooks, *All About Love: New Visions* (New York: Harper Perennial, 2000), xxvii.

184    **"the preoccupying and strong *desire*"**    Barbara L. Fredrickson, "Love: Positivity Resonance as a Fresh, Evidence-Based Perspective on an Age-Old Topic," in *Handbook of Emotions*, edited by Lisa Feldman Barrett, Michael Lewis, and Jeannette M. Haviland-Jones (New York: Guilford Press, 2016), 847.

184    **whether love is an emotion**    Lubomir Lamy, "Beyond Emotion: Love as an Encounter of Myth and Drive," *Emotion Review* 8, no. 2 (2016):97–107. doi: 10.1177/1754073915594431.

184    **undergraduates were asked to rate**    Phillip Shaver, Judith Schwartz, Donald Kirson, and Cary O'Connor, "Emotion Knowledge: Further Exploration of a Prototype Approach," *Journal of Personality and Social Psychology* 52, no. 6 (1987):1061–86. doi: 10.1037/0022-3514.52.6.1061.

187    **"We cultivate love when we allow"**    Brené Brown, *The Gifts of Imperfection: Let Go of Who You Think You're Supposed to Be and Embrace Who You Are* (Center City, MN: Hazelden Publishing, 2010), 26.

187    **The quote that opens this section**    hooks, *All About Love.*

187    **her book *Teaching to Transgress***    bell hooks, *Teaching to Transgress: Education as the Practice of Freedom* (New York: Routledge, 1994).

188    **"Refusal to stand up"**    hooks, *All About Love,* 90–91.

188    **I shared his essay**    Joe Reynolds, personal communication.

188    **"Heartbreak is an altogether different thing"**    Brené Brown, *Rising Strong: The Reckoning. The Rumble. The Revolution* (New York: Random House, 2015), 143–44.

191    **In *The Thin Book of Trust***    Charles Feltman, *The Thin Book of Trust: An Essential Primer for Building Trust at Work,* Kindle edition (Thin Book Publishing, 2008), 9–11.

193    **"For there to be betrayal"**    Suzanne Collins, *The Hunger Games* (New York: Scholastic Press, 2008), 114.

194    **Betrayal is so painful**    S. Rachman, "Betrayal: A Psychological Analysis," *Behaviour Research and Therapy* 48, no. 4 (2010):304–11. doi: 10.1016/j.brat.2009.12.002.

194    **Most betrayals happen among spouses**    Warren H. Jones and Marsha Parsons Burdette, "Betrayal in Relationships," in *Perspectives on Close Relationships,* edited by Ann L. Weber and John H. Harvey (Needham Heights, MA: Allyn & Bacon, 1994), 243–62.

194    **When betrayal is the result**    Jennifer J. Freyd, "Memory and Dimensions of Trauma: Terror May Be 'All-Too-Well Remembered' and Betrayal Buried," in *Critical Issues in Child Sexual Abuse: Historical, Legal, and Psychological Perspectives,* edited by J. R. Conte (Thousand Oaks, CA: Sage, 2001); Jennifer J. Freyd, Anne P. DePrince, and David H. Gleaves, "The State of Betrayal Trauma Theory: Reply to McNally—Conceptual Issues and Future Directions," *Memory* 15, no. 3 (2007):295–311. doi: 10.1080/09658210701256514.

194    **When we're injured by betrayal**    Laurie L. Couch, Kiersten R. Baughman, and Melissa R. Derow, "The After-

math of Romantic Betrayal: What's Love Got to Do with It?" *Current Psychology: A Journal for Diverse Perspectives on Diverse Psychological Issues* 36, no. 3 (2017):504–15. doi: 10.1007/s12144-016-9438-y.

194 **"an institution causes harm"** Carly Parnitzke Smith and Jennifer J. Freyd, "Institutional Betrayal," *American Psychologist* 69, no. 6 (2014):575–87, 578. doi: 10.1037/a0037564.

194 **Factors that contribute to institutional betrayal** Smith, "Institutional Betrayal."

195 **"Cover-ups are perpetrated"** Emphasis modified from original. Brené Brown, *Dare to Lead: Brave Work. Tough Conversations. Whole Hearts.* (New York: Random House, 2018), 135.

196 **In order to try to limit our exposure** Lisa Feldman Barrett, Nathan L. Williams, and Geoffrey T. Fong, "Defensive Verbal Behavior Assessment," *Personality and Social Psychology Bulletin* 28, no. 6 (2002):776–88. doi: 10.1177/0146167202289007; Michael H. Kernis, Chad E. Lakey, and Whitney L. Heppner, "Secure Versus Fragile High Self-Esteem as a Predictor of Verbal Defensiveness: Converging Findings across Three Different Markers," *Journal of Personality* 76, no. 3 (2008):477–512. doi: 10.1111/j.1467-6494.2008.00493.x; David K. Sherman and Geoffrey L. Cohen, "Accepting Threatening Information: Self-Affirmation and the Reduction of Defensive Biases," *Current Directions in Psychological Science* 11, no. 4 (2002):119-123. doi: 10.1111/1467-8721.00182.

196 **Defensiveness blocks us** Sherman, "Accepting Threatening Information."

197 **"a sensation of feeling . . . overwhelmed"** The Gottman Institute, "How Does Flooding Impact Relationship Conflict?" Gottman Institute Facebook page.

197 **"We each have a sort of built-in meter"** John Gottman, *Why Marriages Succeed or Fail: And How You Can Make Yours Last* (New York: Simon & Schuster, 1994), 110.

198 **chronic flooding sets us up** Gottman, *Why Marriages Succeed or Fail.*

198 **"Individuals who are hurt"** Anita L. Vangelisti, Stacy L. Young, Katy E. Carpenter-Theune, and Alicia L. Alexander, "Why Does It Hurt? The Perceived Causes of Hurt Feelings," *Communication Research* 32, no. 4 (2005):443–77, 446. doi: 10.1177/0093650205277319.

199 **Vangelisti and team explain** Vangelisti, "Why Does It Hurt?"

199 **In fact, hurt feelings** Mark R. Leary and Carrie A. Springer, "Hurt Feelings: The Neglected Emotion," in *Behaving Badly: Aversive Behaviors in Interpersonal Relationships,* edited by Robin M. Kowalski (Washington, DC: American Psychological Association, 2001).

199 **"the more intentional an action"** David J. K. Hardecker, "The Distinctive Constitution of Feeling Hurt: A Review and a Lazarian Theory," *European Psychologist* 25, no. 4 (2020): 293–305, 295. doi: 10.1027/1016-9040/a000390.

200 **Our hurt feelings are typically experienced** Mark R. Leary and Sadie Leder, "The Nature of Hurt Feelings: Emotional Experience and Cognitive Appraisals," in *Feeling Hurt in Close Relationships*, edited by Anita L. Vangelisti (New York: Cambridge University Press, 2009); Leary, "Hurt Feelings."

200 **Our reactions to hurt feelings** Laura N. May and Warren H. Jones, "Differential Reactions to Hurt," *Journal of Worry & Affective Experience* 1, no. 2 (2005):54–59; Laura N. May and Warren H. Jones, "Does Hurt Linger? Exploring the Nature of Hurt Feelings over Time," *Current Psychology: A Journal for Diverse Perspectives on Diverse Psychological Issues* 25, no. 4 (2007):245–56; Keith Sanford and Wade C. Rowatt, "When Is Negative Emotion Positive for Relationships? An Investigation of Married Couples and Roommates," *Personal Relationships* 11, no. 3 (2004):329–54. doi: 10.1111/j.1475-6811.2004.00086.x.

200 **When reparation doesn't seem possible** Hardecker, "The Distinctive Constitution"; Edward P. Lemay, Jr., Nickola C. Overall, and Margaret S. Clark, "Experiences and Interpersonal Consequences of Hurt Feelings and Anger," *Journal of Personality and Social Psychology* 103, no. 6 (2012):982–1006. doi: 10.1037/a0030064.

200 **One thing that motivates me** David S. Chester, C. Nathan DeWall, and Richard S. Pond, Jr., "The Push of Social Pain: Does Rejection's Sting Motivate Subsequent Social Reconnection?" *Cognitive, Affective & Behavioral Neuroscience* 16, no. 3 (2016):541–50. doi: 10.3758/s13415-016-0412-9; Lemay, "Experiences and Interpersonal Consequences."

200 **the language of hurt feelings** Leary, "Hurt Feelings."

#11 PLACES WE GO WHEN LIFE IS GOOD

204 **"And I wish you joy"** Dolly Parton, "I Will Always Love You" (1974), recorded by Dolly Parton (RCA Victor, 1974).

204 **talking to Dolly on the *Unlocking Us* podcast** Brené Brown (host), "Brené with Dolly Parton on Songtelling, Empathy and Shining Our Lights," November 18, 2020, *Unlocking Us,* podcast.

204 **Can you believe she wrote** Parton, "I Will Always Love You," Dolly Parton, "Jolene" (1974), recorded by Dolly Parton on the album *Jolene* (RCA Victor, 1974).

204 **In Dolly's gorgeous book *Songteller*** Dolly Parton and Robert K. Oermann, *Songteller: My Life in Lyrics* (San Francisco: Chronicle Books, 2020).

204 **"that was the last I'd heard of it"** Ibid., 105; Dolly Parton, "I Will Always Love You" (1974), recorded by Whitney Houston on the album *The Bodyguard: Original Soundtrack Album* (Arista BMG, 1992); Parton, *Songteller,* 105.

204 **Joy is sudden, unexpected** Laura Cottrell, "Joy and Happiness: A Simultaneous and Evolutionary Concept Analysis," *Journal of Advanced Nursing* 72, no. 7 (2016):1506–17. doi: 10.1111/jan.12980; Barbara L. Fredrickson, "What Good Are Positive Emotions?" *Review of General Psychology* 2, no. 3 (1998):300–319. doi: 10.1037/1089-2680.2.3.300.

204 **Happiness is stable, longer-lasting** Cottrell, "Joy and Happiness"; David G. Myers and Ed Diener, "The Scientific Pursuit of Happiness," *Perspectives on Psychological Science* 13, no. 2 (2018):218–25. doi: 10.1177/1745691618765171.

205 **In *The Gifts of Imperfection,* I quote Anne Robertson** Brené Brown, *The Gifts of Imperfection: Let Go of Who You Think You're Supposed to Be and Embrace Who You Are* (Center City, MN: Hazelden Publishing, 2010).

205 **"She explains that the Greek word for happiness"** Ibid., 80.

205 **"Chairo is something, the ancient Greeks tell us"** Anne Robertson, "Joy or Happiness?," 1999. Previously posed at stjohnsdover.org; link no longer active.

205 **people find experiences of joy difficult to articulate** Matthew Kuan Johnson, "Joy: A Review of the Literature and Suggestions for Future Directions," *The Journal of Positive Psychology* 15, no. 1 (2020):5–24. doi: 10.1080/17439760.2019.1685581.

205 **while experiencing joy** Ibid.

205 **spontaneous weeping** Jack Barbalet, "Weeping and Transformations of Self," *Journal for the Theory of Social Behaviour* 35, no. 2 (2005):125–41. doi: 10.1111/j.1468-5914.2005.00267.x.

206 **"intriguing upward spiral"** Philip C. Watkins, Robert A. Emmons, Madeline R. Greaves, and Joshua Bell, "Joy Is a Distinct Positive Emotion: Assessment of Joy and Relationship to Gratitude and Well-Being," *The Journal of Positive Psychology* 13, no. 5 (2018):522–39, 534. doi: 10.1080/17439760.2017.1414298.

206 **The intriguing upward spiral goes like this** Ibid.

206 **a story about an outing with Ellen** Brené Brown, *Daring Greatly: How the Courage to Be Vulnerable Transforms the Way We Live, Love, Parent, and Lead* (New York: Gotham Books, 2012).

207 **even the most prominent happiness researchers** Belinda Campos, Michelle N. Shiota, Dacher Keltner, Gian C. Gonzaga, and Jennifer L. Goetz, "What Is Shared, What Is Different? Core Relational Themes and Expressive Displays of Eight Positive Emotions," *Cognition and Emotion* 27, no. 1 (2013):37–52. doi: 10.1080/02699931.2012.683852; Ed Diener, Martin E. P. Seligman, Hyewon Choi, and Shigehiro Oishi, "Happiest People Revisited," *Perspectives on Psychological Science* 13, no. 2 (2018):176–84. doi: 10.1177/1745691617697077; Michelle N. Shiota, Belinda Campos, Christopher Oveis, Matthew J. Hertenstein, Emiliana Simon-Thomas, and Dacher Keltner, "Beyond Happiness: Building a Science of Discrete Positive Emotions," *American Psychologist* 72, no. 7 (2017):617–43. doi: 10.1037/a0040456.

207 **Looking at happiness as a trait** Ed Diener, Richard E. Lucas, and Christie Napa Scollon, "Beyond the Hedonic Treadmill: Revising the Adaptation Theory of Well-Being," *American Psychologist* 61, no. 4 (2006):305–14. doi: 10.1037/0003-066X.61.4.305; Ragnhild Bang Nes and Espen Røysamb, "Happiness in Behaviour Genetics: An Update on Heritability and Changeability," *Journal of Happiness Studies: An Interdisciplinary Forum on Subjective Well-Being* 18. no. 5 (2017):1533–52. doi: 10.1007/s10902-016-9781-6.

208 **when people described themselves as calm** Brown, *The Gifts of Imperfection.*

208 **"Anxiety is contagious"** Harriet Lerner, *The Dance of Fear: Rising above Anxiety, Fear, and Shame to Be Your Best and Bravest Self* (New York: HarperCollins, 2004), 113.

209 **"When you are discontent"** "Oprah Talks to the Dalai Lama," *O: The Oprah Magazine,* August 2001.

211 **Several researchers categorize all** Daniel T. Cordaro, Marc Brackett, Lauren Glass, and Craig L. Anderson, "Contentment: Perceived Completeness across Cultures and Traditions," *Review of General Psychology* 20, no. 3 (2016):221–35. doi: 10.1037/gpr0000082.

211 **Contentment is positively correlated** Howard Berenbaum, Philip I. Chow, Michelle Schoenleber, and Luis E. Flores, Jr., "Pleasurable Emotions, Age, and Life Satisfaction," *The Journal of Positive Psychology* 8, no. 2 (2013):140–43. doi: 10.1080/17439760.2013.772221; Melanie T. Davern, Robert A. Cummins, and Mark A. Stokes, "Subjective Wellbeing as an Affective-Cognitive Construct," *Journal of Happiness Studies: An Interdisciplinary Forum on Subjective Well-Being* 8, no. 4 (2007):429–49. doi: 10.1007/s10902-007-9066-1; Barbara L. Fredrickson, "The Role of Positive Emotions in Positive Psychology: The Broaden-and-Build Theory of Positive Emotions," *American Psychologist* 56, no. 3 (2001):218–26. doi: 10.1037/0003-066X.56.3.218; Sylvia D. Kreibig, "Autonomic Nervous

System Activity in Emotion: A Review," *Biological Psychology* 84, no. 3 (2010):394–421. doi: 10.1016/j.biopsycho.2010.03.010.

211    **"All things considered, how satisfied are you"**    Mariano Rojas and Ruut Veenhoven, "Contentment and Affect in the Estimation of Happiness," *Social Indicators Research* 110, no. 2 (2013):415–31, 422. doi: 10.1007/s11205-011-9952-0.

211    **gratitude is good for us**    Courtney E. Ackerman, "28 Benefits of Gratitude & Most Significant Research Findings," PositivePsychology.com, June 22, 2021.

213    **"world's leading scientific expert on gratitude"**    Robert Emmons, "Why Gratitude Is Good," *Greater Good Magazine: Science-Based Insights for a Meaningful Life*, November 16, 2010.

213    **"positive emotions wear off quickly"**    Ibid.

215    **"feelings of tension leaving the body"**    Ira J. Roseman and Andreas Evdokas, "Appraisals Cause Experienced Emotions: Experimental Evidence," *Cognition and Emotion* 18, no. 1 (2004):1–28, 3. doi: 10.1080/02699930244000390.

217    **Sighing serves as a type of reset button**    Elke Vlemincx, Michel Meulders, and James L. Abelson, "Sigh Rate During Emotional Transitions: More Evidence for a Sigh of Relief," *Biological Psychology* 125 (2017):163–72. doi: 10.1016/j.biopsycho.2017.03.005.

217    **"Tranquility is associated with the absence of demand"**    Howard Berenbaum, Alice B. Huang, and Luis E. Flores, "Contentment and Tranquility: Exploring Their Similarities and Differences," *The Journal of Positive Psychology* 14, no. 2 (2019):252–59, 258. doi: 10.1080/17439760.2018.1484938.

217    **"Tranquil environments" provide**    This description refers to the original work of Kaplan and Kaplan as described by Kim and colleagues. Rachel Kaplan and Stephen Kaplan, *The Experience of Nature: A Psychological Perspective* (Cambridge, MA: Cambridge University Press, 1989); Jun Kim, Namyun Kil, Stephen Holland, and Wendi K. Middleton, "The Effect of Visual and Auditory Coherence on Perceptions of Tranquility after Simulated Nature Experiences," *Ecopsychology* 9, no. 3 (2017):182–189. doi: 10.1089/eco.2016.0046.

217    **auditory and visual components**    Robert Pheasant, Kirill Horoshenkov, Greg Watts, and Brendan Barrett, "The Acoustic and Visual Factors Influencing the Construction of Tranquil Space in Urban and Rural Environments Tranquil Spaces-Quiet Places?" *The Journal of the Acoustical Society of America* 123 (2008):1446–57. doi: 10.1121/1.2831735; Robert J. Pheasant, Mark N. Fisher, Greg R. Watts, David J. Whitaker, and Kirill V. Horoshenkov, "The Importance of Auditory-Visual Interaction in the Construction of 'Tranquil Space,'" *Journal of Environmental Psychology* 30, no. 4 (2010):501–509. doi: 10.1016/j.jenvp.2010.03.006; Robert J. Pheasant, Kirill V. Horoshenkov, and Greg R. Watts, "Tranquillity Rating Prediction Tool (Trapt)," *Acoustics Bulletin* 35 (2010):18–24.

217    **Settings that induce high tranquility**    Thomas R. Herzog and Gregory J. Barnes, "Tranquility and Preference Revisited," *Journal of Environmental Psychology* 19, no. 2 (1999):171–81. doi: 10.1006/jevp.1998.0109; Thomas R. Herzog and Kristi K. Chernick, "Tranquility and Danger in Urban and Natural Settings," *Journal of Environmental Psychology* 20, no. 1 (2000):29–39. doi: 10.1006/jevp.1999.0151.

## #12 PLACES WE GO WHEN WE FEEL WRONGED

220    **anger is an emotion that we feel**    Eddie Harmon-Jones and Cindy Harmon-Jones, "Anger," in *Handbook of Emotions*, edited by Lisa Feldman Barrett, Michael Lewis, and Jeannette M. Haviland-Jones (New York: Guilford Press, 2016).

220    **Anger is an action emotion**    Ibid.; Janice R. Kelly, Nicole E. Iannone, and Megan K. McCarty, "Emotional Contagion of Anger Is Automatic: An Evolutionary Explanation," *British Journal of Social Psychology* 55, no. 1 (2016):182–91. doi: 10.1111/bjso.12134.

220    **"from mild irritation or annoyance"**    Charles D. Spielberger and Eric C. Reheiser, "Assessment of Emotions: Anxiety, Anger, Depression, and Curiosity," *Applied Psychology: Health & Well-Being* 1, no. 3 (209):271–302, 281. doi: 10.1111/j.1758-0854.2009.01017.x.

220    **Anger is also a full-contact emotion**    Nelly Alia-Klein, Gabriela Gan, Gadi Gilam, Jessica Bezek, Antonio Bruno, Thomas F. Denson, Talma Hendler, Leroy Lowe, et al., "The Feeling of Anger: From Brain Networks to Linguistic Expressions," *Neuroscience and Biobehavioral Reviews* 108 (2020):480–97. doi: 10.1016/j.neubiorev.2019.12.002.

220    **our propensity for anger and aggression**    Evangelos Vassos, David A. Collier, and Seena Fazel, "Systematic Meta-Analyses and Field Synopsis of Genetic Association Studies of Violence and Aggression," *Molecular Psychiatry* 19, no. 4 (2013):471–77. doi: 10.1038/mp.2013.31.

220    **believe that anger is a primary emotion**    Paul Ekman, "What Scientists Who Study Emotion Agree About," *Perspectives on Psychological Science* 11, no. 1 (2016):31–34. doi: 10.1177/1745691615596992.

224    **"Sometimes owning our pain"**    Brené Brown, *Braving the Wilderness: The Quest for True Belonging and the Courage to Stand Alone* (New York: Random House, 2017), 67–68.

226 **"When someone is angry at you"** Pamela Meyer, "How to Avoid Being Lied To," *Forbes,* August 26, 2010.

226 **known across the globe** The Gottman Institute, "John & Julie Gottman" (website).

226 **"perhaps the most corrosive force"** John Gottman, *Why Marriages Succeed or Fail: And How You Can Make Yours Last* (New York: Simon & Schuster, 1994), 62.

226 **which couples would eventually divorce** John Mordechai Gottman, *What Predicts Divorce? The Relationship between Marital Processes and Marital Outcomes* (Hillsdale, NJ: Lawrence Erlbaum Associates, 1994); John M. Gottman, James Coan, Sybil Carrere, and Catherine Swanson, "Predicting Marital Happiness and Stability from Newlywed Interactions," *Journal of Marriage and the Family* 60, no. 1 (1998):5–22. doi: 10.2307/353438.

226 **Contempt is one of the most damaging** Gottman, *Why Marriages Succeed or Fail.*

227 **"What separates *contempt* from criticism"** Ibid., 79.

228 **"When you communicate with contempt"** Ellie Lisitsa, "The Four Horsemen: Contempt," The Gottman Institute, May 13, 2013 (emphasis added).

228 **Contempt results in distancing** Agneta Fischer and Roger Giner-Sorolla, "Contempt: Derogating Others While Keeping Calm," *Emotion Review* 8, no. 4 (2016):346–57. doi: 10.1177/1754073915610439.

228 **"the contemptuous person is likely to experience"** Carlo Garofalo, Craig S. Neumann, Virgil Zeigler-Hill, and J. Reid Meloy, "Spiteful and Contemptuous: A New Look at the Emotional Experiences Related to Psychopathy," *Personality Disorders: Theory, Research, and Treatment* 10, no. 2 (2019):173–84, 181. doi: 10.1037/per0000310 10 .1037/per0000310.supp.

228 **"our nation is more polarized"** Arthur C. Brooks, "Our Culture of Contempt," *New York Times,* March 2, 2019.

229 **"Contempt makes political compromise and progress impossible"** Ibid.

229 **not that we need to disagree less** Ibid.

229 **to replace negative communication patterns** Gottman, *Why Marriages Succeed or Fail.*

229 **"I might be willing to try"** These are a few representative items from Haidt et al.'s Disgust Scale. Jonathan Haidt, Clark McCauley, and Paul Rozin, "Individual Differences in Sensitivity to Disgust: A Scale Sampling Seven Domains of Disgust Elicitors," *Personality and Individual Differences* 16, no. 5 (1994):701–13, 707. doi: 10.1016/0191-8869(94)90212-7.

230 **These are five items from the Disgust Scale** The original Haidt et al. Disgust Scale was modified by Olatunji et al. Haidt, "Individual Differences in Sensitivity to Disgust"; Bunmi O. Olatunji, Nathan L. Williams, David F. Tolin, Jonathan S. Abramowitz, Craig N. Sawchuk, Jeffrey M. Lohr, and Lisa S. Elwood, "The Disgust Scale: Item Analysis, Factor Structure, and Suggestions for Refinement," *Psychological Assessment* 19, no. 3 (2007):281–97. doi: 10.1037/1040-3590.19.3.281.

230 **"Disgust is a fascinating emotion"** Jonathan Haidt, "The Disgust Scale Home Page."

230 **With disgust, inferiority is not the issue** Rachel S. Herz and Alden Hinds, "Stealing Is Not Gross: Language Distinguishes Visceral Disgust from Moral Violations," *The American Journal of Psychology* 126, no. 3 (2013):275–86. doi: 10.5406/amerjpsyc.126.3.0275.

230 **"The experience of disgust"** Natalie J. Shook, Ronald Thomas, and Cameron G. Ford, "Testing the Relation between Disgust and General Avoidance Behavior," *Personality and Individual Differences* 150 (November 1, 2019), 2. doi: 10.1016/j.paid.2019.05.063.

230 **"intuitive microbiology"** Steven Pinker, *How the Mind Works* (New York: W. W. Norton & Company, 2009), 383.

230 **"arises as a feeling of aversion"** Paul Ekman, "What Is Disgust," Paul Ekman Group (website).

231 **"disgust contains a range"** Ibid.

231 **"All states of disgust"** Ibid.

231 **we often wrinkle our nose** Ibid.

231 **core disgust is thought to protect the body** Spike W. S. Lee and Phoebe C. Ellsworth, "Maggots and Morals: Physical Disgust Is to Fear as Moral Disgust Is to Anger," in *Components of Emotional Meaning: A Sourcebook*, edited by Johnny J. R. Fontaine, Klaus R. Scherer, and Cristina Soriano (New York: Oxford University Press, 2013).

231 **disgust in an interpersonal context** Paul Rozin, Laura Lowery, Sumio Imada, and Jonathan Haidt, "The CAD Triad Hypothesis: A Mapping between Three Moral Emotions (Contempt, Anger, Disgust) and Three Moral Codes (Community, Autonomy, Divinity)," *Journal of Personality and Social Psychology* 76, no. 4 (1999):574–86. doi: 10.1037/0022-3514.76.4.574.

231 **can rapidly lead to dehumanizing** Maria Miceli and Cristiano Castelfranchi, "Contempt and Disgust: The Emotions of Disrespect," *Journal for the Theory of Social Behaviour* 48, no. 2 (2018):205–29. doi: 10.1111/jtsb.12159.

231 **"The disrespect involved in disgust"** Ibid., 221.

231 **"moral disgust is even more dangerous"** Ibid., 221–22.

233 **Another difference that makes disgust more dangerous** Cendri A. Hutcherson and James J. Gross, "The Moral Emotions: A Social–Functionalist Account of Anger, Disgust, and Contempt," *Journal of Personality and Social Psychology* 100, no. 4 (2011):719–37. doi: 10.1037/a0022408; Miceli, "Contempt and Disgust."

233 **"dehumanization is a response to conflicting motives"** Brown, *Braving the Wilderness,* 71–73.

233 **"Dehumanization is a way of subverting those inhibitions"** David L. Smith, *Less Than Human: Why We Demean, Enslave, and Exterminate Others* (New York: St. Martin's Press, 2011), 264.

233 **"the psychological process of demonizing"** Michelle Maiese, "Dehumanization," Beyond Intractability (website), July 2003. Modified by Heidi Burgess, June 2020 (emphasis added).

234 **"Once the parties have framed the conflict"** Ibid.

234 **"most of us believe that people's basic human rights"** Ibid.

236 **"Hatred will always motivate people"** Agneta Fischer, Eran Halperin, Daphna Canetti, and Alba Jasini, "Why We Hate," *Emotion Review* 10, no. 4 (2018):309–20, 314. doi: 10.1177/1754073917751229.

236 **hate is a combination of various negative emotions** Robert J. Sternberg, "A Duplex Theory of Hate: Development and Application to Terrorism, Massacres, and Genocide," *Review of General Psychology* 7, no. 3 (2003):299–328. doi: 10.1037/1089-2680.7.3.299.

236 **We feel hate toward individuals or groups** Fischer, "Why We Hate."

236 **lack of direct contact** Ibid.

237 **"those currents are provided"** Robert J. Sternberg, "FLOTSAM: A Model for the Development and Transmission of Hate," *Journal of Theoretical Social Psychology* 2, no. 4 (2018):97–106, 102. doi: 10.1002/jts5.25.

237 **"When instigators seek to gain traction"** Ibid., 98.

237 **"the more the leaders whip up powerful stories"** Ibid., 102.

237 **"generally have not done anything"** Fischer, "Why We Hate," 315.

237 **"This is what our film tries to grapple with"** Kevin Fallon, "Laverne Cox Is Fighting for Trans People's Lives: We Need Justice 'Right Fucking Now.'" *Daily Beast,* June 15, 2020.

237 **"goal of hate is not merely to hurt"** Fischer, "Why We Hate," 311.

238 **"It is not clear that there is any magic bullet"** Sternberg, "FLOTSAM," 103.

238 **"The self-righteous scream"** John Mark Green (@JohnGreenpoetry), "The Self-Righteous Scream," Twitter post, April 30, 2018.

239 **"Self-righteousness is the conviction"** Cynthia Nordstrom and Susan L. Thomas, "To Change or Not to Change: Examining the Perception of Political 'Waffling.'" *North American Journal of Psychology* 9, no. 2 (2007):359–76, 362.

239 **People who exhibit self-righteousness** Toni Falbo and Sharyn S. Belk, "A Short Scale to Measure Self-Righteousness," *Journal of Personality Assessment* 49, no. 2 (1985):172–77. doi: 10.1207/s15327752jpa4902_13; Nordstrom, "To Change or Not to Change."

239 **self-righteousness is different from righteousness** Zachary K. Rothschild and Lucas A. Keefer, "Righteous or Self-Righteous Anger? Justice Sensitivity Moderates Defensive Outrage at a Third-Party Harm-Doer," *European Journal of Social Psychology* 48, no. 4 (2018):507–22. doi: 10.1002/ejsp.2349.

## #13 PLACES WE GO TO SELF-ASSESS

242 **Pride is a feeling** Joey T. Cheng, Jessica L. Tracy, and Joseph Henrich, "Pride, Personality, and the Evolutionary Foundations of Human Social Status," *Evolution and Human Behavior* 31, no. 5 (2010):334–47. doi: 10.1016/j.evolhumbehav.2010.02.004; Jessica L. Tracy and Richard W. Robins, "The Psychological Structure of Pride: A Tale of Two Facets," *Journal of Personality and Social Psychology* 92, no. 3 (2007):506–25. doi: 10.1037/0022-3514.92.3.506.

242 **Hubris is an inflated sense** Michael Lewis, "Self-Conscious Emotions: Embarrassment, Pride, Shame, Guilt, and Hubris," in *Handbook of Emotions*, edited by Lisa Feldman Barrett, Michael Lewis, and J. M. Haviland-Jones (New York: Guilford Press, 2016); Tracy, "The Psychological Structure of Pride"; Jessica L. Tracy and Richard W. Robins, "The Nature of Pride," in *The Self-Conscious Emotions: Theory and Research*, edited by Jessica L. Tracy, Richard W. Robins, and June Price Tangney (New York: Guilford Press, 2007).

242 **Humility is openness** Christopher Peterson and Martin E. P. Seligman, "Humility and Modesty," in *Character Strengths and Virtues: A Handbook and Classification* (Washington, DC/New York: American Psychological Association/Oxford University Press, 2004); June Price Tangney, "Humility," in *Handbook of Positive Psychology*, edited by C. R. Snyder and Shane J. Lopez (New York: Oxford University Press, 2002).

242 **distinguish hubris from pride** Tracy, "The Psychological Structure of Pride."

242 **"family of pride experiences"** Lisa A. Williams and Joel Davies, "Beyond the Self: Pride Felt in Relation to Others," in *The Moral Psychology of Pride,* edited by J. Adam Carter and Emma C. Gordon (Lanham, MD: Rowman & Littlefield, 2017), 43.

243 **"Hubristic pride may have"** Cheng, "Pride, Personality," 336.

243  **prestige status is earned**  Joseph Henrich and Francisco J. Gil-White, "The Evolution of Prestige: Freely Conferred Deference as a Mechanism for Enhancing the Benefits of Cultural Transmission," *Evolution and Human Behavior* 22, no. 3 (2001):165–96. doi: 10.1016/S1090-5138(00)00071-4.

244  **the person experiencing hubris**  Lewis, "Self-Conscious Emotions."

244  **"does not require respect"**  Cheng, "Pride, Personality," 343.

244  **pushed the term "narcissism" into the zeitgeist**  Brené Brown, *Daring Greatly: How the Courage to Be Vulnerable Transforms the Way We Live, Love, Parent, and Lead* (New York: Gotham Books, 2012).

245  **"For the narcissist"**  Jessica L. Tracy, Joey T. Cheng, Jason P. Martens, and Richard W. Robins, "The Emotional Dynamics of Narcissism: Inflated by Pride, Deflated by Shame," in *The Handbook of Narcissism and Narcissistic Personality Disorder: Theoretical Approaches, Empirical Findings, and Treatments*, edited by W. Keith Campbell and Joshua D. Miller (Hoboken, NJ: John Wiley & Sons Inc., 2011), 333.

245  **folks with trait hubristic pride**  Jessica L. Tracy, Azim F. Shariff, and Joey T. Cheng, "A Naturalist's View of Pride," *Emotion Review* 2, no. 2 (2010):163–77. doi: 10.1177/1754073909354627.

245  **it mirrors the physical patterns of dominance display**  Zachary Witkower, Jessica L. Tracy, Joey T. Cheng, and Joseph Henrich, "Two Signals of Social Rank: Prestige and Dominance Are Associated with Distinct Nonverbal Displays," *Journal of Personality and Social Psychology* 118, no. 1 (2020):89–120. doi: 10.1037/pspi0000181 10 .1037/pspi0000181.supp.

245  *Humility* **is openness**  Peterson, "Humility and Modesty"; Tangney, "Humility."

246  **I can sum up humility with one sentence**  Brené Brown, *Dare to Lead: Brave Work. Tough Conversations. Whole Hearts.* (New York: Random House, 2018).

246  **What humility isn't: downplaying yourself**  Peterson, "Humility and Modesty"; Tangney, "Humility."

246  **The term "intellectual humility"**  Daryl R. Van Tongeren, Don E. Davis, Joshua N. Hook, and Charlotte van Oyen Witvliet, "Humility," *Current Directions in Psychological Science* 28, no. 5 (2019):463–68. doi: 10.1177/0963721419850153.

## CULTIVATING MEANINGFUL CONNECTION

249  **"It is a capital mistake"**  Arthur Conan Doyle, "A Scandal in Bohemia" in *The Adventures of Sherlock Holmes* (London: George Newnes Ltd., 1892), 4.

250  **if we had an Elton John song**  Elton John (composer) and Tim Rice (lyrics), "Circle of Life," recorded by Elton John, on the album *The Lion King: Original Motion Picture Soundtrack* (Walt Disney/Hollywood/Mercury, 1994).

250  **"A set of interrelated constructs"**  Fred N. Kerlinger, *Foundations of Behavioral Research,* 2nd ed. (New York: Holt, Rinehart, and Winston, 1973), 9.

252  **"Near enemies are states that appear *similar*"**  Chris Germer, "The Near and Far Enemies of Fierce Compassion," Center for Mindful Self-Compassion (website).

252  **"The near enemies depict how spirituality"**  Jack Kornfield, *Bringing Home the Dharma: Awakening Right Where You Are* (Boston: Shambhala Publications, 2011), 102.

253  **"The near enemy of love"**  Jack Kornfield, "Love vs. Attachment" jackkornfield.com.

253  **"The near enemy of equanimity"**  Kornfield, *Bringing Home the Dharma,* 104.

254  **introduced the term grounded confidence**  Brené Brown, *Dare to Lead: Brave Work. Tough Conversation. Whole Hearts.* (New York: Random House, 2018).

260  **"Trauma victims cannot recover"**  Bessel van der Kolk, *The Body Keeps the Score* (New York: Penguin Books, 2014), 102.

260  **"The mind needs to be reeducated"**  Ibid., 103.

261  **"the awareness of our body's sensations"**  Prentis Hemphill, personal communication with author, September 2021.

261  **"an unawareness, repression, or denial"**  Prentis Hemphill, Ibid.

261  **"The habits that become embodied"**  Prentis Hemphill, Ibid.

261  **the theory that emerged from my dissertation**  Brené Brown, *Acompañar: A Grounded Theory of Developing, Maintaining and Assessing Relevance in Professional Helping* (doctoral dissertation, 2002).

262  **"Help is the sunny side of control"**  Anne Lamott, "12 Truths I Learned from Life and Writing," TED Talk, April 2017.

263  **in a 1968 speech**  Martin Luther King Jr., "All Labor Has Dignity," in *All Labor Has Dignity*, edited by Michael K. Honey (Boston: Beacon Press, 1968/2012), 167–79.

263  **In their publication *Making Change Happen***  Just Associates, "Making Change Happen 3: Power. Concepts for Revisioning Power for Justice, Equality and Peace," 2006.

263    **"based on mutual support"**    Ibid.

263    **"based on the belief that each individual has the power"**    Ibid.

263    **defined by an ability to recognize**    Ibid.

264    **there are some universal facial expressions**    Paul Ekman, Wallace V. Friesen, Maureen O'Sullivan, Anthony Chan, Irene Diacoyanni-Tarlatzis, Karl Heider, Rainer Krause, et al., "Universals and Cultural Differences in the Judgments of Facial Expressions of Emotion." *Journal of Personality and Social Psychology* 53, no. 4 (1987):712–17. doi: 10.1037/0022-3514.53.4.712.

265    **based on a role play that I did**    Brené Brown (host), "Brené with Aiko Bethea on Inclusivity at Work: The Heart of Hard Conversations (Part 1)," November 9, 2020, *Dare to Lead,* podcast.

# ILLUSTRATION CREDITS

Page vi–vii: Collage based on original art by PRRINT!, using illustrations by Gavin Aung Than

Page 2–3: Kyle Glenn

Page 9: Elizabeth Gilbert

Page 16-17: Alessio Bogani

Page 38–39: Álvaro Mendoza

Page 56–57: Annie Sprat

Page 60–61: Gavin Aung Than

Page 67: Gavin Aung Than

Page 68–69: Kenzie Kraft

Page 88–89 Janine Robinson

Page 90: August Friedrich Albrecht Schenck, *Anguish (Angoisse)* (c. 1878), National Gallery of Victoria, Melbourne, purchased 1880.

Page 98–99: *Dark Elegy,* copyright © 1991 Suse Lowenstein, photo by Karen Walrond

Page 114–15: Aedrian

Page 126–27: Gavin Aung Than

Page 132–33: Steve Cicero

Page 152–53: Katie Chang

Page 154: Maslow's Hierarchy of Needs, redrawn by Gavin Aung Than

Page 162–63: Gavin Aung Than

Page 166: Elle Lappan Photography

Page 182–83: Warren Sammut

Page 202–03: Eddie Pearson

Page 218–19: Laura Vinck

Page 222: WholeHearted School Counseling

Page 223: © 2000 Creative Therapy Associates, Inc., Cincinnati, Ohio

Page 227: Dr. John Gottman and Dr. Julie Schwartz Gottman. The Gottman Institute

Page 240–41: Zoran Milich

Page 249: Gavin Aung Than

Pages 255–59: Gavin Aung Than

Pages 267–70: Gavin Aung Than

# ABOUT THE AUTHOR

BRENÉ BROWN, PhD, MSW, is a research professor at the University of Houston, where she holds the Huffington Foundation–Brené Brown Endowed Chair. She is also a visiting professor in management at the University of Texas at Austin McCombs School of Business. Brown has spent the past two decades studying courage, vulnerability, shame, and empathy and is the author of five #1 *New York Times* bestsellers. She hosts the *Unlocking Us* and *Dare to Lead* podcasts. Brené's TED Talk is one of the top five most-viewed in the world, and she is also the first researcher to have a filmed lecture on Netflix.

brenebrown.com

Facebook.com/brenebrown

Twitter: @brenebrown

Instagram: @brenebrown

## ABOUT THE ILLUSTRATOR

GAVIN AUNG THAN is a *New York Times* bestselling cartoonist and the creator of *Zen Pencils,* a cartoon blog that adapts inspirational quotes into comics. He is currently working on the middle-grade graphic novel series Super Sidekicks. After working in the corporate graphic design industry for eight years, he quit his unfulfilling job and sold his house to follow his true passion: *drawing comics.* He hasn't looked back since.

Twitter: @zenpencils

Instagram: @zenpencils

This book was set in Minion, a 1990 Adobe Originals typeface by Robert Slimbach (b. 1956). Minion is inspired by classical, old-style typefaces of the late Renaissance, a period of elegant, beautiful, and highly readable type designs. Created primarily for text setting, Minion combines the aesthetic and functional qualities that make text type highly readable with the versatility of digital technology.